Abuse and Victimization across the Life Span

The Johns Hopkins Series in Contemporary Medicine and Public Health

Abuse and Victimization across the Life Span

Edited by
Martha B. Straus

The Johns Hopkins University Press
Baltimore and London

For
Harry and Elizabeth

Second printing, 1990

The Johns Hopkins University Press, 701 West 40th Street,
Baltimore, Maryland 21211
The Johns Hopkins Press Ltd., London

The paper used in this publication meets the minimum requirements of
American National Standard for Information Sciences—Permanence of Paper
for Printed Library Materials, ANSI Z39.48-1984.

Library of Congress Cataloging-in-Publication Data

Abuse and victimization across the life span.

   (The Johns Hopkins series in contemporary medicine
and public health)
   Includes index.
   1. Family violence.   I. Straus, Martha B.,
1956–   .   II. Series.   [DNLM: 1. Child Abuse.
2. Elder Abuse.   3. Family.   4. Spouse Abuse.
5. Violence.   HQ 809 A167]
RC569.5.F3A28   1988   616.85′82   87-46306
ISBN 0-8018-3636-0 (alk. paper)

Contents

Acknowledgments

Many people have contributed to this book since it was just a glimmer in my eye. I would like to take this opportunity to acknowledge and say thank you to:

Eli H. Newberger, M.D., without whom this book would not exist. It has been a rare and special privilege to have Eli as a mentor. The idea for this book stemmed from the Harvard continuing education course he produced and directed. I am deeply indebted to him for his compassionate vision of children and families and for his faith and support.

Other members of the Family Development Study: my fellow fellows—Bev Birns, Lora Melnicoe, and Nora Groce; friends and colleagues—Lisa Gary, Joanne Michalek, Susan Schechter, Penny Grace, Betty Singer, Sylvia Krakow, Sue Doucette, Carolyn Newberger, and Stephen Shirk; and administrative staff—Kathleen Scargle and especially Lindsay Fine, who toiled on many drafts of the manuscript.

Chapter authors, for their thoughtful dedication to victims and survivors of family violence and their willingness to contribute.

Wendy Harris, my editor, for her patience and knowledge.

Friends who added to the completion of this project more than shows in these pages—Annie, Molly, Stacey, Tobi, and Brenda.

Dean Levy, special friend and teacher.

My family: Betty, Nathan, Joe, Andi, Sally, Karen, Nadav, and John and Julie Kronenberger, with all my love.

Contributors

Beverly Birns, Ph.D., professor of psychology and director of child and family studies, State University of New York, Stony Brook

Richard Bourne, J.D., Ph.D., associate, Office of the General Counsel, Children's Hospital, Boston, and associate professor, Department of Sociology, Northeastern University

Howard Dubowitz, M.D., assistant professor, Department of Pediatrics, University of Maryland School of Medicine

Harwood Egan, M.D., lecturer in pediatrics, Department of Medicine, Harvard Medical School, and pediatrician, Growth and Nutrition Clinic, Children's Hospital, Boston

David Finkelhor, Ph.D., associate director, Family Violence Research Laboratory, and associate professor of sociology, University of New Hampshire

Terry Fulmer, R.N., Ph.D., associate professor of nursing, Boston College, associate director, Harvard Geriatric Education Center, and gerontological nurse specialist, Beth Israel Hospital, Boston

Lisa T. Gary, M.S.W., project director, Advocacy for Women and Kids in Emergencies (AWAKE), Family Development Study, Children's Hospital, Boston

Nora E. Groce, Ph.D., research associate, World Hunger Program, Brown University, Department of Anthropology

Robert L. Hampton, Ph.D., associate professor of sociology and dean of the college, Connecticut College, and lecturer on pediatrics (sociology), Harvard Medical School

Alexandra G. Kaplan, Ph.D., lecturer in psychiatry, Harvard Medical School, co-clinical director, Counseling Service, Wellesley College, and research associate, the Stone Center, Wellesley College

Susan Schechter, M.S.W., program coordinator, Advocacy for Women and Kids in Emergencies (AWAKE), Family Development Study, Children's Hospital, Boston

Stephen R. Shirk, Ph.D., director, Child Study Center, University of Denver

Frances Sink, Ph.D., clinical psychologist, Department of Psychiatry, Danbury Hospital, Danbury, Connecticut, and consultant, Victim Recovery Study, Children's Hospital, Boston

Martha B. Straus, Ph.D., instructor (psychology), Department of Medicine, Harvard Medical School, and clinical psychologist, Kaiser Permanente, Greenfield, Massachusetts

Carolyn F. Swift, Ph.D., director, the Stone Center, Wellesley College

Bessel A. van der Kolk, M.D., director, Trauma Center, Massachusetts Mental Health Center, consulting psychiatrist, the Cambridge Hospital, and lecturer on psychiatry, Harvard Medical School

Kersti Yllo, Ph.D., associate professor of sociology and coordinator of Women's Studies, Wheaton College, Norton, Massachusetts

Introduction   *Family Violence across the Life Span*

MARTHA B. STRAUS

An interest in human development across the life span coincides with recent social and demographic changes. Students of family violence toil to keep up with the implications of lower birthrates, longer life expectancy, the women's rights movement, rising divorce and remarriage rates, and female-headed households—in short, dramatic changes in the very meaning of family. Some of us plug the data into our computers and uncover provocative correlations that associate all sorts of social changes with high rates of family violence. Others treat endless victims in our hospitals, agencies, or shelters and see these correlations in human terms. What we have not done, though, is to stop and find a common language and context for our work. *Abuse and Victimization across the Life Span* provides this needed communication among students of family violence.

We have been dogged students. Theories and research on abuse and victimization have mushroomed over the past two decades. From the detailed case analysis up through the national survey, we now know as much as we probably need to know about how many people are doing which types of horrible things to whom and at what emotional, physical, and economic expense. However, we have not made much of a dent in prevention or in prescribing the best combinations of treatments for different types of victims or offenders. Social reforms are necessary, and new policies await the fertile foundation now laid out.

Specialization

With the increase in knowledge, though, has come the isolating age of specialization, which has delayed and diverted us from more comprehensive approaches. Each specialty area has within it people who subspecialize—researchers, practitioners, advocates, and historians who are expert in their particular methods—and the various agencies that fund them. The competition for money in recent years has helped build walls between specialties. For example, until very recently the antagonism between the grass-roots activists in the battered women's movement and the professionals in child protection has made any kind of open dialogue difficult, even though battered women and abused children are frequently from the same families. Even within areas, suspicion abounds. Child abuse researchers attempting to study types of intervention, for example, are often viewed warily by clinicians. Those struggling on the front lines with huge caseloads and limited funds wonder why they should take on extra work for research and why money is going to the grant junkies instead of to the victims.

There are also positive and practical reasons for specialization. A carefully defined domain of study or practice has obvious advantages over one that is too broad and inclusive. The expertise of someone devoting her life to helping battered women, for example, is probably greater than that of a generalist in a clinic who sees a little of everything. It is easier to put something small under the microscope and be able to say a great deal about it. In any event, family violence can be an overwhelming problem when considered whole.

However, the specialized literatures of family violence (and the conferences that result) have become increasingly redundant. Moreover, the researchers with their probability levels and the therapists with their countertransference problems have so little in common now that the walls within areas seem higher than ever—even at a time when commerce between professionals would be particularly profitable. Maybe even wider, though, is the gap between clinicians and researchers working in different areas of the life span, who do not attend the same conferences or read the same journals.

Similarities in Family Violence across the Life Span

Communication among professionals in different areas of family violence remains negligible despite obvious similarities in the victimization experience across the life span. As the following chapters describe in greater depth, all victims share a profound belief in their own badness—and an underlying sense that they deserve the violence against them. The loyalty of victims of all ages to their abusers has been noted extensively in the literature on both child abuse and wife battering. Such victims have difficulty believing they are not to blame and that the offender should be held responsible for his or her behavior. This distortion is common in victims of all ages and is generally one of the effects of abuse that is most difficult to threat in therapy. Other effects such as depression, lack of trust, low self-esteem, and impaired social relationships are also common but may be more amenable to intervention. In sum, regardless of age, victims of family violence often share a dependence for their very survival upon someone who harms them. The psychological effects can be devastating at all stages of development.

Another similarity that runs through the recent abuse literature is the theory that offenders act violently because they can get away with it and because they believe it is justified by the end (e.g., quieting the child, getting the wife to keep the house cleaner, stopping the complaints of the elder). All forms of family violence are reduced when strong punishments are put into place—whether or not the offender believes he or she has done anything wrong. Gelles (1974) has also noted that those who commit different types of family violence tend to abuse their power when they perceive they are losing it. Feelings of impotence, for example, may cause a husband or a parent to strike out.

Other characteristics also appear to be common to abusive families: poverty, isolation, rigid patriarchal structure, lack of resources, and alcohol and drug abuse. There is strong evidence that families prone to one type of violence may also be susceptible to others. For example, men who abuse their wives are more likely to abuse their children; battered wives are also more likely to abuse their children; and abused children are more likely to abuse their siblings (Straus 1983). The age-old theory of intergenerational transmission of abuse is generally supported by survey data. Some abused children *do* grow up to become violent adults or victims. However, such descriptions should not be taken as explanations—indeed, many poor, isolated, abused children who fall into the highest risk groups do not become the offenders of tomorrow. The particular individual and social characteristics and me-

diating variables that protect individuals at different stages from per-
petuating violence are described more fully in this book.

Life Span Theories

Knowledge of normal development helps us understand what violence
does to family members. Three theories of life-span development have
emerged over the past several years—the most promising for students
of family violence was described by Gergen (1981), who called it the
aleatoric (autonomous) account. This model focuses on the flexibility
of developmental patterns and emerges from the study of the broad
range of human responses to developmental stresses and opportunities.
Gergen (1981, 34–35) suggested that "existing patterns appear potentially evanescent, the unstable result of the peculiar juxtaposition of
contemporary historical events. For any individual the life course seems
fundamentally open-ended. Even with full knowledge of the individual's past experience, one can render little more than a probabilistic
account of the broad contours of future development." Advocates of
this theory are likely to intervene energetically and hopefully to help a
victim. The other two theories have been criticized for insufficient
data bases and value-laden assumptions in research (Offer and Sashbin
1984) but are worth mentioning because they retain strong followings
among researchers and clinicians alike.

The second life-span theory describes development in a hierarchical
manner and considers it continuous, stable, and cumulative. This
theory is popular among psychoanalytic theoreticians and students of
behavioral constancy. Advocates of this theory would predict that an
abused child is likely to grow up to be either a victim or an offender
in violent relationships.

The third theory, explored in the work of Piaget, Erikson, and
Kohlberg, among others, describes development as discontinuous, unstable, and cyclical. Individuals grapple with similar conflicts at each
stage along the way but may use new skills to resolve old issues.
Advocates of this theory would predict that, with some type of intervention, victims might learn new methods of approaching violent relationships as they get older. Offer and Sashbin (1984) have argued
persuasively that these theories are not mutually exclusive and that no
one theory can describe all aspects of development. Needless to say,
clinical examples can be found to fit all three descriptions.

Each life-span theory contributes to our understanding of what
violence might mean to victims as they develop. On the one hand, as
we grow older we can lay old ghosts to rest with new skills and new

conditions. The abused infant can develop trusting relationships as a toddler, with a different caretaker or with the same caretaker who has learned to nurture. The sexually abused and withdrawn schoolchild can develop better peer relationships through group therapy as an adolescent. On the other hand, with each stage the ghosts can come back to haunt us. A battered wife is made to recall her abuse as a child each time she is hit. A scorned adolescent remembers feeling worthless as a young child. And so on. The life-span perspective takes into account both the continuity of development—personal history as it accumulates—and the resiliency of the human spirit—our ability to use changed situations and maturation to help us continue to grow and develop.

The life-span perspective also describes the developmental tasks of each period and so can help us understand how abuse might impede achievement of those tasks. Obviously, symptoms of abuse vary tremendously—both according to when the abuse took place and with the victim's age at the time of report or treatment. For example, a toddler who is abused at the time he is striving to become more independent may later exhibit separation difficulties when going to school, even if he is not currently being abused. In contrast, a sexually abused twelve-year-old girl who is beginning to struggle all over again with conflicts about being dependent may run away from home or become truant. Symptoms occur in a developmental context; we can use them in our interpretation of how the violence has affected a given individual in a particular period of life.

Finally, in addition to bridging the generation gaps that now exist in the family-violence field, a life-span approach may also close the gaps that yawn between researchers and clinicians. Research in recent years has much to suggest about normal development and about how people grow and change. Such information is invaluable to the frustrated and "stuck" clinician working with an abused patient who is struggling with particular developmental tasks. As a corollary, clinical wisdom abounds and may lead developmental researchers beyond simple associative models to examine the complex process known most generally as growing up. Through such sharing of expertise we can find out what violence does to the human being's natural striving to develop and also how we can help shape a future that is free from violence.

This book is divided into four sections. The first three approach abuse and victimization from a life-span perspective, and the fourth deals with special issues in family violence. Each of the first three parts opens with a chapter on the normal developmental task of that period (Infancy, Childhood and Adolescence, and Adulthood). Subsequent chapters in each section address problems and solutions in research and intervention. The final part (Special Topics) looks at some key issues for the future, including criminalization of family violence, the battered women's movement, disabled people, and social reforms that will diminish violence in our society.

References

Gelles, R. 1974. *The violent home: A study of physical aggression between husbands and wives.* Beverly Hills, Calif.: Sage.

Gergen, K. J. 1981. The emerging crisis in life-span development theory. In *Life-span development and behavior,* ed. P. B. Baltes and O. G. Brim, Jr., 3:31–63. New York: Academic Press.

Offer, D., and Sashbin, M. 1984. *Normality and the life cycle.* New York: Basic Books.

Straus, M. 1983. Ordinary violence, child abuse and wife-beating: What do they have in common? In *The dark side of families,* ed. D. Finkelhor, R. Gelles, et al., 213–34. Beverly Hills, Calif.: Sage.

ONE   *Infancy*

1   *The Mother-Infant Tie:*
Of Bonding and Abuse

BEVERLY BIRNS

A book on violence across the life span logically starts with the mother-infant relationship and the beginning of life. Ironically, public and professional suspicion of the mother in abuse recognizes her close connection to infant and child: How could a mother do that? we ask, horrified. Or perhaps a worse indictment, How could she have stood by and done nothing? Because we assume between mother and child a special intimacy—derived from her having carried the fetus, and given birth, and having served, in the still overwhelming number of cases, as primary caretaker—we assume that behind every violent act toward a child is a mother who has allowed it to happen. But underneath our common beliefs about mothers lie two myths that shape our perception and our policy and impede our search for new and more effective solutions to the escalating problem of child abuse.

Two Myths

The Nuclear Family

Strong beliefs about motherhood have endured for generations, often in the face of contrary evidence. For instance, when little was known about prenatal development, it was commonly believed that if a pregnant woman viewed certain unpleasant sights, her infant might be deformed. With the advent of scientific knowledge about fetal development, we now know that it is not what a pregnant woman sees that harms the fetus, but inadequate nutrition, smoking, disease, and toxic substances such as drugs and alcohol.

Social and psychological myths, however, are harder to disprove and therefore linger even when the evidence contradicts them, and certainly when the evidence is equivocal. In the early and middle twentieth century, middle- and upper-class American families usually consisted of a male breadwinner, a nonemployed mother, and three or four children. Although some women never married, some married couples did not have children, and some families had an "absent father," an employed mother, or both, these arrangements were considered atypical. The prevalent belief was that the nuclear family was the ideal, and to many the only, way to rear children successfully. In the 1950s and 1960s, paternal absence and maternal employment were thought to damage children emotionally. Children raised in lesbian and gay households were not discussed at all—that was beyond the imaginable. The prevalent myth was that normal, healthy children had to be raised in a "traditional" family with a working father and a nonemployed wife, with no other adults in the same dwelling. As recently as the fifties and sixties many considered divorce unthinkable, though of course it happened. Families that included a grandmother or an unmarried uncle or aunt living in the home were also considered unusual.

Currently, newspapers, magazines, scholarly journals, and textbooks on the family all contain data on the changing American family, but the myth persists. If it were true that myths are individual beliefs, then like other personal beliefs they would not be of public interest when they do not harm others. However, myths about the nuclear family influence public policy, which then affects how children will be raised. A recent episode in the state of Massachusetts clarifies this issue and also documents how myths can influence public policy.

The case in point concerned two small boys who had been removed from their mother's care. After careful screening to find the best alternative living situation, they were placed in the care of two men. Shortly afterward the press became aware of this foster home, and reporters and photographers descended on the household. When newspaper stories appeared, the state Department of Social Services (DSS) removed the children, citing as cause the damaging effect of the publicity. Soon afterward the DSS sent out a memorandum clarifying its position on the placement of foster children. The memorandum indicated that prospective foster parents should be interviewed to determine both life-style and sexual preference:

The guiding principle must be the ability of the family to provide a warm, stable, nurturing home for a child on a temporary basis. Accordingly, this administration believes that foster children are served best when placed in traditional family settings, that is with relatives, or in families with married couples, preferably with parenting experience, and with time available to care for foster children (Department of Social Services, Commonwealth of Massachusetts 1986).

While few would question the wisdom of providing children with a warm, stable, nurturing home, the "traditional family" is becoming rare. Furthermore, such traditional families are amply represented among those that physically, sexually, and emotionally abuse their children. Contrary to the beliefs stated in this memorandum, there is evidence that when children are raised in warm, nurturing nontraditional homes, they also thrive. One study conducted by Richard Green (1982) found that children living with lesbian mothers were indistinguishable on measures of sexual identity and self-esteem from children living with heterosexual divorced mothers.

Another example of children successfully raised in nontraditional homes is a case study from Czechoslovakia (Kulchova 1972) describing twins who were grossly neglected, abused, and damaged. When discovered at age three, they required long-term hospitalization to treat their injuries and malnutrition and to evaluate the extent and degree of permanence of their profound retardation. During this period of hospitalization, the Czechoslovakian authorities searched for the family that could best provide the extraordinary care that the twins (who were believed to be permanently retarded) would require when they were released from the hospital. The ideal family consisted of two sisters, one of whom worked full time, who had already successfully "rescued" another child thought to be permanently damaged. The twins progressed so remarkably in the years following their placement that the case is often cited to demonstrate the amazing resilience of children. Clearly the Czechoslovakians do not share our insistence on traditional families headed by heterosexual married couples with mothers at home.

The myth about contemporary families includes mistaken beliefs concerning their economic self-sufficiency: many American families do not have fathers who are earning enough to support the family. Those who believe the myth fault working mothers for seeking employment for selfish reasons (Brazelton 1986). In fact, however, most women work for the same reason men do—to support their families. Now as in the recent past, two-thirds of women work because they are single, divorced, widowed, or married to men who earn less than $15,000 a year (U.S. Department of Labor 1985). Although some mothers have always worked, today 60 percent of all mothers with children under eighteen years of age are in the labor force. Most dramatically, 50 percent of women with children under three are now working, and the percentage of married mothers with children under one year who work is also approaching 50 percent (U.S. Congress, Congressional Budget Office 1985). A major factor that influences women's work-force participation is the rising divorce rate; 77 percent of single mothers of school-age children are in the labor force. In fact, the pattern of father working, mother not employed, and two healthy children describes only about 7 percent of American families. Thus the search for the traditional family may soon become like the search for the holy grail.

Many experts (e.g., Fraiberg 1977) claim that maternal employment has a negative effect on children. Selma Fraiberg states that young children grieve when separated from their mothers for even short periods, and that children in day care come to resemble the institutionalized children described by Bowlby (1952). The most extensive review of the literature to date (Hayes 1982), however, indicates that the influence of maternal employment depends on many factors, including the number of hours worked, whether the mother enjoys working, how much income is provided, and what kind of child care is available. When scientific data, not personal beliefs, are used, the claim that maternal employment has a negative influence on children is simply not supported.

A corollary of the idea that good mothers do not work is the belief that day care is bad for children. Fraiberg's (1977) descriptions of children as being stored in warehouses called day-care centers would bring tears to the eyes of the hardest-hearted adult. Undoubtedly there are day-care centers that not only are unlicensed but are as dreadful as the ones portrayed by the critics of day care. But many other institutions—for instance, nursing homes—that are underfunded, understaffed, or run for profit are equally criticized. The response of nursing-home consumers is to campaign for licensing, better employee training, and higher pay for staff, not to condemn the institutions out of hand. Again, when scientific study rather than personal opinion is provided, there is no evidence that good day care has adverse effects on young children (Scarr 1984). In fact, for some groups of infants and children day care has had markedly beneficial effects (Ramey, Yeates, and Short 1984), and for some there are no differential effects at all. Not surprisingly, professional evaluations of day care make it clear that the effect depends primarily on the quality of the care.

The debate over the influence of maternal employment and day care on both mothers and children reflects a myth about the supremacy of the traditional nuclear family. Working mothers and nonworking mothers in nontraditional families face criticism and obstacles from a society that clings to such myths.

Bonding and Attachment

Child-custody decisions in abuse cases are frequently based upon an assessment of the mother-child bond. This bond is used to describe a special kind of relationship that mother and infant should have. The concept derives from the work of Bowlby (1952) and Klaus and Kennell (1976). In the early 1950s, Bowlby (1952) developed theories based on studies that have altered the way parent-child relationships are described today. Analyzing a massive amount of data on maternal deprivation, he came to believe that by the end of the infant's second year of life the mother-infant relationship is unique and serves as the cornerstone for the development of a mentally healthy adult. The work of Kennell and Klaus on bonding suggested further that this bond is established (or not established) in the first few hours after birth. Although there are many criticisms of their work, much contemporary theory and practice is based on these researchers' ideas about attachment and bonding.

Current bonding theorists (Sroufe 1985; Waters 1978) believe that the special relationship is formed through early care of the infant; once formed, the bond is enduring. This bond develops because mothers are programmed to behave in ways that elicit appropriate infant behavior (Sroufe 1985; Waters 1978). More important, if the bond is not established in the early months, emotional and cognitive damage is certain to occur and perhaps will be irreversible. The nature of this early relationship also predicts later social behavior. A baby who is securely bonded or attached to its mother, the theorists claim, will form good relationships with peers and with other adults. Some recent research has modified the strength of such beliefs.

As early as the 1960s, careful research on attachment behavior indicated that even in homes where the mother provided all the care, some infants became attached early in life to persons other than the mother (Schaeffer and Emerson 1964). In these instances the infant became most attached to those who were most responsive to its nonphysical needs. For example, the father, sibling, or grandparent who "spoiled" the baby by responding to its cries and also played with the child was sometimes the preferred adult.

Today increasing attention is given to fathers' role in the development of their infants and children. Again, the evidence suggests that offspring of primary nurturing fathers can be vigorous, competent, and thriving infants (Pruett 1983). Kotelchuck (1976, 343) further concluded a study on fathers by saying: "Children can and do form active and close relationships with their fathers during the first years of life. Children do not innately or instinctively relate only to their mothers. The presumed uniqueness of the mother-child relationship appears ephemeral." Infants, like others, can love and be intensely attached to more than one person. Thus the first premise of attachment theory, that the mother-infant relationship is unique, must be modified to state that in some families, in some circumstances, the relationship is unique, while in other families it is not.

The second premise, that the relationship must be established during the first two years of life, is also ill founded. The Klaus and Kennell research indicated that the first twenty-four hours were most critical for bonding and that infants who had close physical contact with their mothers immediately after birth gained an advantage that would be reflected in greater intellectual ability in the years to come.

However, attempts to replicate the Klaus and Kennell research have failed. In one careful study (Svejda, Campos, and Emde 1980), mothers who had extra contact with their neonates did not differ in attachment from mothers who did not have this additional contact. Similarly, in another study, Egeland and Vaughn (1981) compared impoverished mothers who were providing good care for their infants with a group of impoverished mothers who mistreated their children. The authors found no significant differences between the two groups either in the delivery or in the amount of contact babies had with their mothers in the postnatal period. Furthermore, mothers of premature babies were not less adequate because of separation at birth. The authors concluded that scientists should be suspicious of assigning single causes to complex problems. Their research also suggests that early separation of mother and infant does not predict later inadequate nurture. At this time the most plausible explanation for the disparity between the Klaus and Kennell studies and those that have followed is the poor design of the original research (Arney 1980).

The interest in attachment in the 1980s is similar in certain ways to the significance attributed to IQ in the forties and fifties. Proponents argue that attachment is a behavior that can be measured and scored and allows for the classification of babies into groups. Like IQ proponents, attachment theorists claim that the characteristic in question reliably measures a quality in the child that reflects experience (not innate qualities) and that it can predict future behavior. For example, the Ainsworth (1969) measure of attachment involves the mother and toddler's entering a laboratory, the entrance of a stranger, the departure of the mother, the departure of the stranger, and the return of the mother. The entire procedure takes about twenty minutes, and the most important responses are the child's reaction to the mother's departure and return. Adherents of the theory claim that based on this small segment of behavior toddlers can be classified as securely or insecurely attached.

This area of research has attracted many productive scientists in the field of child development. The seductiveness of the concept, like that of IQ, is great in a field that tries hard to compete with the physical sciences in predictive ability. It would be very valuable to have measuring instruments that are precise in the same way as electron microscopes or telescopes. But human behavior, like the behavior of other living organisms, is highly dependent on environmental conditions. The claims of attachment theorists, like the claims of the IQ adherents, may appear logical yet may not in fact be true. Researchers who hope to predict behavior at a later stage of development from earlier measures need to consider the relative stability of environmental conditions. For example, low-IQ babies become low-IQ preschoolers only when they remain in situations that are not stimulating. Similarly, low-birth-weight babies with low IQ scores maintain low IQ scores when they live in poor families that fail to provide adequate stimulation (Barrera, Rosenbaum, and Cunningham 1986), whereas early intervention increases their IQ.

The same environmental conditions apply to attachment behavior. Infants in troubled environments may be insecurely attached at one year of age and show problem behavior at three years. But this does not prove that what occurred in the first year of life caused the later problems. An infant in a troubled home at age one will probably still live in this problem home at age three. Problem behavior at three may reflect ongoing negative interactions as well as earlier difficulties. In fact, even the proponents of attachment theory have shown variability in the measure. The same child may be securely attached to one parent and not the other, and when family situations change so do attachment classifications (Sroufe 1985). Attachment theory implies that being deprived of attachment to one mothering figure in the first two years of life causes permanent damage. Yet a child who is insecurely attached during infancy need not be a troubled three-year-old.

The development of attachment continues to be an active area of inquiry (Lamb et al. 1984). For example, in Great Britain, Tizard (1977) studied a group of children who spent their first few years in group care and subsequently were adopted or returned to their biological mothers. The nurseries differed from the terrible institutions of the early part of the century; they consisted of spacious, airy homes that were well furnished and contained excellent toys and resources. The children were taken care of by "nannies" in training, so the adults in their lives frequently changed. The nurses were discouraged from forming a close attachment to any one child because it was believed that changes in personnel would then be harder on the children. Children were cared for by dozens of different adults for varying amounts of time. These children were therefore deprived of the unique relationship that attachment theorists believe is crucial for normal, healthy development. At the age of two the toddlers tested somewhat below age level. However, once they were either adopted or returned to their biological mothers, their development progressed according to their new environment. The children who were adopted into middle-class homes where parents were older, wealthier, and better educated than the biological mothers and were eager to adopt made good progress. At age eight they were of average IQ, and the adoptive parents did not feel they were "problem children." However, their teachers did describe them as more demanding than others. The children who returned to women who gave birth to them fared less well, particularly if these mothers had remarried and had additional children.

Although the development of attachment and bonding has been explored in new research, there are still few answers. Researchers assume that children who start out in life in happy, loving, stimulating homes where both physical and emotional needs are met should be more resilient, even if they are subsequently stressed, than children whose early years are troubled. However, even this logical argument does not explain the resilience of some children. For example, the case of Gena provides a dramatic picture of the deficits of attachment theories. Gena was first admitted to a hospital as a seriously ill infant who failed to thrive. She returned to her mother but was hospitalized a second time several months later because her development was grossly retarded and she seemed near starvation. Her mother was severely depressed; this was her fourth out-of-wedlock baby, and she had almost no external supports. The hospital staff believed that to save Gena's life she should be placed in foster care once she was stabilized. After some weeks in the hospital, however, she was discharged to her mother's care with the assistance of a visiting nurse and other supports. Since that time the mother has had one other child, numerous serious illnesses, and frequent bouts of moderate-to-severe depression. Today, at fifteen, Gena is a healthy, wholesome adolescent who does well in school, takes part in school athletics, and has many friends. What is astonishing is that in spite of severe illness, near starvation, and the depression of her mother, she presents none of the symptoms expected of a child whose "attachment" and development were so seriously compromised during the early years.

Current attempts to analyze the factors involved in forming attachment have generated more heat than light. Proponents claim that the relationship between an infant and a caretaker can be measured independent of the individual infant's characteristics. Critics (e.g., Svejda, Campos, and Emde 1980; Chess 1982; Kagan 1984) claim that individual characteristics of the infants and mothers are undeniably salient to bonding. For example, an infant who is insecurely attached on Ainsworth's measure and who cries and rejects its mother when she returns may well be a child who cries easily whenever stressed. All one can say at this time is that the final answers are not available. It is likely that attachment theory and research will continue to flourish and may contribute to a greater understanding of how maternal behavior promotes or thwarts the development of mentally healthy children. It is unlikely, however, that attachment behavior will ever be understood if we look for linear cause-and-effect relationships. At any one moment a child's behavior undoubtedly reflects biologically programmed factors such as temperament, the care received early in life (which may or may not be tapped accurately by attachment measures), social class, and a very large number of contemporaneous factors including family constellation, general stress level of the family, family conflict, siblings, peers, and important people outside the family.

The mother-infant relationship *is* very important. But children's and adult's mental health cannot be attributed solely to it. It is nonetheless useful to think about what mothers do to foster development in the early years.

Developmental Tasks of Infants and Young Children

The fetus requires favorable conditions in the uterus if it is to have good health and well-being at birth. It needs adequate and appropriate nutrition, a drug- and alcohol-free environment, and the absence of potential maternal hazards such as high blood pressure and infectious diseases, such as AIDS. The human infant, more than other primates is born totally dependent, and it remains dependent on adult care for its very survival. After birth the immediate needs are sufficient oxygen, nourishment, and maintenance of adequate body temperature. Although in the past standard obstetrical care involved removing the newborn from the mother immediately after birth, current practice in many places emphasizes the "bonding" of mother and infant, so that body and eye contact is established as early as possible.

In the early weeks of life, the infant's major task is establishing physiological homeostasis. Patterns of eating, sleeping, and wakefulness that become regular reflect low levels of stress in the infant and foster positive feelings in the adult caretaker. Babies who are easy to soothe invoke more positive feelings than those who are inconsolable (Birns 1965). Although in the distant past aunts or grandmothers were frequently called upon to help new mothers and in the recent past middle-class mothers were happy to have baby nurses assist them in the first difficult weeks, the current trend is "natural mothering," with new mothers intent on "establishing the bond" on their own as soon as possible after birth. According to some (Brazelton 1986), the process of bonding begins during pregnancy when parents share feelings about the baby-to-be. Whatever the long-range implications of these early feelings, there is little doubt that mothers feel better about themselves as mothers if their babies sleep well, eat well, fuss little, and are increasingly awake, alert, and content. Crying babies are a source of stress to mothers and also to other adults.

As babies grow and develop beyond the newborn period, they become more active and also more sociable. Although at birth infants respond to the human face differently than to other visual stimuli, the earliest smiles are not social. But by three or four months, often earlier, babies do smile at faces and recognize and respond differentially to mother, father, and other favored adults. Early object and person recognition is established first in the visual mode. Earliest movements are random and not organized. During the first year of life, however, the infant increasingly becomes an active participant in its social and object world. Piaget describes early development as the increasing coordination of sensorimotor schemata. The baby learns about the world by acting on it. At a few weeks of age an infant stares at a bottle or stares at its mother, but by the time it is a few months old it reaches for and grasps its bottle (and also reaches toward and grasps its mother's, father's, or other caregivers' hair, or nose).

During the first year simple recognition is replaced by action, and the child "learns" by repeating actions and sounds many times. Early play is repetitive and action oriented. A rattle is to shake, a bell to ring, and the early words—dada, mama, or others—are rehearsed for long periods. Before the end of the first year a baby is acquainted with the world of objects and the world of people. It recognizes its mother, its father, and other important people and responds differentially to them according to a hierarchy. By the end of the first year the baby not only is aware of differences in adults but also has favorites.

As the child learns about the people in its world it also learns about objects. It learns to grasp, finger, and hold a variety of items and is also learning that things no longer in view still exist. The understanding of object constancy, carefully studied by Piaget, is acquired by sequential steps. At first the infant gazes at objects as they disappear and makes no attempt to retrieve them. By a series of measurable stages it begins to search for missing items. The baby is learning not only about the properties of objects but also about the predictability of events. Not only does mother leave and then return, but no matter how many times the baby drops a spoon from the high chair, it always lands on the floor. The baby also learns that by pushing buttons all kinds of things predictably happen—noise from a radio, light from a switch. In all, the infant is an active participant.

Another development that begins during the first year of life and becomes even more important during the second year is language acquisition. Infants begin by repeating their own sounds and gradually move toward imitating sounds made by others. Although the earliest sounds are not symbols related to specific objects or actions, the baby slowly learns that all objects and people have names. Many consider language the behavior that most clearly differentiates humans from other primates. Although language acquisition continues throughout childhood and adolescence, the greatest development comes during the first three years of life and is very much a product of the exchanges between baby and caretaker. The babbling of the infant becomes the speech of the three-year-old as adults speak to, repeat, correct, and ask questions of the very young child. Language, most typically acquired through the dialogue of mother and child, provides the key to all later learning.

In addition to learning about people, objects, and words, very young infants are also learning about themselves. Their sense of self is initially based on their sense of mastery—of being able to do their "work," whether that is creeping toward their mothers, grasping a longed-for toy, throwing a ball, or asking for and receiving some milk. The sense of self is also dependent on the views of others. Infants who elicit smiles and cheers, whose new skills are responded to as if they were most significant events, will believe they are treasured and important. Babies whose behavior is unacknowledged or frequently meets a negative response will be less likely to enjoy new skills and to feel valued. In one study the amount of pleasure two-year-olds expressed on different tasks was shown to be a better predictor of IQ in three-year-olds than the children's actual abilities at two (Birns and Golden 1972). Self-esteem or sense of self clearly has its origin in the first two years of life, though it is subject to change throughout the life cycle.

Our views about mothering, or "good enough mothering" (Winnicott 1968), depend on our beliefs about the nature of the child, the goals of child rearing, and the experts' beliefs about how to reach these goals. When behaviorism was the dominant theory in American psychology, the experts believed that the infant was born a "blank slate" and that all behavior could be explained and produced by following simple principles of learning. With the popularization of psychoanalytic theory, the view of the child changed radically, and so did the prescription for good parenting. According to Freud and his followers, at birth the child carries seeds of both love and aggression. Rather than being a blank slate, the infant is born with conflictual instincts that must be resolved to ensure healthy development. In both theories, mothers are primary players.

Maternal Behavior

Although today both behaviorism and psychoanalytic theory play a role in our understanding of human behavior, they differ in their views about determinants of behavior and the goals of child rearing. One example might clarify the different views. According to behaviorism, picking up a baby whenever it cries reinforces the crying behavior. The infant learns that crying brings the mother, and it then cries more often. The mother who wants to reduce crying should therefore provide for the childs' needs, but on schedule and not at the "will" of the child. Psychoanalytic theory advocates gratifying early infantile needs because the child's love for the parent evolves from gratification. It is feelings of love that tame the equally powerful aggressive drives, according to these theorists. These issues have not been resolved for all time, but current expert opinion tends toward the psychoanalytic view of the infant as a "needs-determined" organism, rather than a blank slate whose behavior is primarily determined by parental shaping.

All experts agree that the fundamental requirement of good mothering is to care for and protect the child. Based on what we know of infant development, however, we expect more than just adequate attention to physical needs. We also believe that good mothers are sensitive to their children's emotional needs. They do not attempt to feed an overtired but satiated baby or leave a baby crying for hours because they are otherwise occupied or do not want to spoil it. Very early in life good mothers also talk to and smile at their babies. Most mothers believe that the earliest smiles are for them, and they smile back. These satisfying early interactions are the basis of what Erikson calls "basic trust." It is the sense developed in the earliest months that the world is a safe, predictable place where good things happen.

As the infant's sensory and motor skills develop, the tasks of the caretaker, usually the mother, expand to providing stimulation. The mother supplies objects for the baby to manipulate, space to practice creeping, and a verbal environment. As the mother responds to the baby's initiation of contact and vocalizations, she fosters its emerging sense of self as a separate and valued person. The burgeoning sense of self implies, before it can be stated, that if others like me, then I like me too. When the baby takes its first step, says a new word, or pulls a string to obtain a toy and the mother responds enthusiastically, the child gains a sense of competence and autonomy.

One of the most important roles that the mother plays very early and also later in the child's life is as the facilitator of language. Mothers who imitate their babies' own sounds and repeat the most desired word—usually mama—teach them that words describe objects and also call forth actions. At the beginning, the words babies use may not correspond to conventional meanings. For instance, the baby may say "mama" to everyone or say "dat" when it wants anything and everything. Yet this early dialogue fosters the acquisition of conventional speech. At the end of the first year the baby says only one or two words, but by the end of the third year a child can typically speak in complete sentences.

Mothers and others also teach, albeit not necessarily consciously, a great deal about the expression of emotion. Whereas years ago it was believed that babies respond only to interactions that directly involve them, more recent research indicates that by the age of two toddlers respond to angry verbal interchanges even in strangers and not directed at them (Cummings, Ianotti, and Zahn-Waxler 1985). Similarly, abused toddlers respond to distress expressed by their peers by striking out, a behavior not observed in nonabused toddlers (George and Main 1983). Adults therefore communicate not only positive emotions but negative ones as well, and even toddlers respond to and imitate angry behaviors in others. One of Piaget's anecdotes concerned his daughter, who at eighteen months imitated a temper tantrum she had witnessed the previous day. Although Piaget used the example to demonstrate delayed memory, it also illustrates the impact that expression of strong affect has on the very young child.

Maternal Care

Because most mothers are with their infants in the earliest days and usually remain the primary caretakers, they are responsible for providing both physical and emotional sustenance. Good mothers are affec-

tionate, sensitive, compassionate, generous, and growth fostering. They
can separate their own needs from their infants' needs and have age-
appropriate expectations. This is motherhood at its best, and it provides for optimal infant development. However, early mother-child
interactions are not necessarily so joyful. At times they can become a
struggle for survival or, worse, a long nightmare.

Accurate generalizations about good mothering are available. A
widely cited study by Clarke-Stewart (1973) demonstrates the expected
relationship between "optimal mothering" and competence in very
young children. The author studied thirty-eight pairs of mothers and
babies over a period of nine months when the infants were nine to
eighteen months of age. The study consisted of several observational
sessions, questionnaires administered to the mothers, and infant tests.
Clarke-Stewart identified a composite measure of optimal maternal
care that consisted of sensitivity to the infants' physical and social
needs and responsiveness to these "needs and desires immediately and
contingently" (1973, 4). She further described this care as "not only
warm, loving and nonrejecting, but stimulating and enriching visually,
verbally" (1973, 47).

Clarke-Stewart found that competent mothers who were both warm
and intelligent had children whose competence increased from the first
to the last testing session. Optimal mothers who stimulated their infants verbally had infants with advanced verbal and cognitive skills.
Also, mothers who were themselves happy and loving had children
who were smiling and loving. Although her sample was small and the
infants were all firstborn babies of poor mothers, the study still provides compelling evidence that maternal behavior influences development in measurable ways during this early period. We do not know
from this study whether characteristics of the infants also influenced
the mothers, nor do we have extended longitudinal data. Nonetheless,
we do have evidence that "optimal" mothering influences development positively in this early period. These kinds of data can provide
insights into problems in mothering—in the extreme form, child abuse
and neglect—and guide us in finding solutions.

Abusive Mothers and Mothers of Abused Children

The ambiguous title of this section reflects the lack of clarity in the
field. Many of the early studies as well as some of the current ones use
the terms parent and mother interchangeably. Some titles include the
word parents and then refer to mothers, and sometimes the opposite
is true. Professionals working with abused children often find it is not

possible to be certain about the identity of the abuser. Implicitly, if not explicitly, however, mothers are usually blamed when children are hurt or neglected. Although now, as in the past, mothers are the primary caretakers, they are not necessarily responsible for most of the harm done to children.

Kempe's landmark paper "The Battered Child Syndrome" (Kempe et al. 1962) reported the first attempt to establish the incidence of child abuse nationwide. Hospitals and district attorneys were among the respondents. In all, 302 cases of serious abuse were collected. Kempe was interested in characteristics of injured children and their parents. He found that psychiatric dysfunction, low intelligence, poor marital adjustment, and a history of suffering child abuse were typical of the parents who abused their children. Although Kempe indicated that his findings were preliminary, his paper has become the basis for many of the popular beliefs about abusive parents.

Kempe's study spurred much of the early research in the 1970s on child abuse. In a widely cited review of the literature that followed, Spinetta and Rigler (1972) synthesized existing data to draw a profile of high-risk parents so that preventive efforts could be undertaken. However, Spinetta and Rigler found that their data were limited by small samples and poor methodology. Despite these restrictions, they made sweeping conclusions that continued to emphasize psychiatric factors and to minimize social problems like poverty. For example, Spinetta and Rigler cited defective character, deprivation, lack of love, unrealistic expectations (including role reversal), and frustrated dependency needs as typical of the abusive parent. This review, incomplete and vague as it is, continues to be widely quoted.

In 1974 federal legislation established the Child Abuse Prevention and Treatment Act, which included among its mandates a national study of cases of child abuse. The study, conducted in 1979 and 1980 (National Center on Child Abuse and Neglect 1982), solicited information from child protective services, police, courts, schools, hospitals, and mental health clinics. The report also provided considerable data on the abusing parents. Mothers alone accounted for half of the neglect cases, and both parents for an additional 40 percent. However, mothers alone were responsible for fewer than one-quarter of the abuse cases, and fathers or father substitutes, either alone or with the mother, were involved in two-thirds. Stepfathers were disproportionately represented in all categories, particularly in cases of sexual abuse.

One fact that the National Incidence Study demonstrated unequivocally is that mothers are not the primary perpetrators of child abuse. Since fathers or father substitutes are implicated in 63 percent of all abuse and 90 percent of sexual-abuse cases, studies and treatment programs that focus only on mothers overlook a large portion of abusers, including biological fathers, stepfathers, mothers' boyfriends, and other friends and relatives of the family.

Even today, when many more fathers are engaged in child care than took part ten or twenty years ago, all studies indicate that women remain primary caretakers. It is unlikely that men are directly involved in child care more than a small fraction of the time. Therefore their overrepresentation in abuse is all the more noteworthy. The image of the poor minority mother suffering from psychiatric problems and abusing her child is unfounded according to these data.

Contemporary research asks more specific questions about abusive parents and abused children. Researchers and clinicians no longer view abuse and neglect as a monolithic problem. Accordingly, it will never be possible to come up with one profile of the maltreating parent. Parents who neglect their children because they are depressed and have too few emotional, cognitive, or financial resources are clearly different from those who inflict serious injury on their children, and these in turn are quite different from incestuous parents.

For example, one study (Crittendon and Bonvillain 1984) explored six groups of mothers: middle-class–non-stressed mothers, poor mothers, deaf mothers, retarded mothers, abusive mothers, and neglecting mothers. These researchers wanted to find out if observation in a neutral situation could discriminate which mothers were abusive, neglectful, or at risk for abuse or neglect by virtue of factors such as poverty or sensory or intellectual deficits. The characteristic they chose was labeled maternal sensitivity and consisted of the mother's responsiveness to the child, positive affect, contingency responding, and cooperativeness. They derived this cluster of factors from existing studies that related maternal care to child development (Clarke-Stewart 1973). The researchers then studied mothers presenting a variety of risk factors such as poverty, sensory deficit (deafness), and mental retardation. They found that the groups could be ranked on sensitivity. The least sensitive mothers were the neglectful mothers, and the most sensitive were the middle-class–non-stressed mothers. Although the poor and deaf mothers shared certain attributes, as did the retarded, abusive, and neglectful mothers, there were also ways of characterizing each group. Poor mothers were responsive and affectionate but did not respond contingently to their infants. Abusive mothers were actively involved with their babies but were tense and interfering and would sometimes startle and frighten them. The neglectful mothers were withdrawn and uninvolved, showed little or no affection, and initiated few interactions.

Although this study had only ten mothers in each group and rated them on the basis of very short time samples, it does provide clues about behavioral characteristics among different risk groups of mothers. Reflecting the increasing sophistication of studies of abusive parents, it no longer accepts the idea that maltreating parents share attributes, and it separates abuse from neglect. Also using risk status as the independent variable, the researchers administered a standard procedure to see if groups varied in behavior when the situation was not highly stressful. Although limited to maternal behavior, these kinds of data (which focus on measurable factors rather than ambiguous labels) may be useful in predictive studies. They are also very useful for clinicians who are asked to characterize the interactions of mothers and infants.

Supporting Mothers, Protecting Children

In twenty-five years of research on the causes and treatment of child abuse and neglect, many have tried to describe abusive parents and the conditions under which abuse occurs. It is probably true that being a parent has always been both a joy and at times a hardship, but the circumstances of parenting have changed recently. American families now include divorced, unmarried, and remarried mothers (and fathers) as well as traditional married couples. Half of all American children, in the course of growing up, will live in nontraditional homes, though most will still be raised by their biological mothers. Just as myths about the ideal nuclear family persist, so do myths about the failed family. We know that to *treat* families we have to understand the family's ecological context, including specific psychological problems of individual members and social stresses and supports. However, to *prevent* family violence we have to consider social policy issues.

Poverty

Although the role of poverty in abuse and neglect continues to be debated, we now know that reported abuse and neglect occur more frequently among those with incomes under $7,000 per year. Therefore it is likely that the incidence of child abuse could be reduced by guaranteeing that all mothers can pay for the basic requirements of child rearing, including food, health care, and adequate housing.

Some European countries provide a cash allowance to all parents at the time of a child's birth, thereby rendering assistance to the poor. Support for poor families in this country remains highly controversial.

Within the existing structure, however, several solutions would alleviate some of the poverty. These include welfare payments in all states
sufficient to let mothers and children live above the poverty level;
mandatory child-support payments by all employed nonresident fathers; retaining adolescents in high school so that all youngsters become literate and employable; jobs for women; and conditions of
employment that include child care. Although poverty must be alleviated to reduce child abuse and neglect, that does not mean that all
poor people abuse or neglect their children or that only the poor abuse
or neglect their children. However, it is extremely difficult to provide
adequate care for children if suitable housing, food, and health care
are not readily available and affordable.

Health and Nutrition

Among the factors that limit mothers' abilities to provide for children
are inadequate health care and nutrition. Guaranteed health care would
include birth-control information and devices, abortion when un-
planned and unwanted pregnancies occur, prenatal care, and continued
supervision and health care for all children (Rauch 1983). Healthy
children are easier to care for than high-risk children. Children who
fail to thrive and neglected or abused children receiving regular primary care can be recognized before the problems become acute. Federal programs, such as the supplemental food program for women,
infants, and children (WIC), only begin to address the health needs of
new families (Birns and Noyes 1983). A malnourished mother who
gives birth to a premature or low-birth-weight baby is clearly at risk.
When neither mother nor infant receives adequate medical care, the
health risk is compounded.

Education

Maternal education is a key to abuse prevention. Considerable research
has shown that well-educated women are better able to provide for
their children than poorly educated women (Clarke-Stewart 1973;
Hayes 1982; Scarr 1984). Education also increases job skills and the
likelihood of employment. Educated women are more likely to feel
competent as mothers and therefore to be less stressed. They are also
more likely to find suitable resources when problems arise.

    Education on conflict resolution is also needed. Many children learn
violence instead of language as a tool for solving problems. The schools

should provide training in conflict negotiation and resolution. Children should also be educated for parenthood. Just as we legislate and fund training for computer literacy, so we should provide training for child care and family life. Family-life skills include family planning, sex education, contraception, and child care. We could, for example, without any investment of money, require all high-school students to take care of dependent persons, including young children, the elderly, and the handicapped. This kind of experience, for males as well as females, would expose youngsters to the meaning and responsibility of caring for someone else. By reducing violence among our adolescents and exposing them to nurturing activities, we might well prevent violence within future families.

Day Care

Day care is critical for many mothers of infants. The evidence to date (Scarr 1984; Hayes 1982) indicates that children thrive in good day care but not in poor-quality day care, despite the opinions of many professionals who still see day care as antithetical to the best interests of the child (e.g., Fraiberg 1977). Day care is an important support for mothers and children in a variety of ways. For mothers who work to feed and clothe their families, as most do (U.S. Department of Labor 1985), day care can provide a safe, stimulating, nourishing place for their children. For families that are stressed by the illness of one member or other disorganizing factors, day care can offer respite and prevent additional stress.

The quality of day care is highly variable, however. There are no federal standards or even universal state licensing regulations. But rather than condemning day care because of the many problems associated with it, we must legislate licensing and funding for high-quality day care. We require licensing of physicians, teachers, lawyers, bus drivers, and veterinarians. Similarly, those entrusted with infants should also be educated, licensed, and well paid for the important services they render. When day-care workers are as well trained and are paid as much as car mechanics or high-school physical education teachers, day care will improve greatly.

Family Isolation

Family isolation is widely cited for its association with child abuse and neglect. Although this problem may not appear to be a social policy issue and though it would be hard to legislate a ban on it, local initiatives can help alleviate such isolation. For example, before leaving the hospital, all high-risk mothers should be linked with "mother advocates" or home visitors or a new mothers' support group. No mother should leave the hospital without a telephone in her home and a list of doctors, hot lines, family members, and friends to call in times of stress. This kind of preventive service might be far less costly than treating families for whom no supports are available when coping mechanisms fail.

Mothers as Advocates

It is rare that mothers are asked to serve on boards making decisions about how children shall be reared. For example, it is more likely that pediatricians will be asked to testify before Congress on day care than mothers who use or would like to use day-care programs. Head Start is a model in which planners legislated community involvement in the program. Other services for mothers would benefit from having these consumers involved in policy decisions.

Future Research

Since Kempe's 1962 article and the establishment of the National Center for the Prevention of Child Abuse and Neglect in 1974, we have learned a great deal about child abuse and neglect. Sociologists have provided data on the extent of the problem in nonclinical samples, and psychologists and pediatricians have contributed clinical information on abused children and abusive parents, but many questions remain. We still cannot predict which mothers or which fathers, stepfathers, or mothers' boyfriends are going to abuse or neglect children. We know little about the success of the various interventions that have been tried. We need intensive longitudinal studies of couples, single parents, and families living in all the many ways families do live today before we can begin to make sense out of the changing demographic data.

To better understand and help mothers, we also need to address questions to them. We need to allocate some of the money spent on war and space exploration to research on mothers and families. We should ask women about the sources of strength and of strain in bearing and rearing children. Rather than telling women what is in their and their children's best interests, we need to ask mothers themselves what enhances and what inhibits the joy motherhood can bring.

Mothers may well continue to be the primary caretakers of their children, but as Keniston (1977) wrote in the Carnegie Commission Report, all American families need help. Those of us working with abused children see the failures of the system. Rather than blaming mothers, we need to increase our support for the most difficult and possibly most rewarding job of raising children. Social policy must reflect knowledge as well as the opinions of experts about the mother's role in child development. Many different environments can produce well-functioning, mature adults. There is a great deal we can do to make motherhood, parenthood, and childhood less traumatic and violent.

References

Ainsworth, M. D. S. 1969. Object relations, dependency and attachment: A theoretical review of the infant-mother relationship. *Child Development* 40:969–1025.

Arney, W. R. 1980. Maternal-infant bonding: The politics of falling in love with your child. *Feminist Studies* 6:548–67.

Barrera, M. E.; Rosenbaum, P. L.; and Cunningham, C. E. 1986. Early home intervention with low-birth-weight infants and their parents. *Child Development* 57:20–33.

Birns, B. 1965. Individual differences in human neonates' responses to stimulation. *Child Development* 30:249–56.

Birns, B., and Golden, M. 1972. Prediction of intellectual performance at three years on the basis of infant tests and personality measures. *Merrill-Palmer Quarterly* 18:53–58.

Birns, B., and Noyes, D. 1983. Child nutrition: The role of theory in the world of politics. *International Journal of Mental Health* 12(4):22–42.

Bowlby, J. 1952. *Maternal care and mental health.* Geneva: World Health Organization.

———. 1958. The nature of the child's tie to his mother. *International Journal of Psychoanalysis* 39:350–73.

———. 1982. Attachment and loss: Retrospect and prospect. *American Journal of Orthopsychiatry* 52:664–78.

Brazelton, T. B. 1986. Issues for working parents. *American Journal of Orthopsychiatry* 56:14–25.

Chess, S. 1982. The "blame the mother" ideology. *International Journal of Mental Health* 11:95–107.

Clarke, A. M., and Clarke, A. D. B., eds. 1976. *Early experience: Myth and evidence.* New York: Free Press.

————. 1979. Early experience: Its limited effect upon later development. In *The first year of life: Psychological and medical implications of early experience*, ed. D. Shaffer and J. Dunn. New York: John Wiley.

Clarke-Stewart, K. A. 1973. Interactions between mothers and their young children: Characteristics and consequences. *Monographs of the Society for Research in Child Development* 38:27–32.

Crittendon, P. M., and Bonvillain, J. D. 1984. The relationship between maternal risk status and maternal sensitivity. *American Journal of Orthopsychiatry* 54:250–56.

Cummings, E. M.; Ianotti, R. J.; and Zahn-Waxler, C. 1985. Influence of conflict between adults on the emotions and aggression of young children. *Developmental Psychiatry* 21:495–507.

Department of Social Services, Commonwealth of Massachusetts. 1986. Memorandum on foster care policy, 29 May.

Egeland, B., and Vaughn, B. 1981. Failure of "bond formation" as a cause of abuse, neglect and maltreatment. *American Journal of Orthopsychiatry* 51:78–84.

Fraiberg, S. 1977. *Every child's birthright: In defense of mothering.* New York: Bantam Books.

George, C., and Main, M. 1983. Social interactions of young abused children: Approach avoidance and aggression. *Child Development* 50:306–18.

Green, R. 1982. The best interests of the child with a lesbian mother. *American Journal of Psychiatry and the Law Bulletin* 10(1):56–59.

Hayes, B. 1982. Influence of parent's work on child school achievement. In *Families that work: Children in a changing world*, ed. S. Kamerman, and B. Hayes. Washington, D.C.: National Academy Press.

Kagan, J. 1984. *The nature of the child.* New York: Basic Books.

Kempe, C. H.; Silverman, F. N.; Steele, B. F.; Droegemueller, W.; and Silver, H. K. 1962. The battered child syndrome. *Journal of the American Medical Association* 181:17–24.

Keniston, K. 1977. *All our children.* New York: Harvest.

Klaus, M. H., and Kennell, J. H. 1976. *Maternal-infant bonding: The impact of early separation or loss on family development.* Saint Louis: Mosby.

————. 1982. *Parent-infant bonding.* Saint Louis: Mosby.

Kotelchuck, M. 1976. The infant's relationship to the father. In *The role of the father in child development*, ed. M. E. Lamb, 329–44. New York: John Wiley.

Kulchova, J. 1972. A report on futher development of twins after severe and prolonged deprivation. Cited in Clarke and Clarke (1976).

Lamb, M. E.; Thompson, R. A.; Gardener, W. P.; Charnov, E. L.; and Estes, D. 1984. Security of infantile attachment as assessed in the "strange situation": Its study and biological interpretation. *Behavioral and Brain Sciences* 7:127–71.

National Center on Child Abuse and Neglect (NCCAN). 1981. *Study findings: National Study of the Incidence and Severity of Child Abuse and Neglect.* Washington, D.C.: U.S. Department of Health and Human Services.

Pruett, K. 1983. Infants of primary nurturing fathers. In *The psychoanalytic study of the child*, ed. A. Solnit, 38. New Haven: Yale University Press.

Rauch, H. 1983. Child health policy and developmental continuity. *International Journal of Mental Health* 12(4):43–58.

Ramey, C. T.; Yeates, K. O.; and Short, E. J. 1984. The plasticity of intellectual development: Insights from preventive intervention. *Child Development* 55:1913–25.

Scarr, S. 1984. *Mother care other care.* New York: Basic Books.

Schaffer, H. R., and Emerson, P. E. 1964. The development of social attachments in infancy. *Monographs of the Society for Research in Child Development* 29.

Spinetta, J. J., and Rigler, D. 1972. The child abusing parent: A psychological review. *Psychology Bulletin* 4:296–304.

Sroufe, L. A. 1985. Attachment classification from the perspective of the infant caregiver relationships and infant temperament. *Child Development* 56:1–14.

Steele, B. F., and Pollock, C. B. 1974. A psychiatric study of parents who abuse infants and small children. In *The battered child*, ed. R. E. Helfer and C. H. Kempe. Chicago: University of Chicago Press.

Svejda, M. J.; Campos, J. J.; and Emde, R. 1980. Mother-infant "bonding": Failure to generalize. *Child Development* 51:775–79.

Tizard, B. 1977. *Adoption: A second chance.* London: Open Books.

———. 1979. Early experience and later social behavior. In *The first year of life: Psychological and medical implications of early experience*, ed. D. Shaffer and J. Dunn. New York: John Wiley.

U.S. Congress, Congressional Budget Office. 1985. *Reducing poverty among children.* Washington, D.C.: U.S. Government Printing Office.

U.S. Department of Labor. 1985. Women's Bureau fact sheet.

Vaughn, B.; Egeland, B.; and Sroufe, L. A. 1979. Individual differences in infant-mother attachment at twelve and fifteen months: Stability and change in families under stress. *Child Development* 50:971.

Waters, E. 1978. The reliability and stability of individual differences in infant-mother attachment. *Child Development* 51:208–16.

Winnicott, D. W. 1968. The relationship of a mother to her baby at the beginning. In *The family and individual development*. London: Social Science Publications.

Zahn-Waxler, C.; Radke-Yarrow, M.; and King, R. A. 1979. Child rearing and children's prosocial initiations towards victims of distress. *Child Development* 50:319–30.

2 The Maltreatment of Infants

HOWARD DUBOWITZ AND
HARWOOD EGAN

Infants are vulnerable to maltreatment in some unique ways, owing to several inherent characteristics of infancy. Small size and limited mobility alone put them at risk for serious physical injury, as is borne out by the incidence data (American Humane Association 1986). Infants also lack the cognitive and psychological mechanisms to fend for themselves.

An "ecological" perspective on maltreatment provides a broad view of variables that place an infant at risk. Although infants might unintentionally contribute to their maltreatment, for example, through crying inconsolably, more important contributory factors reside in the context of their families, the community, and the society they live in (Belsky 1980; Garbarino 1977; Newberger and Newberger 1981). This understanding enhances our professional ability to support families in nurturing their infants.

Definitions of the Maltreatment of Infants

In the pluralistic United States, there exists only modest consensus regarding the definitions of child abuse and neglect. Different states, professional disciplines, public agencies, and political persuasions have conceptualized this problem in varying ways. Pragmatic considerations

32

have been important, so that where resources are limited, thresholds for intervention are raised and many cases of probable abuse are screened out. Different forms of abuse and neglect are frequently categorized in these groupings: physical abuse, psychological abuse, physical neglect, psychological neglect, sexual abuse, and societal maltreatment. Although this taxonomy has its uses, particularly for research, the acts are rarely so discrete in real life. For example, excessive spanking has a psychological impact beyond the bruises it may cause. Indeed, the physical signs could well be minor relative to the anxiety and fear engendered.

Physical Abuse

An act that injures an infant is considered physical abuse. At times this is intentional, but more commonly it is committed by a distraught parent who fails to control angry and aggressive impulses. Cigarette burns or multiple fractures are unambiguous examples. Professional concern tends to focus on physical injuries, though most would agree that any spanking, aside from the gentlest tap on the hand, is inappropriate and abusive of the young infant. There exists the inevitable "gray zone" where, for example, roughhousing with an infant could result in injury. If the behavior is not seen as intended to hurt, however, the injury is often diagnosed as "accidental." If ignorance or carelessness is responsible, the action could be seen as neglectful.

Certain cultural practices have defied easy judgment and categorization. For example, it is a popular practice in Middle Eastern cultures for parents to place hot glasses on the backs of their sick infants and children (Asnes and Wisotsky 1981). A negative pressure results as the glass and the trapped air cool, and the suction makes perfectly round purplish bruises, several centimeters in diameter. This is believed to extract the evil spirits responsible for the illness. In the United States this might not generally be seen as abusive, but the treatment would be actively discouraged by health care professionals.

Physical Neglect

Abuse is typically considered an act of commission; neglect, an act of omission. Through ignorance or oversight, the physical needs of the infant might be neglected. Appropriate nutrition and satisfactory health care are widely recognized as fundamental needs, and failure to provide them is seen as physical neglect. In addition, there is an area that falls between commission and omission. Some health-related habits of the pregnant mother are known to harm the developing fetus. An example is the abuse of alcohol, which is thought to impede growth and lead to several congenital anomalies and mental retardation known as fetal alcohol syndrome (Clarren and Smith 1978). The reporting laws in several states mandate that infants born with this syndrome be reported to protective services. Cigarette smoking, however, which also retards fetal growth and affects the airways of young children, has not been construed as a form of abuse or neglect.

A recent development in the area of medical neglect concerns the treatment of handicapped newborn infants. The original Baby Doe was an infant born in Indiana in 1982 with Down's syndrome and a serious congenital defect known as a tracheoesophageal fistula (an abnormal connection between the main air and food pipes). Although medical treatment was available, the parents and the attending physicians concluded that the quality of life expected would be dismal, and they decided to withhold treatment. This decision was unsuccessfully contested in the county circuit court, and the baby died at six days of age. Public concern over the death of Baby Doe led to the involvement of President Reagan, the attorney general, and the Department of Health and Human Services in the area of infant medical care. The appropriate management of such seriously handicapped infants was debated for the ensuing two and a half years by the federal agencies, medical organizations, and citizens' groups and entailed several court proceedings (American Academy of Pediatrics 1985).

Traditionally, these formidable dilemmas of when to treat multiply handicapped infants aggressively and when to resist "heroic" measures have been resolved by parents together with health care providers. Failure to treat these infants is now seen as medical neglect, and the 1985 reauthorization by Congress of the Federal Child Abuse and Neglect Act delegates the oversight of their care to the state child protective agencies. Hospitals are advised to have infant care review boards to guide staff in using "reasonable medical judgment," and states are required to include this area of medical neglect in their programs and procedures for child abuse and neglect. Foreseeably, a report of allegedly inappropriate care will then be investigated by the local child protective agency. In June 1986 the United States Supreme Court rejected the Department of Health and Human Services' intent to rely upon section 504 of the Rehabilitation Act to authorize federal involvement. Although protective service agencies are not barred from intervening, future public policy for multiply handicapped infants remains unclear.

An additional issue of neglect that is gaining public attention is the plight of the homeless in America. More than one-quarter of the homeless population includes families with young children (Coalition for the Homeless 1985; Committee on Government Operations 1986). Adequate shelter is indubitably a critical need of an infant, and failure to provide this could reasonably be considered physical neglect. Attention, however, has been narrowly focused on the behavior of parents or caregivers, and where culpability has been difficult to assign, such cases are typically not construed as constituting neglect or abuse.

Psychological Abuse

Psychological abuse refers to parental behavior that is believed to damage the child's emotional well-being (Kavanagh 1982; Garbarino 1978). Inappropriately high expectations and demands of an infant illustrate what is seen as psychologically abusive. A rejecting parent who repeatedly communicates angry feelings toward the infant is another example.

Child mental health professionals might well consider certain caretaking behaviors damaging to the optimal psychological development of the child. Child protective agencies, however, typically require that a deleterious impact on the child be demonstrated, and be attributable to the abusive behavior, before the case is substantiated as one of psychological abuse. This cause-and-effect pattern is usually very difficult to prove, particularly for infants. Consequently, psychologically abused infants who receive attention from child protective agencies tend to be flagrant cases, often involving serious parental psychopathology or, more frequently, also including other forms of abuse and neglect.

Psychological Neglect

Psychological neglect includes acts of omission that lead to neglect of the child's vital psychological needs (Whitney 1976). For example, infants require affection and cuddling for comfort when upset. Over time, this fosters a sense of security and trust. However, if caregivers are suffering from postpartum depression or illness, they will be less able to respond to babies' cues, and the infants might then fail to thrive as a result of such emotional neglect. As with psychological abuse, child protective agencies require that infants manifest behavior problems directly attributable to the deficiencies in care, and they generally become involved only in severe cases or when other forms of abuse and neglect coexist.

In the United States people take a wide range of approaches to child rearing, so professionals need to be cautious and open minded before being certain that a parental behavior is harmful to a child. However, Polansky's work suggests that there is significant consensus on what people from different backgrounds in the United States consider neglectful (Polansky and Holly 1977).

Sexual Abuse

Even infants are occasionally victims of sexual abuse. Recently, numerous instances of the sexual abuse of children in day-care settings have been uncovered, and while we lack precise estimates of the extent of the problem, we do know that very young children can be sexually misused. Most of such cases entail fondling, digital manipulation of genitalia, and the intimate approximation of adult and infant genitals rather than the more severe forms of abuse involving penetration. Occasionally the presenting signs are those of one of the sexually transmitted diseases such as gonorrhea or chlamydia. The abuse of infants for the production of pornographic materials and for prostitution has also been reported (Campagna 1985). The issue of inappropriate exposure to adult sexual behavior or to pornography, which is significant concerning older children, is less salient during infancy.

Societal Maltreatment

When we consider the needs of infants, there are instances of abuse and neglect in the United States that cannot be attributed to parents' behavior. Societal maltreatment is reflected in practices that are widely pervasive and often institutionalized. One example is the relatively high United States infant mortality rate. Despite the ready availability of "state of the art" neonatal intensive care units in the United States, the probability that a live newborn will celebrate his or her first birthday is higher in sixteen other countries. The increased infant mortality rate among minorities and low socioeconomic groups has also been amply demonstrated (Wise et al. 1985). Mediating factors are thought to include inadequate prenatal care, poor maternal nutrition, and other health-related habits of the mother during pregnancy. Access to prenatal care is an important problem in certain regions; there are areas where a pregnant woman might have to travel a substantial distance to find a source of prenatal care that accepts Medicaid. In most states the federal WIC program, which aims to provide adequate nutrition for poor pregnant women, infants, and young children, reaches fewer than half of those who are eligible (Children's Defense Fund 1986). Impoverished families who cannot feed their children have recently been documented across the country (Physician Task Force on Hunger in America 1985).

There are other examples of societal maltreatment. Families without homes living on the streets, were mentioned earlier. The overwhelmed and underfunded state child protective agencies similarly reflect a failure by our society to seek adequate long-term solutions to some major social and family problems. The lack of guaranteed access to health care for all children in the affluent United States is surely another form of societal neglect of infants. Moreover, as defense spending increases, critical social and health programs are compromised. This too must be seen as reflecting distorted national priorities. Our society, its leaders, and the child protective agencies have yet to confront this realm of societal abuse and neglect.

Infants' Needs

The chain of events leading to maltreatment of infants begins with basic needs that are unique to the infant's physical and psychological state. Maintaining health requires the interaction of biological, psychological, sociological, and anthropological factors (Kleinman 1980).

Physical Needs

Perhaps the most obvious requirement of infancy is physical health. To attain this goal, standards for health care delivery have been established by the American Academy of Pediatrics. For example, a schedule of immunizations over the first two years helps protect against diseases such as polio, measles, mumps, and pertussis.

The infant's rapid growth in head size, length, and weight demands proper nutrition. Infant malnutrition is well recognized in impoverished areas, consequent to both lack of food and inadequate education about nutrition. Standardized growth curves enable health care providers to identify infants at risk for less than optimal growth and to intervene early.

Regular visits to a doctor help ensure good health in other ways. Screening for anemia, lead poisoning, hearing and vision problems, metabolic diseases, and certain infections diminishes morbidity. Chronic iron-deficiency anemia, for example, has been associated with otitis media, poor feeding, and hyperactivity (Oski 1985). Regular monitoring of an infant's development might also help a physician identify a neurological problem and lessen the impact of developmental delay by a referral to an early-intervention program.

Sick infants often need immediate medical attention because they are especially vulnerable to serious infections (e.g., meningitis, pneumonia) with potentially devastating consequences. Proper care demands access to appropriate medical treatment. Attention to basic hygiene and sanitary housing that is warm, uncrowded, and free of rodents and other hazards are important for maintaining health. Lead poisoning associated with chronic intellectual impairment is still a problem in many urban areas.

Injuries are the leading cause of death among children beyond the first year of life (Alpert 1985). As infants mature, households need to be checked for hazards like electrical outlets and medicine bottles. Supervision by a responsible adult who can anticipate dangerous situations and take measures to ensure the child's safety is essential.

Social-Emotional Needs

Fulfilling the infant's need for love and security is essential to healthy emotional growth. To do this, caregivers must accept their infants unconditionally and recognize their strengths as well as their weaknesses. A consistent and dependable environment is the foundation for developing self-esteem and the ability to care for others in future relationships.

Flexible environments that can respond to an infant's changing needs promote growth better than those that are restrictive. Although most children do well in homes that are warm and caring, the infant at three months of age demands a different interaction than the infant at nine months. Caregivers also need to adapt to children's changing developmental patterns over time. Failure to make this adjustment can lead to the breakdown of an infant-parent relationship.

High-Risk Parents

Infant care in this culture is largely provided by the parents. Parenting is a complex process influenced by social and cultural circumstances as well as by attributes of the individual child and parent (Lewis and

Rosenblum 1974; Kohn 1969; Garbarino 1976). Recent thinking about the origins of parents' behavior suggests the importance of a maturational process involving the development of awareness (Newberger 1980). Parental awareness is "an organized knowledge system with which the parent makes sense out of the child's responses and behavior, and formulates policies to guide parental action" (Newberger 1980, 47).

Parenting also requires understanding child development. Sameroff and Feil (1984) propose that this understanding may range from a primitive "symbiotic" level to a level where the child is viewed as a separate individual. Specific deficits in parents' capacities to respond empathically and flexibly to their infants' needs may be a factor in abusive situations (Belsky 1980). Parenting is thus not an inherent ability but derives from a variety of sources including maturation, psychological health, and personal history.

Adolescent Parents

Adolescents have long been viewed as high-risk parents. The increased incidence of premature delivery and other health-related problems for adolescent parents is well documented (McMarney 1985). Although the incidence of child maltreatment by adolescents is high, recent studies show that this may largely reflect environmental factors and lack of family support (Bolton, Laneb, and Hane 1980; Kinard and Klerman 1980). Psychological readiness is also important. Often the psychological needs of the adolescent mother, which include forming an independent identity, may undermine her ability to care for her infant's individual needs. The constraints of crowded housing and limited finances further impinge upon the adolescent's ability to be responsible and assertive. The increasing demands of the maturing infant may also overwhelm the teenage parent, creating additional feelings of jealousy and inadequacy (Adelson and Fraiberg 1980).

Psychological Illness

Few studies claim that a particular psychological illness is directly associated with infant maltreatment. Nevertheless, mental health does have a bearing on the quality of parenting and developmental outcome (Zahn-Waxler and Radke-Yaudm 1984; Beardslee et al. 1983; Kempe et al. 1962). Emotionally disturbed parents can overload infants with inappropriate stimulation or can understimulate them, depending upon the nature of the disturbance. Infants of depressed parents may show abnormal patterns of social interaction as early as three months (Tronick, Cohn, and Shea 1984). Aside from being unavailable and inconsistent, the emotionally disturbed parent may misinterpret an infant's cues for care and interaction, perhaps leading to problems in feeding and sleeping (Pollit, Eichler, and Chan 1975). Parents with thought disorders may attribute unrealistic feelings and motivations to their babies, responding to their own fears rather than the infants' needs. For example, persistent crying might be viewed as harassment rather than as a genuine need for attention.

Personal Background

The personal history an adult brings to the parent role is also important. The literature on abusive parenting suggests that a lack of training with good role models during childhood contributes to a restricted view of child rearing later on and increases the likelihood of abuse or an aberrant response to the demands of caregiving (Steele and Pollock 1974; Park and Collmer 1975). One prospective study indicated that the deficient nurture a mother reported receiving during her childhood was the most consistent predictor of "nonorganic" failure to thrive, a condition associated with poor growth and developmental delay in an otherwise normal infant (Altemeir et al. 1979). As a corollary, positive early child-care experiences promote prosocial nurturing behavior. By contrast, observing aggression or being maltreated may contribute to the adoption of aggressive strategies for coping with parent-child conflicts (Bandura 1973; Feshback 1973; Straher and Jacobson 1981). Research has also suggested that exposure to modeled aggression increases one's tolerance for violence (Berkowitz 1974).

High-Risk Infants

The infant is no longer viewed as being shaped simply by environment. Recent attention has focused on attributes of infants that help determine the level of care they receive (Campos et al. 1983). Individual characteristics such as temperament, physical attractiveness, and intelligence are important variables "that promote differential reactions in other people which feed back to affect further development" (Berger 1985). Such attributes may affect parents' responsiveness, determine the infant's ability to cope with stress, and influence the range of enjoyable sensory experiences. Owing to neurological, maturational, physiological, and physical problems, some infants proceed along different developmental pathways. As a result, such infants are frequently more demanding than their healthy peers.

Temperament

The characteristic style with which infants interact with their environments is commonly referred to as temperament (Rutter 1980). Inherent qualities such as level of energy, liability of mood, intensity of action, persistence, and distractability shape infants' responses to situations such as eating, sleeping, and playing (Carey 1974; Thomas and Chess 1977). In turn, their behavior influences the perception parents develop about them and indirectly the care they receive. Babies who are difficult to soothe, are hyperactive, and cry frequently may generate attitudes and actions that diminish parents' responsiveness. Of particular concern is the infant with a "difficult" temperament (Thomas, Chess, and Bikorn 1982). Described as irregular, avoidant, intense, and slow to adapt, these children demand special qualities of organization and patience in their caregivers. The observed risk for developmental problems, however, while partly constitutional, may also reflect the cumulative effect of adverse parental responses (Bates 1983).

Physical Handicaps

Some authors report a higher incidence of abuse in infants with congenital anomalies (Holman and Kenwar 1975; Glaser and Bentovim 1979; Groce, this volume). Coping with a disabled infant is a long-term task, and physical disability can greatly stress any parent. Some important aspects of disability that could be associated with abuse include its being present at birth (e.g., cleft palate); being life threatening (e.g., congenital heart disease); leading to permanent handicap (e.g., cerebral palsy); substantially interfering with normal routines (e.g. blindness); and distorting physical appearance (e.g., harelip) (Sahin 1979). Becoming attached to an unattractive infant can be extremely hard for parents. A prolonged adverse response to the child's appearance may be an initial indication of difficult parent-infant relations (Bouokydis 1981). A physical handicap may signify failure to the family whose child is perceived as less attractive than they or society are comfortable with (Salvia, Sheare, and Algozine 1975). The grief and sorrow parents suffer may undermine their ability to nurture and to attend to the special needs of their handicapped child. Disabled infants may also have trouble initiating and reacting to communication, which in turn may diminish parents' attempts to communicate. Finally, financial demands and inadequate support systems can add to the stress of the family struggling to accept and manage the long-term nature of an infant's disability. (For a more thorough discussion of disability and abuse, see Groce, this volume.)

Developmental Delay

Developmental delays range from severe intellectual impairment secondary to chromosomal anomalies or serious birth asphyxia to more subtle impairments noted in infants born prematurely or small for gestational age. These infants are probably overrepresented in the population at increased risk for maltreatment (Klein and Stearn 1971). A delayed infant may appear dull, uninterested, and expressionless and may fail to respond with engaging eye contact or clear expressions of enjoyment such as smiling (Gorski, Davidson, and Brazelton 1979; Cicchetti and Sroufe 1976). Parents need to extend themselves more than with the average infant, helping the baby to organize attention and become emotionally engaged (Als, Lester, and Brazelton 1984). Parents have to learn to accept delays in fully differentiated expression, such as laughter, as well as in the appearance of expected developmental milestones (Emde, Gaensbauer, and Harmon 1976). Realizing these limitations often brings disappointment, which may in turn lead to parental withdrawal, apathy, and rejection.

Chronic Illness

Some infants' physical health is jeopardized by congenital problems (e.g., immune deficiency, heart disease) or chronic illnesses developed after birth (e.g., recurrent ear infections, food intolerance). A significant relationship between illness and subsequent maltreatment has recently been demonstrated (Sherrod et al. 1984; Glaser and Bentovim 1979). Hospitalizations, doctor visits, medications, and special diets can leave little time for other aspects of child rearing. Parents may come to view their infants as "sickly," vulnerable, and different, thereby undermining normal parent-infant interaction (Solnit and Provence 1979). In addition, poor growth and delayed development associated with chronic illness can diminish parents' confidence and contribute to a reciprocal process in which both parent and infant "fail to thrive" (Bradley and Casey 1986).

Sociocultural Risk

Support Systems

Social support systems (e.g., marriage, family, neighborhood, work) embedded within a particular cultural context greatly influence the quality of infant care parents provide (Bronfenbrenner 1979). A recent study showed that mothers who had few social supports were less responsive to irritable infants (Crochenberg 1985). These same infants at one year of age were less securely attached to their mothers. Similarly, other studies have demonstrated that supportive environments can diminish the risk associated with adolescent parents (Kinard and Klerman 1980). We might hypothesize that we nurture best when we ourselves are receiving adequate support.

Isolation is cited frequently as a characteristic of abusive families (Garbarino 1976, 1977). Since marriage is the usual source of parental support, single parents are at greater risk for being socially isolated and are possibly more prone to abuse. The continuous demands of infant care can be overwhelming for a parent alone; geography may preclude an extended family's helping with child care. Day care may be too expensive to permit a single parent to work outside the home, and single parents who do work may have too little time to form relationships outside the home. "Role reversal," in which the parent turns to the child for affection, love, and support, is likely to result in neglect of the infant's needs and in parental anger and frustration owing to hopelessly high expectations. Although social isolation may be partly a function of personality disturbances, frequent moves and impoverished neighborhoods may also limit opportunities for social exchange and support (Garbarino and Stocking 1980; Cochran and Broussard 1979).

However, marital discord has also been cited as a common problem within families of abused children (Ory and Earp 1980). Parents' conflict can undermine their confidence as well as diminishing the coping skills needed for stressful situations. Violence between parents is also associated with more abusive forms of child discipline (Feshback 1973; Steinmetz 1977). The infant may become a scapegoat, seen as the reason for a difficult transition into parenthood and thus engendering resentment, frustration, and anger.

Work

For the modern family, the intrusion of parents' work patterns into
family relationships, social activities, and child rearing is a common
problem (Bronfenbrenner and Crouter 1982). The workplace can exert
indirect influence on infant care in a number of ways. Long working
hours may keep parents isolated from each other, and so friends at
work, if available, may become the parent's only sources of support
(Cotterel 1986). Work hours may further conflict with family routines,
leaving working parents little time to spend with their children. Work
schedules and traditional roles also tend to establish one parent, usually the mother, as largely responsible for all child care. Geographical
moves for employment are common and can contribute to isolation by
separating parents from their extended families. Finally, some parents
are severely strained because either they need to work though they do
not want to or they struggle with career and parenting conflicts
(Brazelton 1986).

Unemployment also appears to be an important stressor contributing to infant maltreatment. One study that followed economic change
in two metropolitan areas over a thirty-month period found a significant correlation between reported child abuse and a decline in the
work force (Steinberg, Catalano, and Dooley 1981). In Gil's (1970)
analysis of thirteen thousand cases of abuse, nearly half of the fathers
had been unemployed in the year preceding the abuse, and secondary
analysis of the data found that unemployment was the most significant
factor distinguishing between abusive and nonabusive families. Most
of the research in this area suggests an association between infant
maltreatment and unemployment, probably mediated by family stress.

Cultural Risk

Given the significant incidence of child maltreatment in the United
States, it is necessary to look beyond individual families and examine
influences within American society. The "culture of violence" is both
a major health threat and a way of life for many American children.
Nielsen index figures indicate that by the time of graduation from high
school, the average child will have viewed fifteen thousand hours of
television, including eighteen thousand murders, compared with eleven
thousand hours of formal classroom instruction. The association between viewing violence and increased aggressive behavior has been well
documented (Bandura 1973). Violent television programs reflect the
cultural approval if not enjoyment of violence in United States society.

Another indication of the pervasive acceptance of violence is the large number of parents who use physical punishment to discipline even infants. These data, together with statistics of violent crime in the United States, lend credence to the epigram that "violence is as American as apple pie."

Cultural values are important in determining community standards of acceptable child-rearing practices, and they also influence interpersonal relationships within families. Broad values alone cannot explain the etiology of child maltreatment, but they do contribute to it. Given a stressful family situation, a "difficult" child, and an overwhelmed parent, child maltreatment is more likely in the midst of a violent society.

The following case illustrates how an ecological approach helps redefine our understanding of risk and guides intervention efforts.

Brent was the first child for Mr. and Mrs. C. She was thirty-two years old and a nurse's aide, he was thirty-one and a carpenter. They had been married two years. Mrs. C's pregnancy was complicated only by mild hypertension. Brent was born without difficulty but weighed only four pounds. Like other babies born small for gestational age, Brent had difficulty feeding and was slow to gain weight (infant characteristics). His mother continued to nurse him. At two months of age Brent developed gastroenteritis and was hospitalized owing to a significant weight loss. He was discharged after a week with instructions to feed him slowly and to use a supplemental formula (extra demand on family).

At about the time of Brent's hospitalization Mr. C lost his job (paternal unemployment). Hoping he could find work in the lumber industry, the couple moved to Washington, leaving both their families behind (loss of social supports). Lack of health insurance led Mrs. C to delay Brent's medical follow-up. Mr. C refused Medicaid. At about five months Brent was brought to a local emergency room with vomiting and diarrhea. He was extremely underweight for his age. His poor growth, developmental delay, and extreme irritability led to hospitalization with the diagnosis *failure to thrive*. Mr. C was against the hospitalization, feeling that it was too expensive and that Brent would eat *when he was ready* (parent-child difficulties). Brent remained in the hospital three weeks. During this time he gained some weight.

Following his discharge, social services became involved, and Brent was enrolled in an early intervention program in the next town (social supports put in place.) Both parents seemed pleased with their participation in the program. In addition to receiving some guidance about Brent's hypersensitive nature and feeding difficulties, Mrs. C regularly attended a parent-support group one night a week. Follow-up with the pediatrician showed that Brent was gaining weight, becoming less irritable, and starting to attain expected developmental milestones. After about two months Mrs. C returned to evening work as a nurse's aid, but her husband was still unemployed, since the lumber industry was economically depressed.

Within a few weeks, negative changes were noticed in Brent and his mother at the early intervention center. Mrs. C looked tired and apathetic and expressed little enthusiasm about Brent's progress. Brent was more irritable and seemed to avoid social interaction. In the parent-infant group, Mrs. C seemed unusually frustrated with Brent's failure to respond to her attempts to get his attention. At one point she shook him, saying he was stubborn just like his father. As a result of these concerns, a social worker attempted to make a home visit. Mrs. C refused. When the social worker said she would have to report this to child protective services, Mrs. C allowed her to visit. Mrs. C later revealed that she was embarrassed and afraid people would think she was *unfit* to take care of Brent. She believed that Brent's failure to thrive was her fault and that there was little she could do. It was soon learned she and Mr. C had separated owing to marital discord subsequent to his depression over being unemployed (parental conflict). A teenager baby-sat in the evening while Mrs. C worked. She voiced resentment toward Brent for needing so much attention (single parent). At night when she needed to sleep he would be up crying. She was exhausted and unable to bring him to the early intervention center.

At the suggestion of the social worker, temporary foster placement was arranged (social intervention). This allowed Mrs. C to continue working as well as to bring Brent to the early intervention center. The next month Mr. C finally found employment, and he and Brent returned to the family to live together (economic solvency). Over the following months Brent made considerable developmental progress and continued to grow.

Toward Preventing the Maltreatment of Infants

Currently, intervention is undertaken if child maltreatment is documented by one of the designed protective agencies. Few services are available for the family struggling to cope or the infant at high risk until a report of actual abuse or neglect is substantiated, despite evidence that primary prevention approaches can be effective (Olds et al. 1986). Experts in the field have increasingly drawn attention to the need to develop and implement effective preventive strategies (Cohn 1983).

Infancy is a period especially amenable to primary prevention. During prenatal care, labor and delivery, and much of the infant's first year, the family has extensive contact with health care professionals.

This presents a good opportunity for identifying high risk situations and instituting supports. The interest and excitement around a new baby enable families to accept helpful and constructive services, providing a *window of receptivity*. In addition, early intervention can help the family make a healthy start and diminish the likelihood of later difficulties. Prevention efforts should include the following:

1. Medical, social, and nutritional services in the perinatal period. Currently, fewer than 50 percent of families eligible for nutritional support through the federal women, infants, and children program (WIC) receive this service (Children's Defense Fund 1986). Diminishing the morbidity and mortality associated with high-risk pregnancies requires adequate prenatal care for all pregnant women. As a consequence, several risk factors for infant maltreatment (prematurity, parent-child separations, physical handicaps) can be diminished.

2. Health, social, and educational interventions for handicapped infants and their families following discharge from the newborn intensive care unit. These infants should be considered at risk for maltreatment (Soloman 1979). Through the Baby Doe legislation, the federal government has registered its concern for the optimal care of these babies. This commitment should be extended beyond the first few months of life as their high-risk status continues.

3. Home visitation by professionals, which appears to be an effective early intervention program that is also likely to be cost effective. For example, in one program, prenatal and infancy home visitation by nurses was provided to first-time mothers who were either teenagers, unmarried, or of low socioeconomic status. Though they were among the women at highest risk for caregiving dysfunction, those mothers who were visited by a nurse were implicated in fewer instances of substantiated child maltreatment during the first two years of the baby's life than those who were not visited. In addition, these mothers reported more positive perceptions of their infants and less use of physical punishment than did the comparison groups (Olds et al. 1986). A variation of this model is employing a nonprofessional but skilled mother (or father) with good parenting experience to make home visits to support and guide the family. The home visitor, in turn, is supervised by a professional, such as a public health nurse, knowledgable in the health and developmental needs of infants. During this period the visitor performs a valuable screening function. When support no longer seems necessary, visits are terminated. If problems are evident the service is continued, adding the appropriate interventions. It is not surprising that this service is more likely to be accepted, since it provides support for a family without the stigma associated with abuse (Kempe 1976).

4. Day care, parenting groups, and other community resources. Many families struggle to balance their commitment to their infants with the need or wish to work outside the home (Brazelton 1986). Day care also benefits parents who do not work outside the home but find continuous child care stressful. Good-quality, affordable day care is needed particularly by lower-income families. Parenting groups that offer guidance on child rearing and an opportunity to develop a social network address both the deficits in parenting skills and the social isolation that contribute to infant maltreatment.

5. Education of parents, and especially parents-to-be, in child development and child rearing. The structural changes in the nuclear family and the decreased availability of the extended family have left new young parents, who lack experience and knowledge, without valuable educational resources. Teenagers who become pregnant are even less well equipped to be parents. School systems could play a useful role by incorporating parent training into their curricula. Sex education and family-planning resources might lead to fewer unwanted babies. Television could be used more creatively to offer prospective parents credible role models and supply valuable information about the real work of caring for a developing infant. Public-awareness campaigns can inform parents of the resources available in their communities to assist them in parenting and in coping with difficulties. The media have not fulfilled their vast potential to educate families about child maltreatment and, perhaps more important, about parenting and child development in general.

6. Evaluation of the early intervention programs that exist to learn what works, for whom, and in what circumstances.

7. Improved diagnostic services. Professionals responsible for children need to be better educated to recognize the signs of maltreatment. In the first year or two of life this primarily involves physicians, nurses, and day-care staff. Once indentified, these infants should be reported to the protective agency responsible so that the appropriate interventions can be made. The quality of work performed by child protective agencies must be improved. In large part this relates to inadequate funding and difficult working conditions. It is hardly ethical to screen for and identify maltreated children without the resources to be of assistance. Competent community-based treatment services for children and their families are woefully lacking in many areas. Quality day care, exemplified by the Head Start program, provides a valuable respite for stressed parents and offers children a stimulating and supportive environment. Family support services are also needed to assist parents in times of acute stress. Crisis care programs should offer twenty-four-hour access to telephone and in-person counseling

and ideally should include crisis baby-sitters and nurseries or the option of a temporary homemaker. Beyond the crisis period, many families need longer-term services. Individual, couple, group, and family therapy is also a necessary community resource.

8. Change in social policy. Finally, and most important, we need to recognize the importance of supporting families so they can nurture and protect their children adequately. This priority should be incorporated in federal and state policies and programs that should be sensitive to the needs of families. This would acknowledge the importance of the family as the critical environment for children. It is important that at the national level we should actively pursue strategies to strengthen American families. Although many federal policies and programs directly or indirectly affect families, there is a need for a concerted effort, such as a department of family policy, to coordinate these endeavors and to act as advocates for families when their well-being is in jeopardy. Important areas for consideration include: day-care facilities at the workplace, employment strategies that decrease the number of the unemployed, guaranteed access to health care for pregnant women, infants, and children, paid maternity and paternity leave, and welfare benefits that do not require the father's absence from the home. Infants, children, families, and American society would be the beneficiaries.

References

Adelson, E., and Fraiberg, S. 1980. An abandoned mother and abandoned baby. In *Clinical studies in infant mental health: The first year*, ed. S. Fraiberg. New York: Basic Books.

Alpert, J. 1985. Injuries and injury prevention. In *Pediatric clinics of North America*. Philadelphia: W. B. Saunders.

Als, H.; Lester, B.; and Brazelton, T. B. 1984. Dynamics of the behavioral organization of the premature infant: A theoretical perspective. In *The high risk newborn*, ed. T. Field. New York: Spectrum.

Altemeir, W. A.; Vietze, P. M.; Sherrod, K. B.; and Sandler, H. M. 1979. Prediction of maltreatment during pregnancy. *Pediatrics* 18:205–18.

American Academy of Pediatrics. 1985. *Recent governmental action regarding the treatment of seriously ill newborns*. Elk Grove Village, Ill.: American Academy of Pediatrics.

American Humane Association. 1986. *Highlights of official child neglect and abuse reporting: 1984*. Denver: American Humane Association.

Asnes, R. S., and Wisotsky, D. H. 1981. Cupping lesions simulating child abuse. *Journal of Pediatrics* 99:267–86.

Bandura, A. 1973. *Aggression: A social learning analysis*. Englewood Cliffs, N.J.: Prentice-Hall.

Bates, J. E. 1983. The concept of the difficult temperament. *Merrill-Palmer Quarterly* 26:269–319.

Beardslee, W.; Bemporad, J.; Keiler, M.; and Klerman, G. 1983. Children of parents with major affective disease. *American Journal of Psychiatry* 7:825–32.

Belsky, J. 1980. Child maltreatment: An ecological integration. *American Psychologist* 35:320–25.

Berger, M. 1985. Temperament and individual differences. In *Child and adolescent psychiatry*, ed. M. Rutter. Oxford: Blackwell.

Berkowitz, E. 1974. Some determinants of impulsive aggression. *Psychological Review* 81:165–76.

Bolton, F. G.; Laneb, H. R.; and Hane, B. S. 1980. Child maltreatment risk among adolescent mothers: A study of reported cases. *American Journal of Orthopsychiatry* 30:489–503.

Boukydis, Z. 1981. Adult perception of infant appearance: A review. *Child Psychiatry and Human Development* 2(4): 241–54.

Bradley, H. R., and Casey, P. M. 1986. A transitional model of failure to thrive: A look at misclassified cases. In *New directions in failure to thrive: Implications for research and practice*, ed. D. Drotar. New York: Plenum.

Brazelton, T. B. 1986: Issues for working parents. *American Journal of Orthopsychiatry* 56:14–25.

Bronfenbrenner, U. 1979. *The ecology of human development*. Cambridge: Harvard University Press.

Bronfenbrenner, U., and Crouter, P. C. 1982. Work and family through time and space. In *Families that work: Children in a changing world*, ed. S. B. Hammerman and C. D. Haye, 39–83. Washington, D.C.: National Academy Press.

Campagna, D. 1985. The economics of juvenile prostitution in the U.S.A. *International Children's Rights Monitor* 2(1): 15.

Campos, J.; Barrett, K.; Lamb, M.; Goldsmith, H.; and Stenberg, M. 1983. Social emotional development. In *Handbook of child psychology*, ed. P. Mussen. New York: John Wiley.

Carey, W. B. 1974. Nightwaking and temperament in infancy. *Journal of Pediatrics* 84:756–58.

Children's Defense Fund. 1986. *A children's defense budget*. Washington, D.C.: Children's Defense Fund.

Cicchetti, D., and Rizley, R. 1981. Developmental perspectives on the etiology, intergenerational transmission, and sequelae of child maltreatment. In *New directions in child development: Developmental perspectives on child maltreatment*, ed. R. Rizley and D. Cicchetti. San Francisco: Jossey-Bass.

Cicchetti, D., and Sroufe, L. A. 1976. The relationship of affective and cognitive development in Down's syndrome infants. *Child Development* 47: 920–29.

Clarren, S. K., and Smith, D. W. 1978. The fetal alcohol syndrome. *New England Journal of Medicine* 298:1063–67.

Coalition for the Homeless. 1985. *A crying shame: Abuse and neglect of homeless infants*. New York: Coalition for the Homeless.

Cochran, M., and Broussard, J. 1979. Child development and personal social networks. *Child Development* 50:601–16.

Cohn, A. H. 1983. *An approach to preventing child abuse.* Chicago: National Committee for Prevention of Child Abuse.

Committee on Government Operations, U.S. House of Representatives. 1986. *Homeless families: A neglected crisis.* Washington, D.C. Government Printing Office.

Cotterel, J. L. 1986. Work and community influences on the quality of child rearing. *Child Development* 57(2): 326–74.

Crochenberg, S. R. 1985. Infant irritability, mother responsiveness and social support influences on security of infant mother attachment. *Child Development* 52:857–65.

Emde, E. N., and Brown, C. 1978. Adaptation after the birth of a Down's syndrome infant: A study of six cases. *Journal of the American Academy of Child Psychiatry* 17:299–323.

Emde, R. N.; Gaensbauer T. J.; and Harmon, R. J. 1976. Emotional expression in infancy: A biobehavioral study. *Psychological Issues* 10(1), Monograph 37.

Emde, R. N.; Katz, L. E.; and Thorpe, J. H. 1978. Emotional expression in infancy: II. Early deviation in Down's syndrome. In *The development of affect,* ed. M. Lewis and L. Rosenbloom. New York: Plenum.

Feshback, N. D. 1973. The effects of violence in childhood. *Journal of Clinical Psychology* 2:284–393.

Garbarino, J. 1976. A preliminary study of some ecological correlates of child abuse: The impact of socioeconomic stress on mothers. *Child Development* 47(1): 178–85.

———. 1977. The human ecology of maltreatment: A conceptual model for research. *Journal of Marriage and the Family* 39:721–31.

———. 1978. The elusive "crime" of emotional abuse. *Child Abuse and Neglect* 2:89–99.

Garbarino, J., and Sherman D. 1980. High risk neighborhoods and high risk families: The human ecology of child maltreatment. *Child Development* 51:188–98.

Garbarino, J., and Stocking H. S. 1980. *Protecting children from abuse and neglect.* San Francisco: Jossey-Bass.

Gil, D. G. 1970. *Violence against children: Physical abuse in the United States.* Cambridge: Harvard University Press.

Glaser, D., and Bentovim, A. 1979. Abuse and risk to handicapped and chronically ill children. *Child Abuse and Neglect* 3:565–75.

Gorski, P. A.; Davidson, M.; and Brazelton, T. B. 1979. Stages of behavioral organization in the high risk neonate. *Seminars in Perinatology* 3(1): 61–71.

Holman, R. R., and Kenwar, S. 1975. Early life of the battered child. *Archives of Diseases in Childhood* 50:78–80.

Kavanagh, C. 1982. Emotional abuse and mental injury. *Journal of the American Academy of Child Psychiatry* 21(2): 171–77.

Kempe, C. H. 1976. Approaches to preventing child abuse: The health visitor concept. *American Journal for Diseases of Children* 130:941–47.

Kempe, C. H.; Silverman, F. M.; Steele, B. F.; Droegemuller, W.; and Silver, H. K. 1962. The battered child syndrome. *Journal of the American Medical Association* 17:17–24.

Kinard, E. M., and Klerman, L. V. 1980. Teenage parenting and child abuse. *American Journal of Orthopsychiatry* 50(3): 481–89.

Klein, M., and Stearn, L. 1971. Low birth weight and the battered child syndrome. *American Journal of Diseases of Childhood* 122:15–18.

Kleinman, A. 1980. *Patients and healers in the context of culture: An exploration of the borderland between anthropology, medicine, and psychiatry.* Berkeley and Los Angeles: University of California Press.

Kohn, M. L. 1969. *Class and conformity: A study of values.* Homewood, Ill.: Dorsey Press.

Lewis, M., and Rosenblum, L. A., eds. 1974. *The effect of the infant on its caregiver.* New York: John Wiley.

McMarney, L. 1985. Adolescent pregnancy and childbearing: New data. *Pediatrics* 75:973–75.

Morris, M., and Gould, R. 1963. Role reversal: A necessary concept in dealing with the battered-child syndrome. *American Journal of Orthopsychiatry* 33:298–99.

Newberger, C. M. 1980. The cognitive structure of parenthood: Designing a descriptive measure. *New Directions for Child Development* 7:45–67.

Newberger, C. M., and Newberger, E. H. 1981. The etiology of child abuse. In *Child abuse and neglect*, ed. N. S. Ellerstein, 11–20, New York: John Wiley.

Olds, D. L.; Henderson, C. R.; Tatelbaum, R.; and Chamberlin, R. 1986. A randomized trial of nurse home visitation. *Pediatrics* 78:65–78.

Ory, M. G., and Earp, J. L. 1980. Child maltreatment: An analysis of familial and institutional predictors. *Journal of Family Issues* 1:339–50.

Oski, F. A. 1985. Iron deficiency, facts and fallacies. In *Pediatric clinics of North America.* Philadelphia: W. B. Saunders.

Park, R., and Collmer, C. 1975. Child abuse: An interdisciplinary review. In *Review of child development and research*, vol. 5, ed. E. M. Heatherington. Chicago: University of Chicago Press.

Physician Task Force on Hunger in America. 1985. *Hunger in America: The growing epidemic.* Middletown, Conn: Wesleyan University Press.

Polansky, N., and Holly, C. 1977. *Profile of neglect: A survey of the state of knowledge.* Washington, D.C.: Department of Health, Education, and Welfare.

Pollit, E.; Eichler, A. E.; and Chan, C. K. 1975. Psychological development and behavior of mothers of failure to thrive children. *American Journal of Orthopsychiatry* 45(4): 525–37.

Rutter, M. 1980. Temperament: Concepts, issues and problems. In *Temperamental differences in infants and young children*, ed. G. M. Collins, 286–92. London: Pitman.

Sahin, S. T. 1979. The physically disabled child. In *High risk parenting: Nursing assessment for families at risk*, ed. S. B. Hall Johnson. Philadelphia: Lippincott.

Salvia, J.; Sheare, J. B.; and Algozine, B. 1975. Facial attractiveness and personal and social development. *Journal of Abnormal Child Psychology* 3:171–78.

Sameroff, A. J., and Feil, L. A. 1984. Parental concepts of development. In *Parental belief systems: The psychological consequences for children*, ed. I. E. Sigel. Hillsdale, N.J.: Lawrence Erlbaum.

Sherrod, K. B.; O'Conner, S.; Vietze, P. M.; and Altemeir, W. A. 1984. Child health and maltreatment. *Child Development* 55:1174–83.

Solnit, A. J., and Provene, S. 1979. Vulnerability and risk in early childhood. In *Handbook of infant development*, ed. J. Osofsky. New York: John Wiley.

Soloman, G. 1979. Child abuse and developmental disabilities. *Developmental Medicine and Child Neurology* 21:101–6.

Steele, B., and Pollock, C. B. 1974. A psychiatric study of parents who abuse their infants and small children. In *The battered child*, 2nd ed, ed. R. E. Helfer and C. H. Kempe. Chicago: University of Chicago Press.

Steimetz, S. 1977. The use of force for resolving family conflict: The training ground for abuse. *Family Coordinator* 26:19–26.

Steinberg, L. D.; Catalano, R.; and Dooley, D. 1981. Economic antecedents of child abuse and neglect. *Child Development* 52:975–85.

Straher, G., and Jacobson, R. S. 1981. Aggression, emotional maladjustment and empathy in abused children. *Developmental Psychology* 17:762–65.

Thomas, A., and Chess, S. 1977. *Temperament and development.* New York: Brunner Mazel.

Thomas, A.; Chess, S.; and Bikorn, S. J. 1982. The reality of different temperament. *Merrill-Palmer Quarterly* 28:1–20.

Tronick, E. Z.; Cohn, J.; and Shea, E. 1984. The transfer of affect between mothers and infants. In *Affective development in infancy: Advances in infant development and behavior*, ed. M. Yogman and T. B. Brazelton. New York: Ablex.

Whitney, L. 1976. Defining emotional neglect. *Child Abuse and Neglect* 5(1): 2–5.

Wise, P.H.; Kotelchuck, M.; Wilson, M. L.; and Mills, M. 1985. Racial and socioeconomic disparities in childhood mortality in Boston. *New England Journal of Medicine* 313:360–66.

Zahn-Waxler, C., and Radke-Yaudm, M. 1984. Affective arousal and social interaction: Young children of manic depressive parents. *Child Development* 55:112–21.

T W O   *Childhood and*
               Adolescence

3   The Interpersonal Legacy of Physical Abuse of Children

STEPHEN R. SHIRK

One of the basic tenets of a developmental approach is that the present is placed in the context of the past and the future (Wenar 1982). However, among developmentalists there exists a long-standing debate regarding the significance early experience has for later development (Clarke and Clarke 1976; MacDonald 1985; Sameroff 1975). In recent years this debate has emerged in the context of the maltreatment of children (Elmer 1977; Sameroff and Chandler 1975). Although there is considerable consensus among clinicians that child abuse constitutes a formidable developmental hazard, there appears to be less agreement about its enduring effects. The primary task of this chapter is to consider the impact of physical abuse on social development in early and middle childhood. Of central concern is the connection between children's exposure to physical abuse and their subsequent experience of and behavior in interpersonal relationships.

Toward a Developmental Model of the Sequelae of Child Abuse

Thirty years ago, Heinz Werner (1957, 126) maintained that "wherever development occurs it proceeds from a state of relative globality and lack of differentiation to a state of increasing differentiation,

57

articulation, and hierarchic integration." Werner's orthogenetic principle has been invoked primarily to describe the behavioral and intellectual development of children and adults, but it appears equally descriptive of the evolutionary history of psychological constructs. Child abuse is a case in point. The process of understanding child abuse began when Kempe and his colleagues distinguished inflicted injuries from noninflicted accidental injuries to children and labeled them the "battered child syndrome" (Newberger and Newberger 1982). Since this early global conceptualization of child abuse, the problem has been studied in much greater detail.

Perhaps the most notable advance in understanding child abuse has been the increasing recognition that maltreatment of children is a heterogeneous problem. As Cicchetti and Rizley (1981) pointed out, differentiation of maltreatment "types" stands in sharp contrast to a concept of child abuse based on the assumption that variations in maltreatment are part of a single continuum and differ only in severity. Guided by the assumption of heterogeneity, recent research has begun to distinguish and compare children with different maltreatment histories (Cicchetti and Rizley 1981; Egeland and Sroufe 1981). For example, Egeland and Sroufe (1981) identified four patterns of maltreatment in their high-risk samples: physically abusive, hostile/verbally abusive, psychologically unavailable, and neglectful. Based on this differentiation of the child abuse construct, different patterns of etiology and outcome have been articulated (See, e.g., Egeland and Sroufe 1981; Bauer and Twentyman 1985; Wolfe et al. 1985).

Although discriminating among maltreatment "types" represents a significant conceptual advance, the resulting description is essentially static and omits a developmental dimension. Such a typology assumes that variations in child outcome can be largely accounted for by type and intensity of maltreatment. For example, we might expect higher levels of aggressive behavior from a physically abused child than from a chronically neglected child. Specific types of abuse are assumed to have equivalent effects at different points in development.

Such a concept appears to embrace what Kendall (1984) called the "developmental uniformity myth." In criticizing nondevelopmental models of child therapy, Kendall, Lerner, and Craighead (1984) argue that treatments designed for "children" ignore important developmental differences and result in therapy that is less than optimal, since the category "children" comprises diverse individuals with extremely varied cognitive abilities, emotional capacities, and behavioral repertoires. Consequently, the "same" treatment applied at different points in development is not likely to produce uniform effects. Analogously, the "same" type of maltreatment experienced at different points in development is not likely to produce uniform outcomes. Just as maltreatment is heterogeneous, so "children" are far from homogeneous. An explicit developmental concept of child abuse requires differentiating both types of abuse and types of children.

How does "type" of abuse interact with "type" of child? More specifically, in what way does developmental level mediate the impact of physical abuse? It appears that mediation can be framed in three ways: first, developmental differences in the *experience* of abuse; second, differential *outcomes* resulting from developmental differences at the time of abuse; and third, developmental differences in the *expression* of enduring distress resulting from abuse.

From a cognitive-developmental perspective, children's experiences of maltreatment are shaped not only by the type and intensity of abuse, but also by their own level of development. Traditional positions on the growth of intelligence cast the developing child in a more passive role. Nativism endows the child with innate categories into which sensory stimulation is channeled. Empiricism provides virtually no endowment but a blank slate and subjects the child to the environment. Piaget (1968, 1970) recast the role of the child by asserting that individuals actively participate in the "construction" of experience. In Piaget's framework, knowing an object entails a cognitive action or operation. Consequently, experience is not simply a copy of the "objective" properties of the world but results from an interaction between cognitive operations and "objective" events. The *meaning* of an event does not reside in the event itself but depends on the active interpretation of a knowing subject. Because children at various developmental levels have qualitatively different cognitive tools for interpreting events, the "same" event is likely to produce qualitatively distinct meanings for children at different ages. Piaget focused largely on the development of logical-physical concepts such as space, time, and causality, but in recent years cognitive-developmentalists have applied Piaget's model to children's understanding of the social world (cf. Flavell and Ross 1981; Leahy 1983; Selman 1980).

The cognitive-developmental perspective entails a number of important implications for understanding children's experience of abuse. Among the most important is the notion that children at different developmental levels will experience their maltreatment in qualitatively different ways. Consequently it is likely that they will reconstruct their experience of abuse in distinctive manners. For example, Piaget (1932) proposed that between early and later childhood there is a shift in conceptions of justice and morality. For the younger child, whose relationships are characterized by unilateral respect, parental authority defines right or wrong actions. Thus, the younger child may be more likely to experience abuse by parents as "justified" and possibly deserved. Similarly, a preschooler whose causal reasoning is colored by egocentrism is likely to understand physical abuse in a way that contrasts with the ideas of a preadolescent who possesses less egocentric causal schemata. The preschooler may overattribute the abuse to his or her own actions, whereas the preadolescent may consider other situational or interpersonal causes. Moreover, it is likely that these qualitatively different cognitive constructions of abuse will produce different emotional reactions. Recent clinical research on depression and other affective disorders reveals that each emotion is characterized by distinctive sets of cognitions (Beck 1976; Leahy 1985). For example, for the preschooler who attributes physical abuse to his or her own behavior, guilt may figure more prominently in the affective response than it would for the preadolescent. Therefore the enduring effects of maltreatment are likely to differ, in part, because of developmental differences in children's experience of abuse.

Developmental level is also likely to mediate the enduring effects of abuse for other reasons. From an organizational perspective, each phase of development is characterized by a pivotal task (Erikson 1968; Sroufe and Waters 1977). Perhaps the best-known example of this developmental model is Erikson's (1968) epigenetic stage theory. According to Erikson, development proceeds through a predetermined sequence of "nuclear crises." Each crisis represents a pivotal task or turning point in the development of personality. For example, the pivotal task of infancy is to establish basic trust in others. Developing autonomy is the task of toddlerhood, followed by the growth of initiative and self-reliance in the preschool period. In the elementary-school years, industry and competence represent the pivotal tasks. For Erikson each task is a crisis not because it produces storm and stress for the developing child, but because its resolution leaves an enduring mark on the emerging personality.

Egeland and Sroufe (1981) outlined a sequence of five developmental tasks children face between infancy and kindergarten. These include modulating physiological arousal, forming an attachment relationship, object mastery, autonomous problem solving, and forming peer relationships. Maladaptation in later development is linked to incomplete mastery of these early tasks. Moreover, continuity of adaptation can be defined in terms of relative competence or incompetence across the series of developmental tasks (Egeland and Sroufe 1981).

Consistent with the organizational model is the theory of sensitive periods, which postulates that during certain age periods organisms are most vulnerable to environmental stimulation (MacDonald 1985).

At these times the organization of specific behaviors is relatively more susceptible to environmental influences. Although heightened sensitivity to the environment may serve an adaptive function, it also implies greater vulnerability to disruption. Different sets of behavioral competencies are more vulnerable at different points in development rather than being equally vulnerable across the life span. Thus behaviors associated with an age period's pivotal task should be most susceptible to environmental influence, and disruptions of different developmental tasks should have different behavioral outcomes. From this perspective, the characteristic sequelae of physical abuse should depend upon which developmental task was disrupted by trauma. For example, the enduring effects of physical abuse experienced at age two and at age five are likely to be quite different. At age two, object mastery and autonomous problem solving are pivotal tasks. Characteristic sequelae might include heightened dependency or diminished curiosity. By contrast, at age five the formation of peer relationships is prominent. Traumatic disruption of this developmental task might result in enduring social incompetence or aggression toward peers. From a developmental perspective, the diversity of outcomes found among physically abused children can be partially accounted for by the developmental phase during which they were abused.

The third way developmental level mediates the enduring effects of physical abuse is through reorganizing *symptomatic expressions* of trauma or distress. From this perspective children can be expected to express psychological distress in a manner consistent with their developmental level (Leahy 1985). That is, symptoms of distress are not simply a function of type of trauma or type of conflict but are influenced by the child's level of development. For example, among emotionally disturbed school-age children, the expression of internalized symptoms such as guilt or sadness is related to social-cognitive level (Posner 1983). Children at higher levels of role taking and moral development are more likely to express their distress as *thought symptoms* than are less advanced peers, who are more likely to do so in *action symptoms*. As Posner (1983) noted, symptoms are expressed in a manner consistent with the child's level of development. From this perspective, the enduring effects of physical abuse can be expected to take different forms as the child develops. Distress expressed as disruptive behavior in the preschool child may give way to self-reproach in later childhood. In essence, growth involves a kind of *developmental symptom substitution*. Although the underlying distress may endure, its expression will change with development.

Similarly, Egeland and Sroufe (1981) proposed that maladaptation across the life span will be expressed developmentally. Over time, a child's symptoms will reflect the critical tasks of a given age period. For example, children abused in infancy can be expected to show disrupted attachment relationships. By kindergarten the enduring effects of early trauma will be expressed in disrupted peer relationships. Each developmental period introduces a new challenge for which the physically abused child has been compromised. Early trauma reduces the child's ability to master developmental tasks and is expressed in a predictable sequence of symptoms.

In summary, a developmental approach to child abuse requires both the discrimination of "types" of abuse and a differentiation of "types" of children. Children are far from homogeneous. Consequently, to understand the impact of physical abuse on children, we must consider how developmental level influences the experience, expression, and enduring effects of physical abuse.

Children's Social Development and Physical Abuse

An assumption common to most developmental theories is that the course of individual growth is marked by increasing adaptation to the demands of the social world (Leahy 1985). Among the most formidable changes during the preschool and elementary-school periods is the dramatic expansion of the child's social world. Although the family remains a prominent social context during this period, relationships with peers and with adults outside the family grow more important.

A number of studies have shown that the frequency of social interactions with peers increases substantially during late toddlerhood (Mueller and Brenner 1977). Sequential measures have revealed that during the preschool period there is a significant rise in the complexity and length of such interactions (Guralnick and Weinhouse 1984). During this period there are marked changes in various forms of group relations, including cooperative play (Parten 1932). Rubin, Watson, and Jambor (1978) have shown that this trend continues into kindergarten, with kindergarteners engaging in more group dramatic play than preschoolers. Entrance into elementary school is marked by social exchanges organized around games and more complex tasks (Asher, Oden, and Gottman 1981).

In recent years there has been growing recognition of the significance of childhood social relations for adult mental health. Unpopular children, for example, are more likely to be disproportionately represented later in life in mental health settings (Cowen et al., 1973). Roff, Sells, and Golden (1972) reported a highly positive relationship between low peer acceptance and later delinquency. In fact the consequences of rejection by peers may be more severe than the consequences of low achievement (Cowen et al., 1973). It appears, then, that forming and maintaining relationships outside the family is a pivotal developmental task during the preschool and early school years.

Heightened aggressiveness is frequently cited as one of the enduring, and most serious, effects of child physical abuse (Martin and Beezley 1977), particularly for boys. Early formulations focused on defensive reversals to account for this effect (Galdston 1965). More recently, social learning models have emphasized modeling and imitation in explaining abused children's aggressive behavior (Patterson 1982). A third and noteworthy hypothesis is that abused children's aggressive behavior is mediated by developmental deficits in social cognition and associated lags in their social skills.

Social Cognition

Researchers have recently begun to distinguish three domains of social cognition: moral, societal, and psychological. According to Smetana (1983), the moral domain has been defined as a prescriptive system that focuses on how individuals ought to behave toward others. The societal domain refers to knowledge of social relations, including the conventions that regulate social interaction. Finally, the psychological domain refers to conceptions of persons, including knowledge about thoughts, feelings, and motives.

Models of social-cognitive development share the basic assumption that social understanding is derived from experience in social interaction. Social-learning formulations generally assume that children acquire social knowledge through observational learning in social exchanges (Mischel and Mischel 1976). By contrast, cognitive-developmental models postulate that social understanding results from an interaction between the child's conceptual structures and the structure of the social environment and not directly from learning or maturation (Kohlberg 1969). From this perspective the development of social cognition is best seen as an ongoing process in which the child constructs and tests social conceptions in relation to personal, social encounters (Furth 1978). Finally, both social-learning and cognitive-developmental theories maintain that social cognitions regulate social behavior.

Given the assumption that social cognition develops through social interaction, distortions in abused children's social cognition may result from the disturbed interactions that characterize abusive families. For example, Barahal, Waterman, and Martin (1981, 509) hypothesized that "parallels might exist in the ways in which abusive adults and their children view and feel about themselves, others, and their environment." Based on findings that showed social-cognitive deficits among abusive parents, they predicted that abused children would display a comparably troubled pattern. By contrast, Frodi and Smetana (1984) suggested that abusive social interactions might improve some aspects of social cognition. For example, abused children's social sensitivity might be more advanced than other children's because of their need to monitor adult behavior closely in order to protect themselves. In other words, abusive social interactions might not exert a uniform effect on all aspects of social cognition. A second hypothesis regarding the relation between abusive interactions and children's social cognition involves the role of general intelligence in the growth of social understanding. Previous research has indicated that various measures of social cognition are related to mental age (Leahy and Shirk 1984). Moreover, studies have shown that abuse frequently diminishes intellectual attainment (Barahal, Waterman, and Martin 1981). Consequently, abused children may also evince delays in social cognition because of global intellectual deficits.

One area of social cognitive development that has attracted research is the growth of social sensitivity among abused children. Rothenberg (1970) defined social sensitivity as the ability to accurately perceive and comprehend the feelings and motives of others. In a normative study of elementary-school children, Rothenberg (1970) found that social sensitivity increased with age and was positively related to intelligence. Moreover, children who were highly sensitive were rated more positively by teachers and peers on social adjustment. Camras, Grow, and Ribordy (1983) compared a small sample of abused and nonabused children on their ability to identify facial expressions of emotion accompanied by interactional cues. Abused children were matched with comparison children on age, sex, and race. Mean age for the sample was five years. Results indicated that abused children were less accurate than nonabused children in discriminating emotional expressions. There was a trend (statistically nonsignificant) suggesting that abused children had greater difficulty identifying happiness than anger. As Camras, Grow, and Ribordy (1983) pointed out, previous research has found lower frequencies of positive interactions in abusive families than in nonabusive ones. Abused children may be less frequently exposed to positive expressions of affect and as a result have more trouble discriminating expressive cues of happiness. A second finding was that teachers perceived abused children as less socially competent than comparison children. Camras, Grow, and Ribordy (1983) concluded that abused children's problems in recognizing emotion may be central to their peer difficulties.

Frodi and Smetana (1984) argued that the inferior performance of maltreated children on measures of social cognition may be due to differences in general intelligence. In a study of abused children's ability to discriminate others' emotional expressions, they compared abused children with neglected children and two "normal" comparison groups. One comparison group was matched with the abused group on IQ, while the other was composed of children with above-average IQs. All children were between three and five years of age. Overall, they found that nonabused children with higher IQs demonstrated the greatest ability to discriminate emotional expressions. However, the performance of abused children did not differ from that of the IQ-matched comparison group. As Frodi and Smetana caution, the inferior performance of abused children on social cognitive tasks may not be *directly* attributable to their abusive histories. Instead, their social-cognitive deficits may be linked to general intellectual deficits. Physical abuse may *indirectly* affect social cognition by compromising basic intellectual functions. Of course this hypothesis could be tested by comparing abused and nonabused children of high and low intelligence.

In a study of the social-cognitive styles of abused children, Barahal, Waterman, and Martin (1981) attempted to isolate the contribution of IQ from that of abuse. They compared a group of abused children with a carefully matched group of nonabused children. The mean age in the sample was seven and a half years. Along with other measures of social cognition, they assessed social sensitivity. Their findings indicated that abused youngsters were less able to identify emotional expressions than were controls. This effect was only moderately diminished when IQ scores were covaried with social-sensitivity scores. Therefore these results suggest that the experience of abuse has a unique effect on children's ability to discriminate and identify emotions, an effect that cannot be attributed to general intellectual deficits.

How are the differences in these findings to be reconciled? Though all studies used the same measure of social sensitivity, the mean ages for the children in the samples differed. In the Frodi and Smetana (1984) study, where no effect was found, children were younger than in those where appreciable differences were found. Thus it could be that deficits in social sensitivity do not become significant until the early school years. That is, whereas nonabused children's social sensitivity increases with age, abused children show a slower rate of development, resulting in a relative deficit by elementary school.

In addition to measuring social sensitivity, Barahal, Waterman, and

Martin (1981) found that abused children were more egocentric than nonabused children; that is, they had greater difficulty in taking another's perspective. It has been postulated that role-taking ability underlies a range of social-cognitive activities including moral reasoning, empathic understanding, and comprehension of social interaction (Feffer 1970; Selman 1980). Given their finding of greater egocentrism among abused children, it is not surprising that Barahal, Waterman, and Martin (1981) also found abused children less able to comprehend and integrate social roles. In this connection, Straker and Jacobson (1981) found that abused children were significantly less empathic than nonabused children. Although some of the group differences were attenuated in the study by Barahal, Waterman, and Martin (1981) when IQ was covaried, abused children appear to be more egocentric and less sensitive to social and emotional cues than their nonabused counterparts.

Barahal, Waterman, and Martin (1981) also compared abused and nonabused children on a measure of perceived locus of control. As a construct, locus of control refers to beliefs about the causal locus of events—that is, whether outcomes are within one's control. Barahal, Waterman, and Martin (1981) hypothesized that compared with controls, abused children would perceive the cause of events as external rather than as a consequence of personal action. Results clearly showed that abused children were more likely to believe events were beyond their control, particularly when the events were unpleasant or frustrating. As Barahal, Waterman, and Martin (1981) pointed out, these beliefs may be adaptive in the face of distressing and unpredictable family circumstances. However, their overgeneralization could contribute to a sense of helplessness and depression.

These studies indicate that physically abused children have deficits in a variety of social-cognitive skills. In recent years there has been growing recognition of the significance of age-adequate social cognition for effective social interaction (Berndt 1981; Kendall 1984). For example, Ford (1982) found that socially competent adolescents show greater social-cognitive resources than their less-competent peers. In particular, empathy is a salient characteristic of socially competent adolescents. Similarly Waterman et al. (1981) found that behaviorally disturbed boys demonstrate inferior skills in perspective taking. Although the foregoing studies of abused children did not relate social-cognitive abilities to social competence, research on normal and emotionally disturbed children suggests that social-cognitive deficits may contribute to peer problems.

One area of social cognition that could directly influence the social behavior of abused children is the development of behavioral standards. As Smetana, Kelly, and Twentyman (1984) contended, given the importance of standards in self-regulation, it is important to determine whether abused children develop different standards of behavior than nonabused children. Specifically, they investigated how children who were abused, neglected, or not maltreated judged the permissibility of conventional and moral transgressions pertaining to physical harm, psychological distress, and unfair distribution of resources. The investigators hypothesized that children who had experienced extended abuse or neglect might be sensitized to issues of justice or welfare and thus view transgressions as less permissible than other children. Results only partially supported this hypothesis. Abused children regarded transgressions involving psychological distress as more universally wrong for others than did neglected children, but children who were abused, neglected, or not maltreated did not differ in their judgments about physical harm. The authors concluded that, at least in terms of judgments, children who have been abused do not appear to internalize different standards for behavior (Smetana, Kelly, and Twentyman 1984). The absence of group differences in moral judgment is consistent with the reasoning. It is not clear whether the absence of significant group differences is due to the insensitivity of the measures or to other factors that promote moral development in abused children. It is possible that subsequent positive interactions offset the impact of early maltreatment upon moral reasoning.

Research on abused children's social cognition reveals that the effect of physical abuse is not uniform across domains of social cognition. However, these studies indicate that abused children do show deficits in several critical areas of social reasoning. Most notable are delays in social-cognitive skills that are thought to be essential for understanding social exchanges. However, one of the limitations of existing research has been the emphasis on social-cognitive constructs that are closely related to developmental level.

The use of measures related to developmental level is based on a *deficit model* of psychopathology. Differences between abused and nonabused children are understood primarily in terms of relative delays or advances. What this model fails to consider is that group differences may reflect *distortions* in social cognition. That is, abused children's social reasoning may be qualitatively different from that of their nonabused peers not because of developmental delays, but because of qualitative differences in social experience. For example, expectations for the behavior of caregivers may differ significantly for abused and nonabused children. Such a difference would result not from a delay in normative development, but from the experience of atypical social interactions. Dodge (1980) made a similar distinction in the study of childhood aggression. In contrast to a developmental deficit model, which postulates a relationship between inappropriate aggression and *lags* in social cognition, Dodge (1980) proposed that aggressive children show systematic biases or distortions in their social-cognitive processes. His results indicate that a critical difference between aggressive and nonaggressive boys involves a *bias* in causal attributions that cannot be readily understood as a developmental delay, thus suggesting that it may be fruitful to consider both developmental deficits and characteristic distortions in abused children's social cognition.

A second limitation of existing research is the absence of studies relating social cognition to social behavior among abused children. Results showing deficits in areas of social cognition that are assumed to be essential for social adaptation are consistent with the hypothesis that abused children's peer problems are rooted in social-cognitive difficulties. As Gottman, Gonzo, and Rassmussen (1975) pointed out, however, deficits in social cognition should not be equated with social-skill deficits simply because their manifest content is social and because older children perform better than younger children. Instead, it is important to relate performance on social-cognitive tasks to some measure of social success such as peer acceptance. Research relating abused children's social cognition to their social behavior is clearly needed.

Social Competence and Peer Interaction

The peer interactions of physically abused children are frequently described in the language of maladaptation. Abused children have been characterized as passive or withdrawn (Martin and Beezley 1977) or as negative and oppositional (Kempe and Kempe 1978). Studies of toddlers who have been physically abused reveal disturbances in early interactions with peers. For example, Main and George (1985) found that abused toddlers often reacted to the distress of a peer with physical attack or anger rather than with the concern or sadness frequently observed among nonabused toddlers. Although subsequent positive interactions may remedy the effects of abuse, these children appear to be at risk for peer problems in early and middle childhood.

Research on the relation between physical abuse and peer interaction has been guided by several hypotheses. The first is derived from attachment theory. According to this model, the earliest attachment relationship is a prototype for later social relationships (Bowlby 1969). Disruptions in early attachment resulting from abusive interactions should cause subsequent problems with peer relationships (Egeland

and Sroufe 1981). A second hypothesis is derived from social-learning theory. Abusive and coercive exchanges between parents and children provide a fertile context for observational learning. Abusive families model maladaptive forms of social exchange that children imitate and use on peers (Patterson 1982). A third hypothesis, advanced by Howes and Espinosa (1985), is less direct. Noting that several studies of abusive parents have reported isolation from social supports, they argued that abusive parents may contribute to maladaptive interactions with peers because their children lack essential social experiences with others. Consequently these children have few opportunities to engage with others and develop basic social competencies. In summary, all three models share the assumption that the experience of abuse will interfere with the development of peer competence.

Research on the relation between physical abuse and peer interaction among preschool and school-age children is rather limited. Jacobson and Straker (1982) investigated peer relations of physically abused five- to ten-year-olds. Children were videotaped in triadic interaction during free play. Their behavior was rated along nine dimensions by independent judges. Rating scores were factor analyzed and yielded two components that accounted for approximately 70 percent of the behavioral variance. The authors labeled these factor "social interaction" and "hostility," with the former reflecting positive exchanges and the latter reflecting aggression. Individual children were then assigned scores for each factor. Abused children scored significantly lower on social interaction. No difference was obtained for hostility, though this may be due to an unusual pattern of item loadings on this factor. Jacobson and Straker (1982) concluded that abused children interact less than nonabused children. However, it should be noted that their "social interaction" factor included items relating to both quantity and quality of participation. Moreover, children were observed for only five minutes of interaction following a brief warm-up period. In addition to questions about the reliability of these observations, a more conservative interpretation might be that abused children are slower than nonabused children to initiate peer interactions in novel settings. Such an interpretation would be consistent with the clinical observation that abused children are frequently slow in establishing trust.

Howes and Espinosa (1985) also investigated the peer interactions of abused, neglected, clinic-referred, and normal children in new and well-established play groups. Like the study by Jacobson and Straker (1982), the design called for behavioral observations of peer interaction, but children were observed in somewhat larger groups, and their behavior was sampled for a greater length of time. In addition, the children were all five years of age or younger. Peer interaction was measured by the frequency of positive and negative emotion expressed, positive and negative behaviors directed toward others, exchanges initiated, and complexity of play. For the analysis the children were divided into three age groups: under three, three-year-olds, and four- and five-year-olds. Based on their findings, Howes and Espinosa (1985) concluded that abused children observed in well-established groups are similar to normal children in the complexity and frequency of their interaction with peers as well as in the expression of positive emotion. In newly formed groups, however, abused children are less competent in peer interaction and express less positive emotion than other children. On the basis of these findings, they contended that opportunities for social interaction, inherent in the well-formed groups, benefit abused children. There are a number of reasons to view this conclusion with caution. First, because of sample size, the authors were unable to use the most appropriate statistical test. Thus results reported as main effects may actually reflect interactions. Second, as the authors acknowledge, the effect of group familiarity may be confounded with that of group composition. Clearly, type of partner in peer interaction may influence the overall competency of the interaction. Consequently, the greater difficulty abused children have in newly formed groups may be due to the relatively low social competence of their fellow group members. Similarly, given the age range in this sample, results may be confounded by the age characteristics of the groups—for example, same age versus mixed age. Thus, though the study suggests that abused children are less competent in the absence of social support and familiarity, the results should be viewed with caution.

In a more carefully designed study, Wolfe and Mosk (1983) investigated the behavior problems and social competence of physically abused school-age children. Rather than assuming a direct relation between physical abuse and child disturbance, they hypothesized that negative outcomes may result from exposure to prolonged aversive interactions among family members. To test this hypothesis, they compared physically abused children with children from distressed but nonabusive families and with a nonclinical population. In contrast to previously reviewed studies, social competence was measured through parent ratings on the Child Behavior Profile (Achenbach and Edelbrock 1978). Consistent with their hypothesis, children from both abusive and nonabusive but distressed families obtained significantly lower social-competence scores than nonabused children from the community. Moreover, the two clinic groups did not differ from each other. As Wolfe and Mosk (1983) concluded, lowered social competence does not appear to be specific to abused children, but instead is characteristic of children from problem families in general. A similar result was obtained for behavior-problem scores. It appears that disturbances in children's social development may spring as much from family instability and discord as from specific abusive events. Once again, cautious interpretation of these results seems prudent. First, it is possible that the distressed but nonabusive comparison sample contained undetected abused children, thus attenuating group differences. Second, exclusive reliance on parents' reports as a measure of social competence limits generalizations about children's actual behavior. However, Wolfe and Mosk (1983, 706) recommended that the "negative psychological consequences of child abuse be expanded to include those children raised in highly distressed family environments, in which aversive elements besides physical aggression are operative."

The limited number of studies on how physical abuse affects children's social competence do not provide a firm foundation for understanding, preventing, or resolving abused children's difficulties with peers. Theoretical formulations and clinical observations suggest that peer interaction will be a vulnerable area for physically abused children. Moreover, data suggest that inadequate peer relationships in childhood predict social difficulties in adulthood. Of special significance for abused children is the hypothesis that peer relationships may serve as a therapeutic corrective to maladaptive forms of interaction experienced in the family. Unfortunately, however, the significance of peer interaction for abused children's development has not been matched by a comparable research effort.

Aggression

Unlike social competence, abused children's aggressive behavior has attracted considerable attention from researchers. Much of the interest appears to stem from the "intergenerational transmission hypothesis"—that abused children are at risk for becoming abusive parents. Researchers have therefore begun to look for the antecedents of family violence in the aggressive behavior of abused children. A second reason for concern involves the poor prognosis for children with conduct disorders. Antisocial, aggressive behaviors in childhood portend other problems in adulthood, including alcoholism, psychosis, and crime (Robins 1979). In addition to the personal adjustment problems of aggressive children, aggressive behavior entails a social cost—it creates new victims. From a social perspective, problems with aggression may be one of the most costly disorders of childhood.

Several investigators have examined the aggressive behavior of abused children within their families. For example, Reid, Taplin, and Lorber (1981) compared children from distressed, abusive families, distressed but nonabusive families, and nondistressed, nonabusive families. In this study direct observations of family interactions were made in the children's homes. Children ranged in age from three to fourteen and were largely of lower-class origin. Children from abusive families exhibited higher rates of aversive behavior than children from the other types of families. Most notable was the high frequency of threatening commands and negative physical behaviors (like hitting) in children from abusive families. It is noteworthy that *within* the abusive families, the physically abused children exhibited the highest rates of aversive behavior.

The findings of Reid, Taplin, and Lorber (1981) stand in contrast to the results of Wolfe and Mosk (1983), who found no significant difference in overall level of behavior problems between children from distressed but nonabusive families and distressed, abusive families. Clear differences in measurement strategies probably account for the inconsistent results. Recall that Wolfe and Mosk (1983) used a parent-report measure. The findings based on direct observation add weight to the cautionary note that exclusive reliance on parent-report measures limits conclusions about children's actual behavior.

Burgess and Conger (1978) also examined family interactions in abusive, neglectful, and nonabusive families. Among their results, they found that children in abusive families exhibited less verbal and physical interaction with their parents. In addition, these children showed a trend toward higher levels of aversive behavior. Visual inspection of their data suggests higher rates of aversive behavior among siblings in abusive families than in other families, but these trends did not attain statistical significance.

Abused children also appear to *misbehave* more in their families than their nonabused peers. In a study of parental discipline strategies in abusive and nonabusive families, Trickett and Kuczynski (1986) found that abused children were more aggressive and less compliant than control children. Abused children were more likely than controls to commit transgressions of an antisocial character, including aggressiveness and destructiveness. In addition, abused children tended to accompany their noncompliance with verbal refusals and anger. Not surprisingly, then, abusive parents were less likely than controls to use verbal reasoning as a disciplinary strategy and more likely to use physical punishment.

Patterson (1982) suggested that children's aggression in abusive families can be understood as a synchronous matching of aversive behaviors. Given an aversive intrusion by a family member (parent slaps), there is a dramatic increase in the probability of a counterattack. Patterson (1982) also reported a tendency to match type of counterattack to type of intrusion. Furthermore, aversive exchanges are likely to escalate into extended aversive chains. From this perspective, the aggressive behavior of physically abused children can be seen as part of a coercive family cycle.

A critical question, then, is whether the increased aggressiveness of abused children represents an adaptive, but circumscribed, response to a specific environment or whether it becomes a generalized response that characterizes other social interactions as well. Research on physically abused toddlers suggests that the latter formulation is correct. For example, George and Main (1979) found that abused toddlers physically assaulted peers more than twice as often as controls. Moreover, abused toddlers were the only children in the sample to assault or threaten their caregivers in daycare. Similarly, Egeland and Sroufe (1981) found that abused two-year-olds exhibited more aggressive behavior than controls in a problem-solving situation.

There have been several studies of the aggressive characteristics of abused children in middle childhood. Unfortunately, a number of them rely exclusively on measures of *fantasy* aggression. Others fail to include a comparison group. In a study of the emotional development of physically abused children, Kinard (1980) found that abused children expressed more externally directed fantasy aggression than matched controls. Higher levels of aggressive fantasy were particularly prominent in response to stimuli involving peers. As Kinard (1980) noted, aggression toward other children may represent a displacement of anger toward abusive parents.

In contrast to Kinard's findings, Straker and Jacobson (1981) found no significant difference between abused children and matched controls on fantasy aggression. In addition to the fantasy measure Kinard used (the Rosenswieg Picture Frustration Test), Straker and Jacobson used two other projective measures. They found no significant differences on any of these measures. It is likely, however, that the inconsistent findings of these two studies say more about the questionable validity of fantasy measures of aggression than about the aggressive characteristics of abused children.

Unlike the previous researchers, Reidy (1977) used both fantasy and observational measures of aggression. Abused children were compared with nonabused but neglected children and with children who were not maltreated. The neglect group was included to control for the possible influence of inadequate care upon aggression. Aggressive *fantasy* was measured with the Thematic Apperception Test (TAT). Measures of aggressive *behavior* were observational ratings during free play and teachers' ratings on a behavior-problem checklist. Abused children expressed significantly more fantasy aggression in response to the TAT than either the neglected children or those who were not maltreated. In the free-play setting, abused children behaved aggressively much more often than either neglected children or those who were not maltreated. In school, teachers' ratings revealed that they saw abused children as more aggressive than those who were not maltreated, but there was no significant difference between abused and neglected children. Unfortunately, Reidy (1977) did not include findings on the relationships among his measures of aggression. However, his results suggest that in comparison to normally treated children, abused children are more aggressive in school, in free play, and in their fantasies. These results support the hypothesis that the experience of physical abuse leads to increased aggressiveness that generalizes across situations.

Again, the limited number of studies and their inconsistent findings warrant replication of these reported results. From a developmental perspective, it would be useful to determine whether increased aggressiveness is a consistent consequence of abuse for children at different ages or whether it is more characteristic of certain developmental phases. Given the evidence for sex differences in the expression of aggression and in the stability of aggression over time, the experience of physical abuse could portend different adult outcomes for males and females. Furthermore, considering individual differences in aggressiveness among physically abused children could provide insight into the "protective factors" that buffer some children from the impact of victimization.

The emerging empirical evidence supports the clinical hypothesis that physically abused children are "at risk" for developing heightened aggressive behavior. The preliminary results of this research suggest that for many abused children, aggressiveness extends beyond the context in which it is first experienced and generalizes to other interpersonal contexts. As such, aggressiveness tends to become an interpersonal style. Although this finding should be regarded as provisional until replicated, its implications are ominous when considered in connection with other research on the stability of aggression. Longitudinal studies have shown that aggression is a relatively stable, self-perpetuating behavior (Huesman et al. 1984: Olweus 1979). That is, once a characteristic style of aggressive responding develops, it seems to endure, particularly among males (Huesman et al. 1984). It is likely that aggressive behavior has multiple origins in biology, family, and culture, but it appears that physical abuse must be considered a potent precipitating factor in its development.

Future Directions for Research

As this review indicates, the early preoccupation with etiology has given way to investigations of the sequelae of physical abuse. Within the area of social development, there is increasing evidence to support the clinical hypothesis that physical abuse is a serious developmental hazard. Although more research is needed, studies indicate that the experience of physical abuse interferes with the development of social-cognitive abilities related to social competence. Consequently, abused children appear to be at risk for maladaptive relationships with peers. The magnitude of this risk is emphasized by evidence that abused children are also vulnerable to developing aggressive social behaviors. Previous research indicates that aggressiveness undermines acceptance by peers (cf. Patterson 1982). Furthermore, because peer acceptance is critical for later adjustment, physical abuse exerts an *indirect* effect on later adaptation by undermining social competence. That is, physical abuse entails both *direct* and *indirect* effects on later adjustment. For example, a direct consequence might be heightened aggressiveness, which portends problems like criminal behavior. An indirect effect would be deficits in social cognition that interfere with social competence and result in rejection by peers, which in turn adds its own contribution to maladaptive outcomes.

Normative research has revealed a pattern of relationships among social cognition, social skills, and aggressive behavior (Ford 1982; Pellegrini 1985), but these relationships have not been directly investigated among physically abused children. In fact, this is one of the major limitations of the existing research on abused children's social development. Research on these relationships could open new avenues for intervention with physically abused children.

Finally, despite the growing recognition of the importance of differentiating types of abuse and separating the effects of abuse from general family distress, it does not appear that the importance of distinguishing types of children has been translated into research design. For example, several studies have lumped children from a rather broad age range into a single sample. Often there are no analyses of sex differences. Certainly, problems with subject ascertainment and small sample size make it tempting to ignore developmental level, but this may interact with type of abuse to produce diverse outcomes. From a developmental perspective, greater attention needs to be directed both to the type and intensity of abuse and to the developmental level of the abused child. Failure to consider developmental level implicitly assumes that the impact of abuse overides a multitude of other factors that contribute to children's social development.

Implications for the Treatment of Physically Abused Children

Researchers and clinicians frequently find themselves speaking different languages. For the clinician, group averages and significant statistical effects pale in comparison with the unique histories of individual children and significant therapeutic effects. What, then, do developmental theory and research have to offer the practicing clinician who is faced with treating an abused child? In this section I will consider the *goals* of psychotherapy with physically abused children against the background of developmental theory and research on the effect of physical abuse on children's social development.

During the past decade, mental health professionals have begun to acknowledge the extent to which victims of abuse are seen in clinical settings. Recognition of the burgeoning number of abused children in clinical treatment has led to a reconsideration of the role trauma plays in the development of psychopathology. However, the etiological significance attributed to trauma has oscillated over time. Initially, Freud hypothesized that a range of clinical problems shared a common origin in actual traumas of early childhood. Symptoms represented conversions of traumatic experiences that had been denied expression. This view has been labeled the trauma model. Freud abandoned the trauma model when he developed his theory of infantile sexuality and the oedipal complex. The roots of psychopathology were to be found, he averred, not in actual traumatic events, but in the wishes and fantasies fueled by infantile drives. In essence, the source of psychopathology was internalized in the form of intrapsychic conflicts.

The current revival of the trauma model appears to be a welcome corrective to dynamic formulations that emphasize wishful fantasy and the symbolic expression of internal conflicts. Instead, the trauma model redirects attention to the reality of traumatic experiences and their corrosive impact on development. Yet is it possible that this model of psychopathology entails assumptions that should be tempered by developmental considerations?

Models of etiology invariably imply methods of intervention (Newberger and Newberger 1982). The trauma model is no exception. Historically, when the trauma model dominated Freud's early etiological formulations the goals of treatment were to uncover past traumatic experiences and to release the associated affect that had been denied expression. Uncovering and abreaction were the necessary and sufficient conditions for resolving psychopathology.

One of the potential dangers of reembracing the trauma model resides in its assumption about the goals and methods of treatment. These goals and methods are based upon an etiological model that assumes a *linear* relationship between past traumatic experiences and present symptoms. In its original form, the trauma model suggests it is possible to link early maltreatment directly with subsequent symptoms. For example, present interpersonal difficulties represent an "acting out" or a repetition of the past trauma. Numerous current fomulations about the behavior of abused children are based on this assumption. For example, an abused child's aggressive behavior with peers is seen as a displacement of anger unconsciously felt toward abusive parents. In this example adjustment problems are *directly* tied to past trauma.

In contrast to the linear assumption of the trauma model, developmental theory and research postulate a more complex relationship between the experience of trauma and enduring problems of adjustment. Research on physical abuse and children's social development provides a case in point. For example, problems with peer relations are often attributed to a history of abuse, but research suggests that the relation between physical abuse and problems with peers may involve a number of intervening factors. That is, physical abuse may undermine acceptance by peers by interfering with the development of the social-cognitive skills necessary for social competence. In this case physical abuse exerts an *indirect* influence. Recovering and understanding past traumatic events cannot be expected to be a sufficient corrective to deficits in social cognition or any other developmental deficit resulting from abuse. Although insight into the past may help the child overcome persistent *distortions* of present experience, insight alone will not offset enduring developmental *deficits*. And to this point research suggests that many physically abused children exhibit specific deficits.

Developmental theory provides an alternative model for understanding the relation between a history of physical abuse and persistent problems of adjustment. From this perspective, physical abuse causes enduring effects by disrupting mastery of critical developmental tasks. For example, physical abuse experienced by a toddler might disrupt the development of autonomous problem solving. Consequently the child remains dependent on adults and avoids peers. In turn, the lack of experience with peers causes deficits in social skills. Without appropriate social skills, the child resorts to aggressive behavior to resolve interpersonal conflicts. Although physical abuse may have set in motion a sequence of events that led to a maladaptive outcome, the original trauma is not *directly* responsible for current problems with peers. In this case early physical abuse produced a "domino effect" that was compounded over time. Although abuse was the critical etiological factor, later expressions of maladjustment were shaped by cumulative disruptions in development. Again, one could not expect insight into the early experience of abuse to be a sufficient condition for emotional and behavioral change.

Attention to developmental theory and research on physical abuse and children's social development can serve as a corrective to what might be called the "etiological fallacy" in the treatment of physically abused children—the assumption that insight into the etiology of a problem will produce emotional and behavioral change. The trouble with this approach is that a history of physical abuse can exert indirect effects on current adjustment by disrupting developmental tasks and undermining the acquisition of basic competencies. These developmental failures, in turn, make their own contribution to a legacy of social and emotional adversity. Insight or uncovering will not, by itself, fill in gaps in the child's developmental history. Thus the danger in reembracing the trauma model is that its assuming a direct connection between past abuse and present problems may narrow the goals and methods of treatment for physically abused children. From a developmental perspective, the primary reason for uncovering the past is to let the child benefit from new relationships that can encourage future development.

References

Achenbach, T., and Edelbrock, C. 1978. The classification of childhood psychopathology: A review and analysis of empirical efforts. *Psychological Bulletin* 85:1275–1301.

Asher, S.: Oden, S.; and Gottman, J. 1981. Children's friendships in school settings. In *Contemporary readings in child psychology*, ed. M. Hetherington and R. Parre. New York: McGraw-Hill.

Barahal, R.; Waterman, J.; and Martin, H. 1981. The social cognitive development of abused children. *Journal of Consulting and Clinical Psychology* 49:508–16.

Bauer, W., and Twentyman, C. 1985. Abusing, neglectful, and comparison mothers' responses to child-related and non-child-related stressors. *Journal of Consulting and Clinical Psychology* 53:335–43.

Beck, A. 1976. *Cognitive therapy and the emotional disorders.* New York: Meridian.

Berndt, T. 1981. Relations between social cognition, nonsocial cognition, and social behavior: The case of friendship. In *Social cognitive development*, ed. J. Flavell and L. Ross. Cambridge: Cambridge University Press.

Bowlby, J. 1969. *Attachment and loss.* Vol. 1. *Attachment.* New York: Basic Books.

Burgess, R., and Conger, R. 1978. Family interactions in abusing, neglectful, and normal families. *Child Development* 49:1163–73.

Camras, L.; Grow, G.; and Ribordy, S. 1983. Recognition of emotional expression by abused children. *Journal of Clinical Child Psychology* 12:325-28.

Cicchetti, D., and Rizley, R. 1981. Developmental perspectives on the etiology, intergenerational transmission, and sequelae of child maltreatment. In *New directions in child development: Developmental perspectives on child maltreatment*, ed. R. Rizley and D. Cicchetti. San Francisco: Jossey-Bass.

Clarke, A. D., and Clarke, A. B. 1976. *Early experience: Myth and evidence.* New York: Free Press.

Cowen, E.; Pederson, A.; Babigan, H.; Izzo, L.; and Trost, M. 1973. Long-term follow-up of early detected vulnerable children. *Journal of Consulting and Clinical Psychology* 41:438-46.

Dodge, K. 980. Social cognition and children's aggressive behavior. *Child Development* 51:162-70.

Egeland, B., and Sroufe, A. 1981. Developmental sequelae of maltreatment in infancy. In *New directions in child development: Developmental perspectives on child maltreatment*, ed. R. Rizly and D. Cicchetti. San Francisco: Jossey-Bass.

Elmer, E. 1977. A follow-up study of traumatized children. *Pediatrics* 59:272-79.

Erikson, E. 1968. *Identity, youth and crisis.* New York: Norton.

Feffer, M. 1970. A developmental analysis of interpersonal behavior. *Psychological Review* 77:197-214.

Flavell, J., and Ross, L. 1981. *Social cognitive development.* Cambridge: Cambridge University Press.

Ford, M. 1982. Social cognition and social competence in adolescence. *Developmental Psychology* 18:323-40.

Frodi, S., and Smetana, J. 1984. Abused, neglected, and normal preschoolers' ability to discriminate emotion in others. *Child Abuse and Neglect* 8:459-65.

Furth, H. 1978. Young children's understandings of society. In *Issues in childhood social development*, ed. H. McGurk. London: Methuen.

Galdston, R. 1965. Observations on children who have been physically abused and their parents. *American Journal of Psychiatry* 122:440-43.

George, C., and Main, M. 1979. Social interactions of young abused children. *Child Development* 50:306-18.

Gottman, J.; Gonso, J.; and Rasmussen, B. 1975. Social interaction, social competence, and friendship in children. *Child Development* 46:709-18.

Guralnick, M., and Weinhouse, E. 1984. Peer related social interactions of developmentally-delayed young children. *Developmental Psychology* 20:815-27.

Howes, C., and Espinosa, M. 1985. The consequences of child abuse for the formation of relationships with peers. *Child Abuse and Neglect* 9:397-404.

Huesman, L. R.; Eron, L.; Lefkowitz, M.; and Walder, L. 1984. Stability of aggression over time and generations. *Developmental Psychology* 20:1120-34.

Jacobson, R. S., and Straker, G. 1982. Peer group interaction of physically abused children. *Child Abuse and Neglect* 6:321-29.

Kempe, R., and Kempe, C. H. 1978. *Child abuse.* Cambridge: Harvard University Press.

Kendall, P. 1984. Social cognition and problem-solving: A developmental and child-clinical interface. In *Applications of cognitive developmental theory,* ed. B. Gholson and T. Rosenthal. Orlando: Academic Press.

Kendall, P.; Lerner, R.; and Craighead, W. 1984. Human development and intervention in childhood psychopathology. *Child Development* 55:71–82.

Kinard, E. M. 1980. Emotional development in physically abused children. *American Journal of Orthopsychiatry* 50:686–95.

Kohlberg, L. 1969. Stage and sequence: The cognitive-developmental approach to socialization. In *Handbook of socialization: Theory and research,* ed. D. Goslin. New York: Rand McNally.

Leahy, R. L. 1983. *The child's construction of inequality.* New York: Academic Press.

———. 1985. The costs of development: Clinical implications. In *The development of the self,* ed. R. Leahy. New York: Academic Press.

Leahy, R., and Shirk, S. 1984. The development of social cognition: Conceptions of personality. In *Annals of child development,* ed. G. Whitehurst. London: JAI Press.

MacDonald, K. 1985. Early experience, relative plasticity, and social development. *Developmental Review* 5:99–121.

Main, M., and George, C. 1985. Responses of abused and disadvantaged toddlers to distress. *Developmental Psychology* 21:407–12.

Martin, H., and Beezley, P. 1977. Behavioral observations of abused children. *Developmental Medicine and Child Neurology* 19:373–87.

Mischel, W., and Mischel, H. 1976. A cognitive social learning approach to morality and self-regulation. In *Moral development and behavior,* ed. T. Lickona. New York: Hold, Rinehart, and Winston.

Mueller, E., and Brenner, J. 1977. The growth of social interaction in the toddler play group: The role of peer experience. *Child Development* 48:854–61.

Newberger, C., and Newberger, E. 1982. Prevention of child abuse: Theory, myth, practice, *Journal of Preventive Psychiatry* 1:443–51.

Olweus, D. 1979. The stability of aggressive reaction patterns in human males: A review. *Psychological Bulletin* 85:852–75.

Parten, M. B. 1932. Social participation among preschool children. *Journal of Abnormal and Social Psychology* 27:243–69.

Patterson, G. 1982. *Coercive family process.* Eugene, Oreg.: Castalia.

Pellegrini, D. 1985. Social cognition and social competence in middle childhood. *Child Development* 56:252–64.

Piaget, J. 1932. *The moral judgement of the child.* London: Routledge.

———. 1968. *Structuralism.* New York: Harper and Row.

———. 1970. *Genetic epistemology.* New York: Columbia University Press.

Posner, J. 1983. Symptom formation in children from a cognitive developmental point of view. Ph.D. diss., New School for Social Research.

Reid, J. B.; Taplin, P. S.; and Lorber, R. 1981. A social interactional approach to the treatment of abusive families. In *Violent behavior: Social learning approaches to prediction, management, and treatment,* ed. R. Stuart. New York: Brunner/Mazel.

Reidy, T. J. 1977. The aggressive characteristics of abused and neglected children. *Journal of Clinical Psychology* 33:1140–45.

Robins, L. N. 1979. Follow-up studies. In *Psychopathological disorders of childhood*, ed. H. Quay and J. Werry. New York: John Wiley.

Roff, M.; Sells, S. B.; and Golden, M. 1972. *Social adjustment and personality development in children.* Minneapolis: University of Minnesota Press.

Rothenberg, B. 1970. Children's social sensitivity and the relationship to interpersonal competence, intrapersonal comfort, and intellectual level. *Developmental Psychology* 2:335–50.

Rubin, K.; Watson, K.; and Jambor, T. 1978. Free play behaviors in preschool and kindergarten children. *Child Development* 49:534–36.

Sameroff, A. 1975. Early influences: Fact or fancy? *Merrill-Palmer Quarterly* 20:275–301.

Sameroff, A., and Chandler, M. 1975. Reproductive risk and the continuum of caretaker causality. In *Review of child development research*, vol. 4, ed. F. Horowitz. Chicago: University of Chicago Press.

Selman, R. 1980. *The growth of interpersonal understanding.* New York: Academic Press.

Smetana, J. 1983. Social-cognitive development: Domain distinctions and co-ordinations. *Developmental Review* 3:131–47.

Smetana, J.; Kelly, M.; and Twentyman, C. 1984. Abused, neglected, and nonmaltreated children's conceptions of moral and social-conventional transgression. *Child Development* 55:277–87.

Sroufe, A., and Waters, E. 1977. Attachment as an organizational construct. *Child Development* 48:1184–99.

Straker, G., and Jacobson, R. S. 1981. Aggression, emotional maladjustment, and empathy in the abused child. *Developmental Psychology* 17:762–65.

Trickett, P., and Kuczynski, L. 1986. Children's misbehaviors and parental discipline strategies in abusive and nonabusive families. *Developmental Psychology* 22:115–23.

Waterman, J.; Sobesky, W.; Silvern, L.; Aoki, B.; and MacCaulty, M. 1981. Social perspective taking and adjustment in emotionally-disturbed, learning disabled, and normal children. *Journal of Abnormal Child Psychology* 9:133–48.

Wenar, C. 1982. *Psychopathology from infancy through adolescence.* New York: Random House.

Werner, H. 1957. The concept of development from a comparative and organismic point of view. In *The concept of development*, ed. D. Harris. Minneapolis: Minnesota Paperbacks.

Wolfe, D., and Mosk, M. 1983. Behavioral comparisons of children from abusive and distressed families. *Journal of Consulting and Clinical Psychology* 51:702–8.

Wolfe, D.; Jaffe, P.; Wilson, S.; and Zak, L. 1985. Children of battered women: The relation of child behavior to family violence and maternal stress. *Journal of Consulting and Clinical Psychology* 53:657–65.

4   Sexual Abuse in the Lives of Children

FRANCES SINK

The perception of childhood as a time of sheltered innocence carries considerable weight in American society. It is a perception founded on cultural values, religious teachings, and a certain degree of national self-esteem. This sentimental viewpoint has made it difficult for advocates to gain appropriate attention for the plight of the many children who live in homes that are neglectful, abusive, and exploitative. Public denial and ignorance of child exploitation are entrenched in our society and stem in part from the idealization of childhood.

Sexual abuse, considered by many the most severe form of child maltreatment (e.g., Garrett and Rossi 1978; Giovannoni and Becerra 1979), has been the most denied and the least understood form of abuse in childhood. Because the subject is heavily infused with emotion and moral judgment, it has been difficult to address sexual abuse frankly as the widespread social problem it is. Furthermore, the causes and effects of sexual abuse have been distorted by public myths and misguided social theories grounded more in narrow, judgmental attitudes than in scientific enlightenment.

Because of the abhorrence the idea of incest or sexual abuse of children engenders, early theories attempting to describe such abuse and its origins reflected a cultural need to deny and minimize the problem. Many professionals viewed incest as a serious but rare form of family pathology occurring in socially isolated families. Popular images of impoverished families inbreeding in backwoods communities abounded. Sexual abuse outside the family was presumed to result from abductions or seductions by child molesters who preyed upon unsuspecting children on playgrounds or sidewalks. The message was consistent that sexual abuse was not the problem of the typical American family. Given a cultural climate of denial and disbelief, large numbers of victims were unable or unwilling to disclose their abuse. Until recently, professionals shared in the silence and did not act to expose the abuse or protect the child.

A new social awareness about sexual victimization of children had its beginnings in other movements of social concern in the 1960s and 1970s. Battered and neglected children became a target of public concern in the 1960s. When protective action through mandated reporting of abuse cases was legislated in many states in the early 1970s, sexual abuse also began to be reported more frequently to child protective authorities. Simultaneously the rape crisis movement focused attention on the impact of rape by offering rapid, sensitive intervention for women victims following sexual assaults. As a result, mothers with sexually abused children also began to seek services in rape crisis centers. Over time, the special needs of child sexual abuse victims became apparent—distinct from physical abuse or adult sexual assault—and a new population for specialized attention and care began to emerge.

Public awareness about child sexual abuse grew most in response to the efforts of several courageous women who began to write individually and collectively to educate others about their histories of sexual abuse as children and about the impact of that abuse on their adult development (Allen 1980; Armstrong 1978; Butler 1978). Through their retrospective reports these women shared their childhood experiences not only of abuse but of others' failure to believe them and to intervene. As a group, these articulate and impassioned women were able to draw attention to the plight of children in abusive situations. They began to engender support and action not only for adult survivors of abuse but also for young children not able to speak for themselves.

In the 1970s reports of child sexual abuse increased dramatically. The American Humane Association's nationwide data collection system reported increases from 1,975 reports in 1976 and 4,327 in 1977 to 22,918 in 1982 (AHA 1986). Protective service agencies and the courts were inundated with reports of suspected abuse. It became increasingly apparent, however, how little was known about sexually abused children, their families, or their abusers. In the face of a new public demand for information and services, the denial of sexual abuse as a serious social concern began to give way to questions about the dynamics of abuse, its effect on child development, and the appropriate social response.

Scope of the Problem

With a history of secrecy and misunderstanding surrounding child sexual abuse, its magnitude as a cultural problem has remained disguised for many years. In 1979 David Finkelhor, a sociologist at the University of New Hampshire, published the first findings to suggest that the problem might be larger in scope than previously presumed. In a sample of 796 college students from six New England colleges and universities, he found that 19.2 percent of the women and 8.6 percent of the men reported histories of sexual victimization. These numbers were impressively large compared with prior estimates. He also found that his participants reported widely diverse types of sexual abuse and marked differences in their reactions to the abuse, ranging from claims that it had no impact to reports of a major effect on development (Finkelhor 1979).

Subsequent studies have confirmed that sexual abuse is not the uncommon, isolated experience of a few children but rather is a major risk in childhood. In fact, as researchers have refined their methods to increase the sensitivity and depth of their questions, the number of women who have been willing to discuss histories of abuse has risen dramatically. The belief that official reports of abuse far underestimate the problem, because of the secrecy surrounding the abuse itself and the improbability that a report will ever be made, has been validated. Russell (1983), reporting on a household sample of 930 women in San Francisco, found that in face-to-face interviews 38 percent acknowledged histories of sexual abuse before eighteen years of age. Wyatt (1985) found that 45 percent of a Los Angeles household sample of 248 women reported sexual abuse before the age of eighteen.

Although the term child sexual abuse is used as a global reference to experiences that involve children in inappropriate and unwanted sexual interactions, the specifics of the sexual abuse experiences are far more heterogeneous than homogeneous. The acts themselves vary on a severity continuum from unwanted kissing and touching to forcible intercourse. Genital touching is a predominant form of abuse. Exhibitionism and voyeurism, taking nude photographs, and exposure to pornography are also reported as forms of sexual abuse. The child's experience of abuse also varies not only with the severity of the acts themselves, but also with their frequency and duration. Many individuals report one abusive encounter, but for others the abuse goes on for months or years.

Although some abuse is violent, resulting in physical trauma, frequently the abuser uses authority and physical restraint to gain compliance. Consequently there are often no physical signs of abuse. Those who do not understand why children comply rather than run or scream misperceive the power of adult authority in the eyes of many children, especially when the authority figure is a significant adult in the child's life. Sexual abusers of children tend to be people the child knows who, through kinship or an assigned caretaking role, have access and authority in the child's daily life. Fathers, stepfathers, uncles, brothers, and grandfathers are among the most frequent perpetrators. Abuse by mothers is infrequently reported but does in fact occur. It is likely that male socialization and specific aspects of the male's relationship to children create a greater vulnerability to sexual exploitation.

As Finkelhor's 1979 study also pointed out, both boys and girls are sexually abused in large numbers. The ages of children at risk for abuse vary widely. Retrospective studies place onset predominantly during prepubertal years. However, with more services for children available, children abused at younger ages are being identified, even infants, toddlers, and preschoolers (Friedrich, Urquiza, and Beilke 1986; Gomes-Schwartz, Horowitz, and Sauzier 1985).

Looking for factors that might place a child at greater risk for sexual abuse directs attention to the child's family life (Finkelhor and Baron 1986). Unlike the situation in physical abuse, poverty, poor education, and parental stress do not necessarily increase a child's vulnerability to sexual abuse. Instead, risk arises in those situations where an abusive male has access to potential child victims. This occurs most frequently in the family context, where the safety of children is presumed rather than enforced. Although much attention has been focused on father-daughter abuse, other male family members form a significant percentage of abusers (Russell 1986). Uncles are frequently identified as abusers. Brothers are responsible for some of the more physically forcible forms of abuse. However, fathers and stepfathers are responsible for the most enduring and psychologically severe forms of abuse.

A higher vulnerability to sexual abuse exists for children who live without their biological mother or father at some time during childhood. Also, children who live with their biological mothers but with stepfathers have been found to be strikingly vulnerable to abuse, by the stepfather or someone else. It appears that sexual abuse is more likely when a potentially abusive male is present within the family or

extended family and there is a disruption in the protective features of
the family that would ordinarily prevent such abuse. The disruption
may be caused by parental absence, parental incapacitation, or changes
in parenting roles and functions within the family.

The Dynamics of Child Sexual Abuse

Sexual victimization of children, especially within the family, has been
the focus of theories of family dynamics and interactions. Unfortunately, most theories to date start their explanations at a point beyond
the actual abuse, examining instead the interactions and relationships
among members of the incestuous family. In doing so, they have
frequently made assumptions that confuse the causes of abuse with the
reactions to the abuse. For sexual abuse to occur, there must be a
person motivated toward sexual contact with a child. The behavior of
the child victim, mother, siblings, and even an entire family system
must be viewed in context, distinct from the abuser's motivations and
actions. When the problem of incest is viewed first as a family problem, without such distinctions, attention is deflected from the abuser
and his responsibility for his own actions. In many ways the explanations for abuse that have focused on the child's or the family's role in
the abuse have been more sympathetic toward the abuser than toward
his victim.

The Child's Role in Sexual Victimization

Historically, it has been proposed that children may contribute to their
own abuse. Psychiatrists Bender and Blau (1937), in one of the earliest
psychiatric reports on child sexual abuse, described child victims as
"unusually attractive and charming personalities." They noted that
even though the children spoke of fear of physical harm, enticements
by their abusers, and actual physical force used to gain compliance,
they believed (for reasons that are not clear) that these factors alone
could not account for the frequency of repetition of the sexual acts.
With a surprising insensitivity to the children they studied, these
authors observed, "It is not remarkable that frequently we considered
the possibility that the child might have been the actual seducer rather
than the one innocently seduced" (1937, 514).

Subsequent writers on incest have also suggested that children col-
luded in their abuse, accepting their fathers' advances as expressions
of affection (Kaufman, Peck, and Tagiuri 1954) or as revenge against

an unloving mother (Sloane and Karpinski 1942). Even the well-known Kinsey report on female sexual development (Kinsey et al. 1953) observed that repetitious preadolescent sexual contacts with adults in the same household occurred "because the children had become interested in the sexual activity and had more or less actively sought repetitions of their experiences" (p. 118). Kinsey et al. acknowledged that 80 percent of the sample reporting sexual contacts with adults indicated being "emotionally frightened or upset." Nonetheless, these researchers took the position that "it is difficult to understand why a child, except for its cultural conditioning, should be disturbed at having its genitalia touched, or disturbed at seeing the genitalia of other persons, or disturbed at even more specific sexual contacts" (p. 121). They blamed adults' warnings about abuse and "hysteria" about sexual offenders for causing the children's anxious and fearful reactions.

Blaming children for their own victimization is not a thing of the past. It is an attitude that still frequently arises as an impediment to holding abusers accountable for their exploitation of children. Abusers who do not outright deny their actions will resort to blaming the child in their own defense.

In response to those who blame children for their abuse Finkelhor (1984) and Russell (1986) have both argued that it is illogical to postulate consent in children given the discrepancy in power and status involved in the abusive relationship or in any relationship between children and adults. If anything, "seductive" children would warrant extra protection and care, given their added vulnerability—not adult exploitation.

Further, victims of abuse, when asked as adults, consistently fail to recall wanting sexual involvement as children, and they are adamant about the negative impact of abuse, particularly where incest was involved (Finkelhor 1979; Russell 1986; Herman 1981). In some cases the initial approaches an adult used may have involved an element of positive sexual arousal for the child. More often than not, however, such feelings accentuated ambivalence, confusion, and self-blame in the victim, particularly if the sexual exploitation continued.

Additional evidence against victim blaming is a growing body of literature suggesting that abusers, even those who become incestuous abusers, begin their molestation while they are still youths (Becker and Abel 1984; Groth 1979). Furthermore, they may seek involvement with multiple victims simultaneously or sequentially. Given this pattern, it is highly unlikely that any one victim can be held accountable in cases of child sexual abuse (Russell 1986).

Some important contributions have been made correcting the misperceptions of children's role in their abuse. Summit (1983) and Bur-

gess and Holmstrom (1978) developed theories about why children
are so frequently compliant and silent. Summit's sexual abuse accommodation syndrome describes the typical reactions to abuse in children, including secrecy, helplessness, accommodation, delayed
unconvincing disclosure, and retraction of the disclosure. These reactions reflect children's efforts to cope with an overpowering and at
times threatening abusive situation in the absence of adequate protection and support from their environment. The pressure from the abuser
or the family not to disclose abuse is highlighted by Summit as central
to explaining the child's behavior. Burgess and Holmstrom similarly
describe an accessory-to-sex syndrome that delineates the central role
of pressure and secrecy in controlling the child's response to abuse.
Children's reactions can be interpreted accurately only in the context
of the abuse, where they are pressured into secret sexual activity and
then must withstand the tension of keeping the secret of the abuse. It
is also important to note that the sexualized behavior in some children
subsequent to abuse emerges in treatment as a symptomatic by-prod-
uct of abuse, not a causative factor (Krieger et al. 1980; de Young
1982).

The Role of the Family in Child Sexual Abuse

The families of child victims have also been implicated as causing the
child's abuse. A series of qualities of incestuous families have been
delineated, all of which are proposed to contribute to the occurrence
of abuse. In many families there is a lack of generational differentiation. Blurred role boundaries allow the victim daughter to become a
central female figure in the family (Lustig et al. 1966). Mothers of
incest victims are frequently described as incapacitated through mental
illness or physical disability or as physically or emotionally unavailable
(Herman 1981). Family members are often unusually anxious about
separation and loss, and rigid requirements of interdependency keep
them trapped in dysfunctional patterns. Alliances are formed within
families excluding those members not privy to secrets. Such alliances
persist for irrational but enduring reasons and can prevent members
from paying attention to a child's need for protection (Karpel 1980).
    Clinical observations about incest are based on studies of families
where incest has ultimately been disclosed and the family or a family
member has been referred for treatment of serious mental health concerns. Consequently it is not possible to know whether the observations apply to the full range of incestuous abuses. Nonetheless, there
probably is merit to the finding that in situations of ongoing incestuous

abuse, the family's failure to protect children can occur for many reasons.

Unfortunately, while these observations are valid contributions to understanding why some families respond to knowledge or disclosure of incest with denial or failure to protect the child, they do not explain why the incest occurs in the first place. Describing incest as "a family group survival pattern" (Lustig, et al. 1966) or as a "family affair" (Machotka, Pittman, and Flomenhaft 1966) perpetuates the idea that families cause incest. What must be more accurately portrayed is that families must react to incest and that many are ill equipped to act effectively either to confront the abusing person or to protect the child.

Overemphasizing the roles of children and families in cases of incest can only be expected to obscure the perpetrator's responsibility for the abuse. Finkelhor (1984) has proposed a model of four preconditions for sexual abuse, the first condition being an individual who is motivated to abuse a child sexually. The motivation to abuse includes three components: emotional congruence, meaning that sexual interaction with a child fulfills an important emotional need; sexual arousal such that the child can be a source of sexual gratification; and blockage, whereby other sources of sexual gratification are not available or are less satisfying.

The second precondition of abuse is the abuser's ability to overcome internal inhibitors. Without motivation to abuse, disinhibition alone is not sufficient to create abuse. But for the motivated individual disinhibition can result from alcohol, impulsivity, or mental or emotional impairment. One must account for why the social taboos against sex between adults and children fail to control the adult's behavior. The disinhibition condition for abuse must be present, since even persons sexually motivated toward children will not act if inhibited by social, moral, or psychological taboos.

The third precondition involves overcoming external inhibitors and concerns conditions outside the abuser that control his access to a child. Certainly supervision within the family, among neighbors, and with peers is a critical dimension of the child's protection. The more isolated, undersupervised child is also more vulnerable, given a motivated and disinhibited abuser. It stands to reason that mothers who are incapacitated physically or emotionally will be less able to create a naturally protective network for their children. Unlike some families where other members become involved in supplemental child care and supervision, mothers who are isolated and lack adequate external supports may in fact be completely dependent on the abusing individual for parenting support, thereby increasing his access to children.

Although access to children is a precondition for abuse, it does not follow that mothers and other family members should be held responsible for abuse. Many child protection programs focus on reducing access to the child as the primary form of intervention. One can see, however, that this approach does not address the motivation and disinhibition of abusers.

The fourth precondition for abuse is overcoming the child's resistance. Finkelhor suggests that some children are naturally protected from abuse by a "front of invulnerability" that conveys that they will not go along with abuse or keep it a secret—that they will say no, and cannot be intimidated. Other children, because of their immaturity, naïveté, or emotional neediness, are more vulnerable to relationships that are at first nurturing but then become abusive. In many cases, however, whatever the child's predisposition, the abuse occurs without the use of force to gain the child's compliance and secrecy. Abusers skillfully play upon children's dependencies and loyalties, particularly their fears that harm or distress will result for themselves, their families, or even the abuser if they disclose the abuse.

The historical blaming of children and families for allowing abuse has had two serious consequences. First, victims have been made to feel guilty for their alleged role in the abuse. Second, abusers have not been given the message that they must accept responsibility for their behavior and gain control over it. Treatment programs for incest victims and their families far outnumber programs for abusers. The number who abuse repeatedly without being stopped is alarming. In individual cases, questions about a child's credibility or a mother's possible motives for making "false allegations" receive far more attention than data suggesting that large numbers of men repeatedly fail to control their impulses to sexualize their relationships with children.

Although the sexual abuse itself is an event or a series of events between a child and an abuser, the relationship between the child and the abuser within the family and the community establishes its meaning for the child. Children's responses are also formed by others' reactions to the abuse. To understand causation one must examine the abuser's motives and psychological functioning. To understand the process subsequent to the abuse—the secrecy, denial, and ongoing failure to protect a child once abuse is disclosed—one must examine the relationships among the people involved.

Impact of Abuse

The psychological consequences of sexual victimization have been a topic of debate in the psychiatric literature for years. Many studies have examined small numbers of children of diverse ages in mental health settings without regard for their widely varied abuse experiences or the time elapsed since the abuse and its disclosure. Consequently, although children have exhibited a variety of symptoms, it has been difficult to determine whether the symptoms are specific to abuse or instead reflect preexisting psychological problems. Additionally, assumptions have been made about how children who have been abused should behave if they were in fact traumatized. It is not surprising that such studies fail to converge in their findings (Browne and Finkelhor 1986).

Only recently, with better understanding about the diversity of sexual-abuse experiences, have studies been able to explore the different psychological outcomes for children. Both effects of child sexual abuse and more enduring patterns of vulnerability are apparent. Gomes-Schwartz, Horowitz, and Sauzier (1985) examined 112 preschool, school-age, and adolescent children, most of whom had been sexually abused in the year before their evaluation. As a group, these children had more behavioral problems and signs of emotional harm than children in the general population. Among preschoolers, 20 percent showed impairment in their cognitive development and social skills and exhibited severe stress reactions. School-age children (seven to thirteen years) exhibited the most serious psychological disturbances, with 40 percent showing signs of aggression, impulsivity, destructive behavior, and severe fearfulness. Among adolescents, 24 percent were symptomatic with anxiety, depression, and obsessive concerns, and 21 percent showed dependent, inhibited qualities. Age-appropriate sexuality was also significantly disturbed in 27 percent of the four- to six-year-olds and 36 percent of the seven- to thirteen-year-olds, whose behavior included masturbation, excessive sexual curiosity, and exposure of the genitalia.

Friedrich, Urquiza, and Beilke (1986) studied a sample of eighty-five children aged three to twelve who had been sexually abused in the preceding twenty-four months. Behavior problems were examined for patterns of internalizing or externalizing symptoms (e.g., depression, withdrawal, and sleep problems, or aggression, cruelty, delinquency, and hyperactivity). Sexual behavior was also examined. Approximately 35 percent of the boys and 46 percent of the girls exhibited internalizing symptoms, and 36 percent of the boys and 39 percent of the girls exhibited externalizing symptoms. In particular, aggression, depression, and social withdrawal were most frequently noted for both males and females. Sexual problems were also common in the younger girls and the older boys.

Disruption of social functioning is most common among sexually abused adolescents and young adults. Herman (1981) interviewed forty pyschotherapy patients who had been victims of father-daughter incest and found that 33 percent had attempted to run away as adolescents. Her comparison group of twenty therapy patients whose fathers had been seductive toward them but not overtly incestuous had a runaway rate of less than 5 percent. Russell (1986) found that incest victims were at serious risk for being victimized again by sexual assault, including rape and attempted rape. Compared with nonvictimized women, they also bore children earlier, were more likely to be separated or divorced (at the time of Russell's study), and were more likely to have no religious preference and to have defected from their religious upbringing. Twice as many victims as nonvictims were unemployed.

Self-reports of serious psychological trauma from incest are also frequently accompanied by reports of subsequent psychological distress in young adulthood and later. Herman, in her in-depth research on adult victims of incest who were in psychotherapy, found significant levels of depression, impaired self-concept, and relationship disturbances in the women she studied. Russell's sample reported a range of long-term effects. These included negative feelings and attitudes toward men in general and the perpetrator specifically, negative feelings about their own self-worth and their bodies, and increased fear, anxiety, depression, and mistrust of others. Overwhelming evidence has accumulated indicating that childhood sexual abuse is consistently associated with serious mental health problems (Browne and Finkelhor 1986).

Efforts have been made to discern those aspects of the abuse experience most clearly associated with trauma. Three variables consistently emerge: the severity of sexual acts involved in the abuse; the use of force in gaining the child's compliance; and the relationship of the abuser to the child.

Severe types of child sexual abuse are associated with more severe psychological symptoms (Russell 1986). Extreme abuse includes completed or attempted intercourse, fellatio, cunnilingus, analingus, and anal intercourse. Least severe acts include unwanted kisses and touching. The possible effect of frequency and duration of the abuse is less clear than the increasing negative impact of more intrusive forms of sexual contact. Use of force to gain the child's compliance with abuse also contributes significantly to self-reported trauma (Finkelhor 1979; Russell 1986). Finally, incestuous abuse by fathers or stepfathers has been associated with more reported or observed trauma than abuse by others inside or outside the family (Finkelhor 1979; Friedrich, Urquiza, and Beilke 1986; Russell 1986).

Making sense out of the factors associated with abuse remains a more formidable task than isolating the factors themselves. Both short-term and long-term impact studies document a significant percentage of victims who do not respond in the direction researchers predict. How is it that some individuals come through less scarred? Why is abuse more important for some than for others? Placing child sexual abuse in a broader context helps us understand the variability in children's responses to it.

Antecedent Conditions in the Child

For individual children, the abuse interacts with preexisting conditions of their development, including their specific strengths or vulnerabilities. The "steeling" effect, a kind of temperamental resistance to stress, has been noted in some children who cope in spite of significant environmental strain (Garmezy 1983). Other children who are more anxious or insecure may react more to the stress of abuse and show more symptoms.

Developmental level will also influence the psychological meaning the abuse has for the child. Young children are extremely sensitive to violation of the stability and predictability of their caretaking environment, so abuse can disrupt their developing sense of interpersonal trust and safety. Older children will be more concerned with the moral meaning of the abuse ("he's bad; I'm bad") or the effect of the abuse on their identity and self-concept ("why me?").

Conditions of the Trauma

As studies have noted, the severity of the sexual abuse is significantly related to its impact on victims. At the most severe level, for some children the encounter with sexual abuse constitutes a psychic trauma. It is a negative and stressful event or series of events too anxiety-producing to cope with or understand. The experience is one of terror and unpredictable danger. The consequences constitute a form of post-traumatic stress reaction, including fearfulness, a pervasive sense of danger, a sense of being trapped, and reenactment and visualization of the abuse (Terr 1981). For some children, powerful negative emotions associated with sexuality, men, or situations perceived as threatening can be incapacitating and may result in persistent avoidant or phobic responses throughout development or in later life stages.

When abuse is recurrent, the need for defenses to "survive" psychologically is paramount. The most distressed children perceive the abuse as inescapable pain at the hands of those on whom they are wholly dependent. In addition to producing pronounced symptoms of posttraumatic stress, severe sexual abuse impairs development of effective coping strategies. Child victims experience dissociation from their feelings and may forget events or deny that they occurred. These coping strategies can help a child survive trauma, but they may not be adaptive in other stressful situations the child encounters later in life.

Relationship Trauma

The disruption of a safe and predictable relationship with a caretaker can be damaging for the child even when the sexual abuse is not severe. The child's feelings of betrayal can be lasting and may permanently destroy that relationship.

Sexual abuse can also damage the child's relationships with other family members. Victims may view their mothers as uncaring or as unavailable and passive. Expecting protection and nurturance from their parents, abused children are at first surprised and disbelieving if they find themselves unsupported. For such children their trauma also involves grief over their lost dependency. In many cases negative feelings generalize to affect other relationships beyond the family in later life.

Environmental Mediators

Studies of childhood resiliency and coping (Garmezy 1983; Murphy and Moriarty 1976) consistently point to the role of the family in mediating the impact of trauma and stress in the life of the child. Children need parents to intervene during stressful times and buffer them from trauma. Parents offer comfort and reassurance by showing that the environment will be responsive and that adults will protect children. Parents can also act as interpreters of events by putting traumatic situations in perspective and providing hope that things will eventually be better.

Unfortunately, sexual abuse and its disclosure create such severe environmental strain on parents too that often their response is not therapeutic or sensitive to the needs of the child. Following disclosure, families are in turmoil and often become highly unstable. Mann (1981) observed that parents and children hold widely divergent concerns and priorities for action subsequent to sexual assaults. Parents react by being angry and punitive, whereas children are more vulnerable and frightened. It has also been noted (Russell 1986) that children who are victims of incest are least likely to be offered support when they need it most.

Some children find parent "substitutes" outside their families. These children are better able to balance the feelings of betrayal by parents. They may then get the nurturance they need, escape from family pressure, and have alternative role models to emulate. Abused children who have safe, predictable adults in their environment appear to fare better than those who do not.

Proposed Response to Sexual Abuse

Child sexual abuse is complex, and professional responses to it vary widely. Therapists, pediatricians, protective service workers, law enforcement officials, attorneys, legislators, and social policymakers have all developed their own responses to the aspects of sexual abuse they must deal with. Some approaches are more oriented toward victims, others toward perpetrators; some are more therapeutic in their response, others more adversarial. The potential for conflict is greatest between therapeutic and adversarial responses to child sexual abuse where the mental health system and the legal system intersect and overlap. Repeatedly, as both systems have attempted to deal with the massive increase in reported cases of abuse, methods and goals of common legal practice and of psychological procedure have clashed.

Increasing numbers of sexual abuse cases are being tried in the criminal and civil courts to determine the guilt or innocence of alleged abusers and, where appropriate, to punish the offenders and protect the child victims. Society's reliance on the courts to provide a remedy for sexual abuse is relatively new and evolving. Retrospective reports of adults who were abused as children indicate the infrequency with which their abuse was ever made public, much less prosecuted (Finkelhor 1979; Herman 1981; Russell 1986). Now, however, as more children are being asked to participate in court as victim-witnesses to their own abuse, the courts are being criticized for their inappropriate expectations that child witnesses be able to function like little adults and to tolerate settings, procedures, and styles of questioning beyond their developmental capabilities.

Significant concerns are also expressed in the legal system about mental health practices and procedures. The bases for expert psychological opinions about sexual abuse have been criticized as inadmissible and irrelevant, since the slow and interpretive nature of diagnostic interviewing differs significantly from accepted legal procedures. Mental health experts also voice concern about the further trauma that in-depth interviews and testimony will cause some children; such thera-peutic concerns have also been seen as impediments to investigating or prosecuting a case.

These mutual complaints have led to improvements in practices in both the mental health system and the legal system. Legal experts are paying more attention to the developmental needs of child witnesses in many court settings (Berliner 1985; Lloyd 1985). Similarly, mental health experts have begun to objectify the process of interviewing and evaluating child victims in order to meet legal standards (White et al. 1986). A distinct role for psychological evaluation and psychotherapy with abused children as separate from legal proceedings is also being clarified (Sink 1988).

Beyond new procedural developments that make it more likely that courts and treatment providers can work cooperatively, there nonethe-less remain psychological and social dimensions of child sexual abuse that create such exceptional circumstances for the courts that solutions are not readily apparent. The areas of concern are delays in the child's disclosure of abuse, irregularities in the child's report of abuse, the child's need for safety and protection, the child's retraction of a disclo-sure of abuse, and the abuser's denial of responsibility (Sink and Graef 1985). In these areas the conflicting procedures and goals of the ther-apeutic and the legal responses to sexual abuse become more obvious. Each of these concerns highlights the social and psychological com-plexities of sexual abuse that can stymie the legal system and make treatment take longer.

Delay in Disclosure

A child's reluctance to disclose sexual abuse and to seek help from family or others is common. In a study of 156 cases of sexual abuse of children conducted at Tufts New England Medical Center in Boston (1984), 76 percent involved significant delays in disclosure. Among those were children who had been threatened and warned not to tell of their abuse and also children who feared their families' response to disclosure.

Abused children's failure to report their abuse and seek help is difficult for many people to comprehend. When one appreciates the complicated psychological and interpersonal realities surrounding abu-sive situations and the fact that the problem solver is in fact a child rather than an adult, their actions become more understandable. Al-though it is a sad commentary on family and societal protection of children, in many cases a child's silence after abuse begins to look adaptive and self-protective when seen in light of the rage and lack of resources the child must contend with after disclosure.

Overt threats against the safety and well-being of children or their loved ones can prevent disclosure for many years; some never tell at all. Children are acutely aware of power differences between themselves and adults. Even without threats they fear they will not be believed about the abuse, especially if the adult is a trusted member of the family or community. Children also worry that if they are believed, their disclosure will bring their family emotional harm, disruption, and social cost for which they will be blamed. The abuser's authority and status and family loyalties, coupled with the victim's total dependence, create a situation where the child fears that telling could increase their vulnerability and loss—making matters worse rather than better. Consequently, children become resourceful in their own efforts to avoid further abuse. They minimize its emotional impact and keep the secret. Frequently, however, they then suffer significant psychological stress and developmental disruption.

In the judicial system, concerns are raised about the motives of a victim who comes forward significantly after the alleged offense. The legal system does not focus on previous impediments to the child's disclosure. Instead, children may be accused of false allegations, instrumentally motivated or encouraged by a vindictive parent. Although empirical studies find the numbers of false allegations of abuse low (Sink 1987), the possibility is frequently raised in court in the defense of the alleged abuser. The exceptional circumstance of bitter child-custody litigation, where the motives of vindictive and polarized parents are highly suspect to attorneys and clinicians alike, unfortunately has resulted in the frequent legal argument that children are lying about abuse, especially when they have been slow to disclose it.

The Child's Report of Abuse

The court expects a witness to be able to make consistent spontaneous reports, elaborated with sufficient details to place the accused at the time and place of the crime with cause to do harm. Child victims of sexual abuse, both developmentally and psychologically, are often unable to be witnesses to their own abuse in this traditional manner. Because of the court's limited experience with child witnesses, children's responses to the usual questioning has been misinterpreted.

Even young children can describe events with consistency and clarity in terms of what happened to them and who was involved, but they use language and concepts appropriate to their developmental level. Their ability to elaborate their reports of abuse with details about dates, times, and frequencies is poor. Therefore one must evaluate the genuineness of children's reports using available contextual information and their emotional state as guides. With a very young child, an interviewer needs to formulate questions in a manner that accommodates the child's limitations in language understanding and expression. Play materials such as dolls and drawings can help verbally limited children demonstrate where and how they were abused.

Many challenges to children's reports of abuse have been successful because the court's understanding of child development is inadequate. When children are questioned with words and language constructions beyond their abilities, they become confused and can be led into contradicting their own statements. On the basis of such demonstrations in the courtroom, their reliability as witnesses has been questioned. Objections of coaching have been raised when children give age-appropriate reports of who abused them and what occurred but cannot offer elaborating information. When play techniques have been used to help a child disclose abuse, the child's ability to distinguish fact from fantasy has been questioned. In many instances children lose their credibility because they do not respond in court like adults.

The process by which disclosure comes about also raises questions about the child's reliability as a reporter. In some cases children's fears concerning disclosure are so strong that initially they deny abuse when questioned directly. Disclosure may occur only after adequate assurance that they will be safe, as will their loved ones, and that they are not to blame for their abuse or the disruptions the disclosure may cause. In other cases children have repressed memories of their abuse because of intolerable, frightening, and overwhelming feelings associated with it. In the course of play therapy in a safe, supportive setting, children may recover memories of abuse as they begin to work through and master their emotions. These memories emerge in a partial, halting fashion, and there may continue to be periods of denial until the entire experience is reconstructed.

When inconsistencies in children's statements about their abuse are embedded in the therapeutic context, they are easily viewed as part of the process of recovery and integration after trauma. From the legal perspective, however, the children's hesitations and self-contradictions in discrete interviews are not viewed sympathetically, but rather are seen as evidence of their unreliability as witnesses.

Empirical work on children's memory for traumatic events and their vulnerability to suggestion constitutes a new area of psychological study (Goodman 1984). Existing data indicate that adults as well as children may be vulnerable to suggestion or to contamination of their memory in particular circumstances (Loftus and Davies 1984). Although there is no adequate reason to assume that children are incompetent reporters, this concern remains pronounced in the courts. Efforts to adapt court proceedings to the developmental needs of children or to allow psychological experts to interpret children's reports for the court meet with resistance out of concern that such changes also reduce legal standards for evidence and compromise the rights of the accused. The adult standards for testimony will continue to be beyond the capacity of many child witnesses, allowing many sexual abusers to be better protected by the legal system than their victims.

The Child's Need for Safety and Protection

Ensuring safety is an important element of therapeutic intervention during the initial stages of a child's recovery. Actual harm or threats of harm during the abuse leave children preoccupied with safety. Fears of repeated trauma and retaliation are common. Even when physical protection can be guaranteed, children's psychological sense of vulnerability causes acute anxiety symptoms. It is common for preoccupation with aggression and powerlessness to predominate in their fantasies and their play. Protective separation from the abusing person and often the family is essential following the disclosure until the child's anxiety and fearfulness can be assessed.

Children whose compliance was gained through coercion or misuse of authority feel particularly vulnerable in the presence of their abusers. Herman (1981) found that adults who had been child victims reported they could not be near their abusers, even as adults, without feeling vulnerable or expecting to be asked to perform sexual acts again.

Given the context of enduring vulnerability, it is understandable that the right of an alleged abuser to face his accuser in court has prevented many children from testifying about their abuse. When it is in a child's best interest to be protected from contact with the abuser, court testimony and cross-examination in his presence will invariably be too traumatic. In such cases the welfare of child victims has not been a priority of the judicial system as it works to protect society more generally. In court, safety and protection for the victim are guaranteed only if a guilty verdict can be attained and is followed by sentencing or restraint from contact with the victim. This sequence and timetable frequently fail to meet the immediate safety needs of child victims.

Efforts are currently being made in many states, through legislation and reform in judicial proceedings, to incorporate more pragmatic child protective measures into the judicial proceedings. For example, videotapes of a child's testimony are being used in an attempt to reduce the number of times a child must attend court proceedings and be interviewed in the presence of the alleged abuser. In cases where potential trauma to the child is predicted from contact with the abuser, closed-circuit television during the child's testimony is being tried as a means of physically separating the victim from the alleged abuser while still allowing a degree of visual contact. Whether the courts will ultimately find this type of confrontation between the alleged offender and the victim constitutionally sufficient to protect the rights of the accused remains to be tested.

Given the large number of child victims now coming forward, the need to help child witnesses testify in court is more obvious and has gained support. The timing of the court proceeding in the child's recovery process still requires attention to allow that investigation of the alleged crime and the court proceedings take place at a point when the child feels sufficiently safe and supported to participate. Efforts to balance the needs of the child against the rights of the accused must continue.

Retraction of Abuse Complaints

When children disclose abuse, their intention is to stop the abuse and regain safety and protection. They may be unaware that their disclosure can severely disrupt their lives. The unexpected family turmoil that ensues can make them regret saying anything, and they may refuse to speak further about the abuse. Children can also feel pressured to withdraw their complaints and may then retract their accusations completely.

Children who withdraw their complaints may be attempting to put the abuse (and its associated stress) behind them. They are often responding to the desires of their parents, who want them to forget it. If parents become skeptical about the value of prosecution, especially when the process becomes lengthy, children lose therapeutic allies and become unable to work with the legal system on their own. In many cases, however, support for the child's disclosure is tenuous at best from the outset. Particularly in incestuous families, children are blamed for the crisis and disruption caused by their disclosure. Loyalty may divide family members into those who believe the child and those who support the abuser. If children become alienated from their families and see more problems than relief coming out of their report, they are likely to take back their disclosure.

Children need therapeutic allies who will attend to the new pressures and will support them in their courageous action to stop the abuse. Children and their parents must be reminded that the sexual abuse, not the child's disclosure, is the cause of the family disruption. In incestuous families the children need additional support to understand that the crisis surrounding the disclosure of abuse is a necessary step toward remedying the situation that allowed the abuse to occur.

Courts have not recognized the pressure placed on children to retract their allegations of abuse. They do not treat retractions as a sign that the child and family need more support if they are to continue in a court proceeding. Instead, retractions are too quickly taken as evidence that the original allegation was false. As discussed earlier, empirical studies find that false allegations are rare. Nonetheless, when a child retracts an abuse allegation or refuses to testify, the charges are usually dropped.

Denial of Abuse

It is rare that men with the potential to sexually abuse children acknowledge their vulnerability and seek therapeutic assistance out of their own motivation. More often, circumstances force them into treatment for abuse even as they are denying it. Their denial then becomes the first therapeutic hurdle. Intensive group treatment with other sexual abusers has been found to challenge their denial most effectively. Abusers vary in their insight and ability to progress toward accepting responsibility for their behavior and recognizing the pain they have caused their victims. Therapeutic change is founded on overcoming such denial and will not occur without it.

In sharp contrast to therapeutic work, the legal system supports the abuser's denial of wrongdoing as a legitimate stance. The presumption of innocence until proved guilty that protects the wrongfully accused also protects the rightfully accused. Men accused of sexual offenses are advised by their counsel not to participate in evaluations or treatment programs or to make statements that might be incriminating. Consequently, the prosecution of an abuse case can successfully delay, for an indefinite period, any efforts to reach the abuser therapeutically.

Therapists attempting to work with incestuous families often find that polarized, divisive court proceedings undermine treatment efforts. The crisis precipitated by disclosure is often useful to help families acknowledge their need for support and intervention. However, the adversarial system pits members against each other, sabotaging therapy.

Abusers also use the legal system to vindicate themselves. Because criminal convictions are rare in sexual abuse cases, abusers use their acquittal of charges as "proof" that the child was lying. With this "proof," abusive fathers seek and often attain, again from the courts, permission for renewed contact with their children despite protests from the children and concerns from therapists about the children's well-being and protection. Beyond that, abusers can effectively end any evaluation, treatment, or protective intervention begun with a child and other family members, claiming that there is no need to continue since it has been "proved" that no abuse occurred. When the legal system is misued and manipulated, resulting in further exploitation of children, the conflicting outcomes of therapeutic and legal approaches to intervention in abuse are most obvious and unsettling.

Prevention of Child Sexual Abuse

The societal response to sexual victimization of children is complicated socially, psychologically, and politically. In the abstract, the sexual molestation of children is a serious cultural taboo and as such is prohibited without exception in the moral, religious, and civil codes of our culture. In actuality, however, research findings on the incidence of abuse are beginning to suggest that sexual exploitation in childhood is common. How can a discrepancy of such magnitude exist between stated belief and behavior.

Unfortunately for the children involved, massive societal denial has contributed significantly to the failure to acknowledge sexual abuse as a child protection problem of major proportions. Even today, as sexual abuse gains public attention, the strength of the denial continues to create significant resistance to social change. An obvious example is the emergence of a more legalistic response to reports of abuse that begins with questioning the child (or adult) reporter's credibility rather than with protective action and advocacy. The criminal courts, with their stringent standards for evidence and witness credibility, have provided a peculiar arena for child protection decisions. The criminalization of sexual abuse may, in fact, perpetuate the social attitude of disbelief and divert attention from reasoned judgments about a child's best interests.

The development of an adequate child protection policy for sexual abuse cases has also been severely curtailed by limited (and often inaccurate) understanding of the incidence and dynamics of sexual abuse. Perceptions of sexual abuse and incest as rare and embarrassing social perversions certainly prevented any serious social attention or advocacy for many years. Failure to build an adequate theory of the motivation to abuse has allowed a disproportionate amount of attention to focus on the victim's behavior and on family response rather than on the sources of the abuse.

Although there is reason to believe that victims of abuse and their families may be more amenable to intervention than the abusers themselves, policy, program, and funding decisions still must recognize sexual abusers as a population worthy of study and intervention.

In ideal circumstances, the response to abuse is multilevel and multifaceted. The child victim needs protection from further physical or psychological abuse, and in a significant number of cases, psychological treatment is necessary for recovery. The family needs support in protecting the child and addressing the reality of the abuse, especially if loyalty to the abuser causes doubt and conflict that diminish attention to the child. The abuser needs to be held accountable for his behavior. Abusers who can respond to treatment must be identified. The widely varying standards concerning punishment should be made more uniform and predictable.

The viability of the criminal courts as a realistic arena in which to decide the complex child protection and social issues in sexual abuse cases requires careful evaluation. A system heavily weighted toward protecting the rights of alleged offenders cannot provide simultaneous support and protection for child victims. Continued refinement with mental health collaboration is indicated.

Misunderstandings about the nature of sexual victimization of children have persisted for a long time. Now, with greatly expanded information about the scope of sexual abuse as a major social concern, there is a clear challenge to go beyond abstract commitment to the incest taboo and move toward responsible action. In a civilized society, the sexual victimization of children and adults cannot be tolerated. Social advocacy and public education about sexual abuse in all its aspects must continue until public denial and ignorance are replaced by social responsibility for our children.

References

Allen, C. V. 1980. *Daddy's girl.* New York: Wyndham Books.

American Humane Association (AHA). 1986. *Annual report: Highlights of official abuse and neglect reporting.* Denver: American Humane Association.

Armstrong, L. 1978. *Kiss daddy goodnight: A speak-out on incest.* New York: Pocket Books.

Becker, J., and Abel, G. 1984. *Methodological and ethical issues in evaluating and treating adolescent offenders.* Washington, D.C.: National Institute of Mental Health.

Bender, L., and Blau, A. 1937. The reactions of children to sexual relations with adults. *American Journal of Orthopsychiatry* 7:500–518.

Berliner, L. 1985. The child witness: The progress and emerging limitations. National Legal Resource Center for Child Advocacy and Protection, Washington, D.C.

Browne, A., and Finkelhor, D. 1986. Impact of child sexual abuse: A review of the research. *Psychological Bulletin* 99:66–77.

Burgess, A. W., and Holmstrom, L. L. 1978. Accessory to sex: Pressure, sex, and secrecy. In *Sexual assault of children and adolescents*, ed. A. W. Burgess, A. N. Groth, et al. Lexington, Mass.: Lexington Books.

Butler, S. 1978. *Conspiracy of silence: The trauma of incest.* San Francisco: New Guild Publications.

de Young, M. 1982. Innocent seducer or innocently seduced? The role of the child incest victim. *Journal of Clinical Child Psychology* 11:56–60.

Finkelhor, D. 1979. *Sexually victimized children.* New York: Free Press.

———. 1984. *Child sexual abuse: New theory and research.* New York: Free Press.

Finkelhor, D., and Baron, L. 1986. Risk factors for child sexual abuse. *Journal of Interpersonal Violence* 1:43–71.

Freidrich, W. N.; Urquiza, A.; and Beilke, R. L. 1986. Behavior problems in sexually abused young children. *Journal of Pediatric Psychology* 11:47–57.

Garmezy, N. 1983. Stressors of childhood. In *Stress, coping and development in childhood*, ed. N. Garmezy and M. Rutter. New York: McGraw-Hill.

Garrett, K., and Rossi, P. 1978. Judging the seriousness of child abuse. *Medical Anthropology* 3:1–48.

Giovannoni, J., and Becerra, R. 1979. *Defining child abuse.* New York: Free Press.

Gomes-Schwartz, B.; Horowitz, J.; and Sauzier M. 1985. Severity of emotional distress among sexually abused preschool, school-age, and adolescent children. *Hospital and Community Psychiatry* 36:503–8.

Goodman, G. S. 1984. The child witness: Conclusions and future directions for research and legal practice. In *The child witness*, ed G. S. Goodman. Special issue of the *Journal of Social Issues* 40:157–75.

Groth, N. 1979. *Men who rape: The psychology of the offender.* New York: Plenum Press.

Herman, J. 1981. *Father-daughter incest.* Cambridge: Harvard University Press.

Jones, D. 1987. Reliable and fictitious accounts of sexual abuse in children. *Journal of Inter-personal Violence.* In press.

Karpel, M. A. 1980. Family secrets. 1. Conceptual and ethical issues in the relational context. 2. Ethical and practical considerations in therapeutic management. *Family Process* 19:295–306.

Kaufman, I.; Peck, A. L.; and Tagiuri, C. K. 1954. The family constellation and overt incestuous relations between father and daughter. *American Journal of Orthopsychiatry* 24:266–77.

Kinsey, A. C.; Pomeroy, W. B.; Martin, C. E.; and Gebhard, P. H. 1953. *Sexual behavior in the human female.* Philadelphia: W. B. Saunders.

Kreiger, M. J.; Rosenfeld, A. A.; Gordan, A., and Bennett, M. 1980. Problems in the psychotherapy of children with histories of incest. *American Journal of Psychotherapy* 34:81–87.

Lloyd, D. 1985. Practical issues in avoiding confrontation of a child witness and the defendant in a criminal trial. National Legal Resource Center for Child Advocacy and Protection, Washington, D.C.

Loftus, E., and Davies, G. 1984. Distortions in the memory of children. In *The child witness*, ed. G. S. Goodman. Special issue of the *Journal of Social Issues* 40:51–67.

Lustig, N.; Dresser, J.; Spellman, J.; and Murray, T. 1966. Incest: A family group survival pattern. *Archives of General Psychiatry* 14:31–40.

Machotka, P.; Pittman, F. S.; and Flomenhaft, K. 1966. Incest as a family affair. *Family Process* 6:98–116.

Mann, E. M. 1981. Self-reported stresses of adolescent rape victims. *Journal of Adolescent Health Cases* 2:29–33.

Murphy, L. B., and Moriarty, A. E. 1976. *Vulnerability, coping and growth: From infancy to adolescence.* New Haven: Yale University Press.

Russell, D. 1983. The incidence and prevalence of intrafamilial and extrafamilial sexual abuse of female children. *Child Abuse and Neglect* 7:133–46.

———. 1986. *The secret trauma: Incest in the lives of girls and women.* New York: Basic Books.

Sink, F. 1987. True and false allegations of sexual abuse: A critique of the evidence. Paper presented at the Third National Family Violence Research Conference, University of New Hampshire.

———. 1988. A hierarchical model for evaluation of child sexual abuse. *American Journal of Orthopsychiatry.* In press.

Sink, F., and Graef, G. 1985. In the courtroom or the clinic: Intervention problems and solutions with childhood sexual abuse. Paper presented at the sixty-second annual meeting of the American Orthopsychiatric Association, New York.

Sloane, P., and Karpinski, E. 1942. Effect of incest on the participants. *American Journal of Orthopsychiatry* 12:666–72.

Summit, R. C. 1983. The child sexual abuse accommodation syndrome. *Child Abuse and Neglect* 7:177–93.

Terr, R. C. 1981. Forbidden games. *Journal of the American Academy of Child Psychiatry* 20:741–60.

Tufts New England Medical Center, Division of Child Psychiatry. 1984. *Sexually exploited children: Service and research project.* Final report for the Office of Juvenile Justice and Delinquency Prevention. Washington, D.C.: U.S. Department of Justice.

White, S.; Strom, G.; Santilli, G.; and Halpin, B. 1986. Interviewing young sexual abuse victims with anatomically correct dolls. *Child Abuse and Neglect* 10:519–29.

Wyatt, G. E. 1985. The sexual abuse of Afro-American and white women in childhood. *Child Abuse and Neglect* 9:507–19.

5   *Abused Adolescents*

MARTHA B. STRAUS

The special problems of abused adolescents have only begun to be addressed, despite evidence that adolescents constitute a significant and increasing proportion of child abuse cases. Of known child abuse cases 25 percent concern twelve- to seventeen-year-olds. Adolescent abuse is twice as prevalent as abuse of children under six years old (National Center on Child Abuse and Neglect 1981). These data suggest that adolescents may be more vulnerable to abuse than are infants and small children. The *National Incidence Study* further revealed that 192,000 adolescents were known to be maltreated in this country in 1980, and most studies estimate that the actual incidence is much greater than reported. The effects of adolescent abuse are also severe: 24 percent of all fatalities and 41 percent of all serious injuries reported in cases of child abuse occur in children between twelve and seventeen. Twice as many cases involving girls as boys are reported, in contrast to the more equal balance between the sexes among preteens. Moreover, the *National Incidence Study* concluded that adolescent girls are one-third again as likely to be abused as those under twelve. It is evident, then, that teenage girls are at risk for physical and sexual abuse in ways not fully appreciated in either the clinical or the research literature on child abuse. Journals devoted to the study of adolescence contribute little more to our understanding of adolescent abuse.

It is probable that adolescents are abused for different reasons than younger children—particularly if there is no previous history of child abuse. Conflict is generally heightened in families with teenagers, and the developmental tasks of this period create new problems. Hoekstra (1984) noted that adolescent abuse can best be understood as a crisis in the life cycle of the family. Resolving the crisis and the symptomatic abuse, Hoekstra suggested, involves helping the family mature to the next stage of development. Indeed, the rebellious "identity crisis" of the adolescent is often timed to collide with the insecure "midlife crisis" of her parents (Erikson 1968), precipitating painful family changes that members may resist (Garbarino and Gilliam 1980; Haley 1980; Stierlin 1974). Although the period of adolescence is disruptive for many families, the abusive parent views an adolescent's move toward greater independence with intense frustration and anger.

Adolescents also respond to abuse in ways that distinguish them from younger children. The dearth of research on adolescent victims is probably the result of behavior that shifts attention away from the abusive incidents and onto the victims themselves. For example, delinquency, running away, truancy, drug and alcohol use, schizophrenia, prostitution, teen pregnancy, juvenile homicide, parricide, and suicide have *all* been associated with abuse of adolescents. While abuse itself does not cause all the social problems of adolescence, these youngsters are turning up with notable regularity in studies of disturbed teenagers that did not begin as research on abuse. In other words, the correlations between abuse and many of the more serious problems of adolescence appear to be strong, albeit fashioned through selective posthoc analyses. Controlled studies of adolescent victims and longitudinal research in this area of practice have been sorely lacking.

Despite the number of situations in which disclosure is possible, abuse of adolescents often goes undetected and untreated. Many groups of professionals come into frequent contact with abused adolescents, including child protective workers, runaway/crisis shelter staff, juvenile court and probation officers, police, family court attorneys and judges, predelinquent diversion counselors, residential treatment staff, community mental health and child guidance therapists, teachers and school administrators, and primary-care physicians (Fisher and Berdie 1978). It is not coincidental that the professionals in these settings tend to be extremely busy, encountering daily insurmountable struggles, since disturbed adolescents often exert dervishlike energy in bringing attention to their plight. However, it is not impending burnout that causes professionals to focus on the task at hand (e.g., teach the teen, adjudicate the shoplifter, do the school physical, listen to complaints about unfair curfew). Rather, these necessary tasks are evident and the abuse may not be.

Adolescents usually do not look like "victims" in the ways that younger children do. Abuse of teenagers does not typically involve broken bones, spiral fractures, subdural hematomas, or other extreme injuries generally associated with physical child abuse. Adolescents do not usually act like "victims," either. They are often as big as adults (or even bigger), and they may try to appear more mature than their years. They have a verbal and behavioral repertoire that often includes outrageously provocative gestures. While they may not always use restraint, they are presumed to have better impulse control than young children and so to be more responsible for their relationships with others. Further, adolescents are mobile and can participate independently in school and extracurricular activities, so they should have access to external social supports if they really need them. In sum, the discrepancies between power and resources so critical to the definitions of abuse employed by professionals (e.g., Finkelhor 1983) are not apparent on first glance in adolescent cases and so may be overlooked altogether.

Even when adolescent abuse cases are recognized, therapeutic interventions are limited. There are insufficient resources to treat abused adolescents (Lipsitz 1977), and knowledge is incomplete about what treatments are most effective (Farber and Joseph 1985; Lourie 1979). Furthermore, the symptoms of distress that adolescents display even when they are recognized as victims often require immediate attention. Treatment of psychological problems has to be secondary to other types of intervention (e.g., detention, special education, group care). Shelters, hospitals, and child protective services all come into contact with adolescents who have experienced similarly severe violence against them (Farber et. al. 1984). However, interventions are based upon the symptoms the adolescent displays and not the underlying abuse. Since abused adolescents are often masters of crisis, it is also typical for those cases to take disproportionate amounts of professional time just in the "handling." For example: an abused runaway is placed in a shelter and offered therapy, only to be moved before treatment gets under way. The move can be precipitated by time constraints (many shelters and group homes are temporary), by violation of rules (alternative placements are strict), or by a repeat of the running away (abused runaways tend to run in the face of both intimacy and conflict). All these real scenarios have one truth in common: they will require crisis intervention once again, and treatment for the psychological effects of the abuse may be mentioned but will not, for many reasons, take center stage.

An Ecological Model

In approaching issues of treatment (or research or prevention), an ecological perspective on adolescent abuse is particularly helpful. Abused adolescents have such a wide experience of victimization, and respond to it with such variety of emotions and behaviors, that there could never be a monolithic intervention. The practitioner, therefore, must have available an array of approaches from which to select the most suitable. An assessment of the complete ecosystem of the abused adolescent will necessarily include an understanding of the background characteristics of the abusive parents and of the abused adolescent (ontogenic development); the particular interaction among family members (microsystem); the family's relationship to the community and to helping agencies (exosystem); and the larger cultural fabric into which the individual, the family, and the community are inextricably woven (macrosystem). Although data collection on so many levels may appear cumbersome and impractical, the information obtained from this kind of analysis can often help to detect and divert impending crises while creating a violence-free situation for the adolescent. Such a theoretical approach may also help release researchers and policymakers from the complex web of variables associated with abused adolescents that often snags well-intentioned efforts.

Ontogenic Development

Adolescents may wittingly or unwittingly contribute to their abuse. This can take the form of oppositional acts or sarcastic and disrespectful behavior (e.g., skipping school, violating curfew, talking back, stealing, lying) that would annoy the most tolerant parent. In fact, it is hard not to be sympathetic with many abusive parents when they describe the irritation they have endured. Although there is no justification for abuse, the parents' testimony suggests the impressive array of provocations many adolescents possess. However, other adolescents may also display "abuse-eliciting characteristics" (Belsky 1980) that can place them at risk no matter how obedient they may seem. These include, for example, poor impulse control, depressive withdrawal, low self-esteem, irritability, accident proneness, magical thinking, hypersensitivity, and a variety of developmental disturbances. Such characteristics make teenagers more difficult to raise and can drive parents to violence if they already respond poorly to the stress of their children's adolescence.

The effects of abuse are severe whether the adolescent is provocative or compliant to begin with. Perhaps more than any other group, teenagers can communicate their distress through a wide variety of attention-seeking symptoms. Farber and Joseph (1985) summarized the emotional and behavioral effects of adolescent abuse. These included six patterns of adolescents reaction: acting out (running away, theft, drug abuse, provoking behavior, and truancy); depression (low activity, social isolation, fluctuations in weight, fatigue, and low self-esteem); generalized anxiety (lack of trust, rationalizing and manipulating, poor concentration, impaired identity development, and academic failure); extreme adolescent adjustment problems (alcohol use, school misconduct, and inaccessibility of feelings); emotional-thought disturbance (homicidal actions, disorders of speech, hypomanic symptoms, and thought disorders); and helpless dependency (homicidal and suicidal ideation, difficulties with siblings, and family role problems). Many abused adolescents exhibit combinations of these patterns at the same time or in succession. If one symptom or set of symptoms does not elicit help, then there will be an escalation into greater disturbance, or a significant change in the symptom constellation, or both. For example, an abused adolescent who acts depressed and does poorly in school may become suicidal or run away if the abusive situation is not identified.

The role of self-destructive behaviors in abused adolescents has received particular attention, especially in light of the recent publicity about adolescent suicide. Most abused adolescents show signs of depression and behave self-destructively whether or not they are actively suicidal or also exhibit other symptoms. They typically exercise poor judgment in protecting themselves from obviously dangerous situations. For example, it is common for these youngsters to experiment with drugs in a random, take-anything manner, to wait alone on dangerous streets, to get sexually involved in an indiscriminate fashion, or to provoke fights with others bigger and stronger than they are. Green (1976) observed that younger children often internalize the hostility of their abusive parents and come to believe that they deserve it. Their self-hatred and low self-esteem then become the nucleus for subsequent self-destructive behavior. These observations are consistent with the clinical picture for older children and adolescents as well.

Abused adolescents are also outwardly aggressive and turn up in large numbers among the growing ranks of status offenders and juvenile delinquents (McCord 1979). Some clinicians call their aggression "masked depression" (Carlson and Cantwell 1980; Stott 1982). These adolescents will act out their sad and helpless feelings by appearing angry and destructive. In the psychodynamic view, acting out is a defense against underlying feelings of hopelessness and low self-esteem (Blos 1962; Burks and Harrison 1962; Chwast 1974). In both early and later formulations, acting out is defined as displacement into action that allows partial gratifications of repressed impulses (Cary 1979). Even parricide in abusive families can be viewed as a culmination of unsuccessful efforts to displace rage against an abusive parent onto some other object. Events coalesce such that, for the adolescent, no alternative symptoms or "cries for help" will be heard clearly enough (Post 1982). Acting out distress need not be the most effective communication of anger about abuse. Toolan (1962) suggested that suicidal gestures can have an aggressive undertone expressing the fantasy: "You'll be sorry when I am dead; you'll see how badly you've treated me," and many abused and suicidal adolescents have largely aggressive fantasies about dying.

Whether the abused adolescent communicates distress through self-destructive and suicidal behavior or through oppositional and delinquent acts, it is clear that the abuse will also have deep and deleterious effects upon normal development. Just at the time when feelings of competence and consistency are most necessary to enable them to move to independence, abused adolescents are faced with overwhelming feelings of inadequacy and confusion. Almost regardless of the strengths with which these adolescents have entered this period, it is likely that abuse will impede the development of important age-related communication and problem-solving skills, placing them at a great disadvantage with peers. For example, they may be slower in attaining the abstract reasoning ability that Piaget described as formal operational thought. It is important for adolescents to learn to consider possible ways a particular problem might be solved—the foundation of logical and flexible thought. They therefore need to have available compelling situations and models for different methods of problem solving. This is as true for conflict resolution as it is for other dilemmas. Some abused adolescents experience the use of force and power against them as the *only* solution to all problems, and their reasoning will reflect this limiting perception.

Similarly, the development of one's own identity as a person (what Erikson called ego identity) requires a perception of the self as separate (despite important emotional ties to others) and a feeling of internal consistency that are both more difficult for abused adolescents to attain. Autonomy and "wholeness" cannot be experienced in the context of abuse. Since adolescents focus so many of their concerns upon the physical aspects of themselves, it follows that they will have further trouble forming this constructive identity while their bodies are being physically or sexually violated.

There is some controversy about whether effects of adolescent abuse differ depending upon time of onset. Lourie (1979) theorized that there might be differences among those whose abuse begins in childhood and continues into adolescence; begins as spanking in childhood but becomes more severe and violent in adolescence; and begins in adolescence. Garbarino and Gilliam (1980) suggested that, with the exception of sexual abuse, abuse beginning in childhood is more psychologically damaging than abuse beginning in adolescence. Galambos and Dixon (1984) provide preliminary support for this view, noting that adolescents who had been abused since childhood had more severe adjustment problems than adolescents who were abused more recently, marked particularly by an extremely external locus of control (they perceived that luck, chance, fate, and powerful others had more control over events than they did). Other evidence suggests, however, that all abused adolescents, regardless of severity or time of onset, react similarly to the violence. For example, in research using Lourie's three groups, Farber and Joseph (1985) found that all abused adolescents had ego deficits and demonstrated emotional and behavioral reactions that made groups indistinguishable from one another. Ultimately, the duration of the abuse may be less important than the fact of the disturbed adolescent-parent relationship in determining psychological adjustment.

Parents of abused adolescents resort to violence out of a variety of needs and frustrations that are important to understanding the abuse. Many clinical investigators have noted that these parents have not themselves had the experience of being mothered as adolescents. The emotional deprivation and anger that result are perhaps responsible for the role reversal often observed in such families. These parents expect to be cared for by their children rather than to care for them (Green 1976; Spinetta and Rigler 1972). When the adolescent is unable to comply with this unrealistic demand, the parent responds with violence. A dramatic example of this role confusion is the case of an abusive mother of a teenage girl who forced her daughter to have an abortion, then got pregnant herself. She was violent when her daughter would not stay home from school to care for her and the infant.

Parents of abused adolescents can also be fatalistic about their ability to influence their children without violence. As they see the child becoming more independent and increasingly out of their reach, they come to feel "externally controlled" and are more likely to resort to force instead of establishing contingency-based punishments for misconduct (Levenson 1973; Yates, Kennelly and Cox 1975). In this reaction, they come to look more like parents who abuse pre-adolescent children.

The intergenerational-transmission hypothesis, so popular in the family violence literature, appears to have some clinical support for families with abused adolescents as well. Parents who abuse their adolescents were frequently abused themselves as teenagers and in these cases the contemporary dynamics become clearer in the context of the parents' painful (and violent) attempts to individuate from their own families of origin (Duke and Duke 1978; Minuchin, Montalvo, and Guerney 1967).

However, a factor that distinguishes recent-onset adolescent abuse from long-term child abuse is often the relatively benign history, provided by parent and adolescent alike, of the years before the child's twelfth birthday. The social and economic stresses associated with child abuse are often absent, and a relatively idealized childhood emerges. In its purest form, the child was obedient and performed adequately in school. The parents may have had some marital problems, but these were kept under control, and each had a relationship with their child that they look back on with nostalgia. They may even report their own childhood as happy and say that their parents got strict only when they were bad as teenagers—though they were never as bad as their own offspring are now. These parents view themselves as once competent and as more lenient than their own parents were. They are suddenly stymied and unable to use the old solutions for resolving conflicts. In turn, they may disagree about how to manage the new problems, fueling the conflict that is then diverted onto the adolescent, often in the form of abuse.

The Microsystem

Research on the functioning of families where adolescents are abused has yielded some interesting theories. Galambos and Dixon (1984) suggested that abusive families function differently depending upon whether the violence is short term (onset in adolescence) or long term (onset in childhood, continuing into adolescence). Parents who begin abusing their offspring at young ages are more often separated, divorced, or single than parents who first abuse their offspring in adolescence. Generally, perpetrators of long-term child abuse earn half the income that short-term abusers earn. In addition, these researchers indicate that long-term abusers are more transient than short-term abusers. The general picture of long-term abusers is clearly spelled out in the child abuse literature: relative poverty, marital instability, and transience, complicated by the low availability of personal resources to cope with life stress. In contrast, short-term abusers appear to be more settled and stable and are more often middle class. There is also some evidence that while both parents may be abusive, fathers are more often responsible for abuse beginning in adolescence (Garbarino and Gilliam 1980).

Another theory, proposed by Pelcovitz (1984) and supported by clinical observation, categorizes adolescent-abusing families into three groups: cases of childhood onset where there is also a history of violence in the family of origin; authoritarian families where rigid parenting styles are characterized by denial of family conflict; and overindulgent families where a pattern of permissive parenting is coupled with sporadic violent attempts at control. This last type is also characterized by a parent's early loss of a parent. Much has been written about the family dynamics in cases of childhood onset and the long-term dysfunction that can be expected. Relatively less has been shared about family structure and functioning in cases of short-term abuse.

The authoritarian adolescent-abusing family is marked by inflexibility. Family members relate to one another in such an unyielding way that any change is felt as a threat to the survival of the family and produces intense anxiety and associated regression. An adolescent's efforts at separation and individuation are equated with desertion and betrayal of the family. As a result, family preoccupations with the selfishness and "badness" of the victim are prominent, and parents work hard to prevent their adolescents from getting privileges that might be associated with maturity or responsibility. Adolescent symptoms are viewed suspiciously and angrily by other family members when they are not denied altogether; even serious suicide attempts may be passed off as "more showboating" on the part of the adolescent. It is more likely that abused adolescents from inflexible families will resort to suicide or running away as dramatic means of restructuring the family. Often they will sacrifice themselves, believing that one way or another everyone would be better off without them. In fact the symptoms in these rigid families reflect the need for a family reorganization that permits the family to remain together in a more flexible arrangement.

By contrast, the overindulgent abusive family is marked by a dramatic inconsistency. Rules change from day to day and are enforced randomly. Parenting functions range from passive and permissive acceptance of the adolescent's behavior to especially punitive styles. This chaotic structure is particularly stressful for adolescents, who search for limits even as they strive for independence. The communication style of these families can be characterized by endless negotiation with little resolution. Many therapy hours can be spent establishing a curfew or the exact chores the adolescent is expected to complete each week, only to have the rules ignored by all members. In these families parents are unable or unwilling to define generational boundaries clearly, and the child, who is set up to act out in this situation, is then abused for overstepping an arbitrary line. The adolescent has learned to act out and "ask for it" through both overt and covert messages from her parents. Johnson and Szurek (1952, 323) suggested that "antisocial acting out in a child is unconsciously initiated, fostered and sanctioned by the parents who, through a child's acting out, achieve gratification of their own poorly-integrated forbidden impulses." It is possible that the parent's early loss of a parent described by Pelcovitz perpetuates an unresolved struggle into the next generation. The rage attendant on the premature death of a parent is unconsciously projected onto the adolescent, whose acting out enables its forbidden expression. Abused adolescents in overindulgent families tend to display symptoms that bring in external authority—truant officers, the courts, mental health workers—to control family members and to help them cope with their crisis of adolescence.

Another feature common to all short-term abusive families is a highly conflicted marital relationship. The choice of a spouse may have been influenced greatly by fantasies and perceptions of people in the parent's family of origin. Interactions between the spouses vary in how anger is expressed—even in the inflexible families it can be quite open, but more often it is aired indirectly, and the adolescent is abused instead. The parental relationship often centers on dependency conflicts in which one spouse or the other is threatened with being hurt emotionally or physically. The threat of separation is always present, and often one parent is overwhelmed and depressed. Chief among the conflicts is a difference of opinion about how to manage the adolescent. Each parent will blame the other for the family stress leading to the violence. Abusive parents will accuse their mates of being too permissive or unavailable. Clearly the parents are not working in concert to provide age-appropriate expectations or limits. However, they do at times resort to "pseudocoalitions" (Hogg and Northman 1979) under stress created by the adolescent. The teenager may question her parents' inconsistent behavior (perhaps to find limits or to test them), which in turn will cause them to unite temporarily against their "audacious" adolescent. Abusive parents are often invested in minimizing their disagreements. This denial is usually carried off on an abstract and emotional level and bears with it a message to the adolescent that punishment is forthcoming. In this manner children divert the marital conflict onto themselves and take the brunt of the aggression that is unconsciously directed at a spouse.

Since abuse of adolescents is often the result of family dysfunction and not the array of social problems that characterize child abuse, it may, in fact be more amenable to family treatment. However, outsiders in the exosystem need to be aware of these dynamics and must be prepared to make contact with the families in a way that offers them support and alternatives to the violence.

The Exosystem

Perhaps more than any other victim group, the abused adolescent comes into contact with community agencies as a matter of course. Whereas victims of long-term abuse may be served by the child protective system, abused adolescents are more likely to reach the interventions of the juvenile justice system, the alternative youth services network, and the mental health system (Fisher and Berdie 1978).

The Juvenile Justice System

A significant number of adolescents who are part of the juvenile justice system have been abused. In one review of the literature on juvenile offenders, Pate (1986) concluded that between 40 and 90 percent of youths in trouble with the law have been abused—often repeatedly or brutally. In the past decade, several reputable longitudinal studies have concluded that children who witness and experience violence in their homes are at high risk for delinquency. Given that more than four million adolescents come into contact with law enforcement agencies every year (Monahan 1976), this association is particularly noteworthy. Moreover, abused offenders are significantly more likely to commit crimes involving interpersonal violence than are their nonabused delinquent peers. Adolescent victims may be unusually well trained in using force to obtain a desired end. A thorough abuse-screening program should become part of the intake procedure for all adolescents charged with delinquency. This needs to be done privately and individually with each family member. Links to protective, community-based, and therapeutic resources should be established as part of dispositional planning. Juvenile offenders who have been abused need more than due process. They also merit protection, treatment, and education in conflict resolution. Family counseling may also be necessary to enable the delinquent to return successfully to the community.

The Alternative Youth Services Network

Deinstitutionalization has diverted large numbers of status offenses—
the majority of arrests—out of the legal system and into other community-based programs. Status offenses are acts committed by minors
(e.g., truancy, running away, being beyond parental control, promis-
cuity) that would not be considered crimes if committed by an adult
but that subject children to the jurisdiction of the juvenile court (Allin-
son 1978). While diversion may be beneficial from a legal standpoint,
the increase in status offenders has created an enormous problem for
the alternative youth services network. However, this network, including runaway shelters, crisis hot lines, storefront counseling, and other
more traditional community services such as YMCAs, is often the most
effective for abused adolescents in crisis and is the most common
source of identified cases.

Abused adolescents run away from home to shelters in large numbers. The National Statistical Survey of Runaway Youth reported that
733,000 adolescents ran away from home in 1975 (Opinion Research
Corporation 1976). More recent studies indicate that as many as 78
percent of all runaways have been abused, suggesting that some abused
adolescents choose to escape destructive and dysfunctional family dynamics in order to get help for themselves and their families (Farber
et al. 1984). However, alternative youth shelters frequently have difficulty maintaining supportive services and therapeutic intervention.
Training programs for crisis counselors and youth shelter workers need
to incorporate an assessment of violence in the home and need to teach
workers how to document the family's difficulties with conflict resolution so that a treatment referral can be made. Before a runaway
teenager can return home, the maltreatment that may have precipitated the escape must be addressed. Moreover, links to child protective
agencies, to the juvenile courts, and to the community mental health
system must be established. Too often, the alternative youth services
programs do not coordinate their services with those of other agencies.
The abuse of adolescents needs to be labeled in the place where they
seek help. Without coordination of services, this abuse will continue
to be subsumed by labels like "status offender," which place the blame
for the problem on the victim.

The Mental Health System

Abused adolescents whose behavior does not earn them the label delinquent or status offender may still reach interventions in the mental
health system. One study (Farber and Joseph 1985) looked at abused
adolescents identified by more traditional referral sources (e.g. pedia-

tricians, educators, friends, and neighbors) and seen in a mental health setting. Of seventy-seven abused adolescents studied, 70 percent had difficulties in academic performance, 52 percent had sleeping problems, 31 percent admitted to drug abuse, 35 percent reported aggressive (though nondelinquent) behavior, and 23 percent had engaged in self-destructive, reckless behavior. Many of the adolescents had homicidal thoughts (41 percent), 13 percent had made suicidal gestures, and an additional 38 percent had suicidal thoughts. In other words, the mental health system may encounter those abused adolescents to whom the label "mentally ill" can best be applied. The abused teenager who appears at a child protective agency, a hospital, or a community mental health center is more likely to be also labeled an "abused child" than those seen in the criminal justice system. The abuse label may earn them more sympathetic treatment by providers in the community.

There are numerous combinations of therapeutic interventions that can assist adolescent victims. These include individual, group, and family therapy, if necessary in conjunction with out-of-home placement (in the care of a relative, friends, shelter, or foster home) and even the juvenile court probation department. For example, an abused teenager may need to stay with her maternal aunt while working out problems with her parents in family therapy, developing problem-solving skills in a group (to learn how to avoid setting herself up for abuse and other dangers in the future), and meeting monthly with her probation officer to ensure that she is attending school. Regardless of the treatment program, the goal is to establish and maintain a safe life for the adolescent through the best combination of services and agencies.

There are also natural supports in the exosystem that are worth mentioning. Social isolation from the extended family and the community, a variable widely cited in the child abuse literature, can also describe the family of the abused adolescent. These families need to be linked up with neighborhood and community activities (e.g. community centers, YMCAs, social clubs, PTAs), religious or cultural organizations, and self-help services (e.g. parent-support groups, parental-stress hot line numbers). In this manner the social isolation and attendant stress can be alleviated while supportive models are offered to parents struggling to cope with a difficult adolescent.

The Macrosystem

Although abused adolescents and their families need a responsive exosystem, contemporary social policies and values have led to inadequate and fragmented services throughout the United States. Studies on the plight of abused teenagers have called for an analysis of community resource networks designed to ameliorate problems of adolescent abuse and neglect (Fisher and Berdie 1978). Once strengths, weaknesses, and service gaps are identified, then strategies for technical assistance to communities can be developed. Coordinated services for abused teenagers will provide an important first step in addressing not only abuse but also many of the urgent contemporary problems of adolescence.

The abused adolescent, the family, and the community are all stitched together, in part, by the philosophy and policies within the social fabric. At the most basic level, it is almost a cliché to note that our social policies condone violence. However, it is still important to keep in mind that the tendency to resort to force in dealing with conflicts in adult-child relationships is endemic to our thinking (Gil 1979). A destructive message can be conveyed to adolescents simply through the prevailing social, economic, and political order. In this context, the unveiled resentment of adults toward the challenges posed by the next generation is just a reflection of social policies that also harm adolescents.

The symbolic and practical importance of federal policy in molding the behavior of private citizens toward adolescents should not be underestimated. Forms of approved abuse—including corporal punishment in schools, mistreatment of teenagers in protective, therapeutic, or correctional institutions, and abuse in the foster care and juvenile justice systems—suggest that reforms are needed before we can convey the message that, as a society, we do not tolerate abuse (Zigler 1983).

Although many communities have an array of services that might help abused adolescents and their families, these services are rarely coordinated, and those who might benefit may not know such help is available. In particular, child protective agencies need to become more involved with the problems of abused adolescents. Protective interventions that work with families of younger children are not suitable and need to be replaced with services that families of teenagers will use— in their schools, churches, and places of employment. Additionally, specialized training in adolescent and midlife development would offer a broader context to service providers who may view child and adolescent abuse similarly. Ultimately, comprehensive federal policy addressing the particular needs of families with adolescents, including health, education, and employment, would help provide a framework for the local effort.

The media also form a kind of social policy by reinforcing negative and violent attitudes toward adolescents. Media coverage confers status on certain events, people, or problems. Such "agenda setting" (Muenchow and Gilfillan 1983) is more obvious in the news, but it extends to fictional programs as well. Television may show excessive violence, but not towards those most likely to be victimized. Children, adolescents, the poor, and minorities are still underrepresented for portrayal, realistic or otherwise. Gerbner (1980) pointed out that both television news and dramas tend to devalue children and adolescents by grossly underestimating their sheer presence in American society. Newspapers also tend to relegate coverage of the "family" to the back of the paper. It is evident that the media's attitude is that "children aren't news" and are certainly not "hard" news (Muenchow and Gilfillan 1983, 227). The conflict between the media's goals of entertainment and education is likely to persist. The relative dearth of education on commercial television can only perpetuate a cynical distortion in beliefs about real events in the lives of adolescents today.

Policies to prevent adolescent abuse cannot await broader social reform, which in the long run seems necessary. However, we cannot ignore the relation between social reform and the quality of life for adolescents and families. Despite the current mood of fiscal austerity toward programs to help teenagers we need to persuade policymakers that denial and ignorance will, in a short time, be more costly than changes now seem. Such social changes can in turn assist communities in providing necessary services, enable families to endure the stress of the period of adolescence, and offer alternatives to individual parents and adolescents so that they may live free from violence.

References

Allison, R., ed. 1978. *Status offenders and the juvenile justice system.* New York: National Council on Crime and Delinquency.

Belsky, J. 1980. Child maltreatment: An ecological integration. *American Psychologist* 358(4): 320–35.

Blos, P. 1962. *On adolescence.* Glencoe, Ill. Free Press.

Burks, H. L., and Harrison, S. I. 1962. Aggressive behavior as a means of avoiding depression. *American Journal of Orthopsychiatry* 32:416–22.

Carlson, G. A., and Cantwell, D. P. 1980. Unmasking masked depression in children and adolescents. *American Journal of Psychiatry* 137:445–449.

Cary, G. L. 1979. Acting out in adolescence. *American Journal of Psychotherapy* 33(3): 378–390.

Chwast, J. 1974. Delinquency and criminal behavior as depressive equivalents in adolescents. In *Masked depression,* ed. S. Lesse. New York: Jason Aronson.

Duke, D. L., and Duke, P. M. 1978. The prediction of delinquency in girls. *Journal of Research and Development in Education* 11(2): 18–33.

Erikson, E. 1968. *Identity: Youth and crisis.* New York: Norton.

Farber, E. D., and Joseph, J. A. 1985. The maltreated adolescent: Patterns of physical abuse. *Child Abuse and Neglect* 9:201–06.

Farber, E. D.; McCoard, D.; Kinast, C.; and Baum-Faulkner, D. 1984. Violence in families of adolescent runaways. *Child Abuse and Neglect* 8: 295–99.

Finkelhor, D. 1983. Common features of family abuse. *The dark side of families*, ed. In D. Finkelor, R. Gelles, et al., 11–17. Beverly Hills, Calif.: Sage.

Fisher, B., and Berdie, J. 1978. Adolescent abuse and neglect: Issues of incidence, intervention and service delivery. *Child Abuse and Neglect* 2: 173–92.

Glambos, N. L., and Dixon, R. A. 1984. Adolescent abuse and the development of personal sense of control. *Child Abuse and Neglect* 8:285–93.

Garbarino, J., and Gilliam, G. 1980. *Understanding abusive families.* Lexington, Mass.: Lexington Books.

Gerbner, G. 1980. Children and power on television: The other side of the picture. In *Child Abuse: An agenda for action*, ed. G. Gerbner, C. J. Ross, and E. Zigler. New York: Oxford University Press.

Gil, D. 1979. Unraveling child abuse. In *Critical perspectives on child abuse*, ed. R. Bourne and E. Newberger. Lexington, Mass.: Lexington Books.

Green, A. 1976. Self destructive behavior in battered children. *American Journal of Psychiatry* 135(5): 579–82.

Haley, J. 1980. *Leaving home.* New York: McGraw-Hill.

Hoekstra, K. O. 1984. Ecologically defining the mistreatment of adolescents. *Children and Youth Services Review* 6(4): 285–98.

Hogg, J., and Northman, E. 1979. The resonating parental bind and delinquency. *Family Therapy* 6(1): 21–26.

Johnson, A. M., and Szurek, S. 1952. The genesis of antisocial acting out in children and adolescents. *Psychoanalytic Quarterly* 21:322–43.

Levenson, H. 1973. Perceived parental antecedents of internal, powerful others, and chance locus of control orientations. *Developmental Psychology* 9:260–65.

Lipsitz, J. 1977. *Growing up forgotten.* Lexington, Mass.: Lexington Books.

Lourie, I. 1979. Family dynamics and the abuse of adolescents: A case for a developmental phase specific model of child abuse. *Child Abuse and Neglect* 3:967–74.

McCord, J. 1979. Some child-rearing antecedents of criminal behavior in adult men. *Journal of Personality and Social Psychology* 37(9): 1477–86.

Minuchin, S.; Montalvo, B.; and Buerney, B. 1967. *Families of the slums.* New York: Basic Books.

Monahan, J. 1976. *Community mental health and the criminal justice system.* New York: Pergamon Press.

Muenchow, S., and Gilfillan, S. 1983. Social policy and the media. In *Children, families, and government*, ed. E. Zigler L. Kagan, and E. Klugman. Cambridge: Cambridge University Press.

National Center on Child Abuse and Neglect. 1981. *National incidence study.* Washington, D.C.: U.S. Government Printing Office.

Opinion Research Corporation 1976. *National statistical survey of runaway youth.* Princeton, N.J.: Opinion Research Corporation.

Pate, M. E. 1986. If we don't want violence, let's do something about abuse. *Justice for Children* 1(4): 16–17.

Pelcovitz, D. 1984. Adolescent abuse: Family structure and implications for treatment. *Journal of the American Academy of Child Psychiatry* 23(1): 85–90.

Post, S. 1982. Adolescent parricide in abusive families. *Child Welfare* 61(7): 445–55.

Spinetta, J., and Rigler, D. 1972. The child-abusing parent: A psychological review. *Psychological Bulletin* 77:296–304.

Stierlin, H. 1974. *Separating parents and adolescents: A perspective on running away, schizophrenia and waywardness.* New York: Quadrangle Books.

Stott, D. H. 1982. *Deliquency: The problem and its prevention.* New York: Spectrum.

Toolan, J. M. 1962. Suicide and suicide attempts in children and adolescents. *American Journal of Psychiatry* 118:719–22.

Yates, R.; Kennelly, K.; and Cox, S. 1975. Perceived contingency of parental reinforcements, parent-child relations and locus of control. *Psychological Reports* 36:139–46.

Zigler, E. 1983. Understanding child abuse: A dilemma for policy. In *Children, families, and government,* ed. E. Zigler, L. Kagan, and E. Klugman. Cambridge: Cambridge University Press.

THREE: *Adulthood*

6 How Normal Is Normal Development? Some Connections between Adult Development and the Roots of Abuse and Victimization

ALEXANDRA G. KAPLAN

Claude Bernard, as quoted by Vaillant (1977, 36), said: "We shall never have a science of medicine as long as we separate the explanation of the pathological from the explanation of normal, vital phenomena." Accordingly, in this chapter I shall attempt to trace connections between normative patterns of adult psychological development and some of the key personality dynamics associated with abuse and victimization. The frequency of physical, emotional, and sexual abuse in contemporary society suggests that such abuse is rooted in patterns of behavior that, when expressed in more benign forms, are considered normal and developmentally appropriate aspects of psychological growth.

Reaching such conclusions, however, requires a careful consideration of the type of developmental theory that would best illuminate the search. Two aspects stand out most prominently. First, the roles of victim and abuser are highly correlated with gender, especially in adulthood, in that most abusers of adults are male and most adult

---

I would like to acknowledge the helpful comments on an earlier draft of this chapter by Judith Jordan, Jean Baker Miller, Irene Stiver, and Jan Surrey.

127

victims are female. By contrast, virtually all prevailing theories of adult development offer one central developmental pathway that is then applied, albeit sometimes with minor modification, to women and men alike. Such theories, including those of Freud, Sullivan, and Erikson, attempt to describe *adult* development, but more realistically they are derived, implicitly or explicitly, from the male experience (Miller 1984). When attempts are made to understand women on the basis of these theories, it is frequently noted that women do not "fit." However, typically not the theories but women are found to be deficient. Either women are seen as lacking something they should have—whether it is a penis or a fully developed superego or an identity outside a hetero-sexual relationship—or they are seen as having something that is not appropriate. This usually falls within the realm of relational style; they are seen as either too dependent on others or too intrusive with them. Although in the long run, to quote Sullivan from another context, "We are all more simply human than otherwise," the biased nature of exsiting developmental theory suggests that it is best at this time to consider female and male development separately in order to under-stand gender-specific behaviors within a framework derived from the experiences of each gender. Therefore what will best meet the demands of the task set forth is a model of psychological development that considers separately the developmental pathways of women and men. The initial basis for such a perspective can be found in the "self-in-relation" perspective on women's psychological development being articulated at the Stone Center, Wellesley College, which will serve as the framework for this chapter. The developmental concepts that fol-low are drawn from the Stone Center *Work in Progress* series, in papers by Miller (1984), Jordan (1984), Kaplan (1984), and Stiver (1985).

Second, despite the current popularity of "stage" theories of adult development, we know that women can be victims of abuse at all phases of adulthood, and adult men of all ages are capable of being abusers. Thus the perspective most useful for the present task would be one, such as that proposed by the Stone Center, that focused on the core continuities rather than on the discrepancies of adult development.

The "Self-in-Relation" Model of Women's Development

The "self-in-relation" model of women's development posits that, for women, the core self-structure is a relational self that evolves and matures through participating in and facilitating connection with oth-ers and through attending to the components of the relational matrix, especially affective communication. These processes begin in the early years of life and are linked to two qualities of the early mother-daughter relationship. Because most primary caretakers are women, girls gain a growing sense of self through perceiving similarity and establishing identification with the nurturing adult, and specifically with the adult's nurturing capacities. In addition, girls learn that their sense of self is enhanced and developed by moving *into* relationships; that personal growth occurs in and is fostered by connection with others. As girls mature, they continue to value relationship as an avenue for growth, and they specifically develop those capacities that will enhance connection and contribute to the development of self and others. This does not mean that they are "doing for others," but rather that they are seeking empowerment through what is ideally a mutual process of affirmation and empathic understanding. By contrast, situations that decrease connection, are strongly lacking in mutuality or empathy, or are experienced as potentially harmful to others can diminish women's sense of their own efficacy and threaten the viability of their core self-structure.

This model of personal growth through active participation in a mutually empathic process of connection can highlight patterns of adult women's development as reported by first-person accounts in the anthology by Ruddick and Daniels (1977). These writings are all organized around the women's experiences of work and love, Freud's hallmarks of maturity. Women's core relational sense involves an intricate interconnection between love and work. Within this perspective, work is defined as the use of one's power and resources for economic, personal, or interpersonal goals, and love is defined as a capacity for empathic, mutual sharing combined with a deep feeling of emotional connection with others. Using these definitions with a self-in-relation model, the basis for positing that work and love are intertwined should be clear. The experience of participating actively in loving, mutually enhancing connection with another is precisely what best empowers women toward the fullest use of their power and resources in their work.

Under optimal conditions of mutually empathic relationships, women's sense of their own capacity for connection serves as a base for the maximal use of their power and resources at home or in the labor force. Working and loving enhance one another. However, this condition is rarely achieved. Rather, for reasons that go beyond the scope of this chapter, women's enhancement is often experienced as a threat to others, and in the absence of this relational validation, women come to believe that acting "for themselves" will be destructive to others. As a result they may then lose touch with their own sources of motivation, so that they find that choices "just happen." Or they may consciously or unconsciously lay aside their own desires out of fear that such pursuits will hamper their relational world— as indeed they might. In this pattern, working and loving stand in opposition to one another.

There is yet a third model, which suggests a dialectical tension between the poles of working and loving. Each is experienced in relation to the other, in a creative opposition in which each pole both draws on and builds on the other. The experiences of many of the women portrayed in the Ruddick and Daniels volume illustrate these themes. All the women whose lives will be discussed, who are well educated and employed in professional fields, have a work/love life where shades of figure and ground may change, but both remain active and development is reflected in an increasing synthesis between the two or in new awarenesses of tension or conflict.

Marilyn Young, for example, writes about her self-image "just happening to change" while she was a graduate student in history at Harvard. She had recently married, and she recalls that "subtly, I became not a graduate student who happened to be a wife, but a wife and mother who was finishing up her degree. Even now I don't know why or how this happened" (Ruddick and Daniels 1977, 221). It was many years before she took an active professional role. Another woman, Ruddick, who experienced a work paralysis while working on her philosophy dissertation at Harvard, found that her felt freedom to work was released following childbirth: "I began to organize my thesis almost the day I learned I was pregnant," she wrote, "and for the first time in a decade I developed non-philosophical interests which brought new life to my philosophical work. Why should new parenthood, which subtracts enormously from the time available nonetheless make work more likely? One explanation is that pregnancies and childbirth constitute success. Moreover, for me, infant care was in itself inspiring work which bred a general self-confidence. Pregnancy and motherhood enabled me to feel, and therefore to be more intellectually competent on no grounds other than my proven capacity to do the work that women have always done" (p. 140). She linked her work paralysis to her earlier separation of work and love: "In college I learned to avoid work done out of love. My intellectual life became increasingly critical, detached, and dispensable. . . . I used to think that I needed to recover the inseparability of work and love common among children, natural to me as a school girl" (p. 136).

Many of these women experienced profound conflict when their core relational self met the realities of isolation, intense competitiveness, and discrimination in a top graduate program. The positions many of these women were relegated to—part timers, lecturers writing only at home—further inhibited their work because of their relative isolation. Rorty, who for a combination of reasons was writing at home, reflected that "the regular companionship of colleagues working in roughly the same area is not only a support but a virtual necessity. Even what seems like solitary work is often social in nature; one has to take the last paragraph down the hall and try it out on someone" (p. 48).

As the women moved into middle adulthood, generally the dialectical tension between love and work moved toward some stage of synthesis, though more for some women than for others. For Keller, for example, the conflict was between "my sense of myself as a woman and my identity as a scientist." She states that this conflict "could only be resolved by transcending all stereotypic definitions of self and success. This took a long time, a personal analysis, and the women's movement" (p. 89). For her, at the time she was writing, the tension between woman and scientist had become "not so much a source of personal struggle as a profound concern." For Gilbert the process was more of acknowledging, with pride, the full extent of her wish for employment hitherto subordinated to caring for the needs of others. In her words, "to give myself to my work—to admit that I loved it as much as husband and children, needed it as much, perhaps more, was the most terrifying admission I could make. Only after many years have I come to realize that the challenge of work is in the daring to use my whole self in the struggle for growth. Without that growth, I would be living an unlived life" (p. 318).

For another woman, Lasoff, who became a writer at the age of forty-seven after having been a homemaker, a sort of synthesis was reached by writing about the serious drug problems of one of her children. Parenting and writing drew from and added to each other: "I came to writing through Bev. For an assignment I wrote about an incident involving Bev and me when she had taken an overdose and was hospitalized. I sent the story to the New York Times. Instead of getting rejected it was accepted and published on the Op Ed page. As I began to get involved in that work I found myself able to deal more rationally with my daughter and her problems. My life was no longer pinpointed on hers. Three years have passed since I made my commitment to writing, and it is also three years since my daughter finally made her own commitment to getting well" (p. 209).

Another view of the interplay of work and love, this time for elderly women, is provided in an anthropological study of a Jewish Socialist Community Center in Los Angeles (Meyerhoff 1980). For these women, immigrants without much formal education, work and love have always both centered on the home. This "work of loving," which continued into their later years, enriched and enlivened the women. Meyerhoff stressed that from the perspective of the elderly aging is a *career,* not a series of losses as it is considered when younger people study the aged. Thus women were able to continue in their work of caring, for "there is always someone to take care of."

Men's Self-development

Studies of male development suggest some basic differences from the female developmental paradigm described above. That is, under current social conditions, how one experiences the other, and the nature of the connection between self and other, seem to be different in certain ways for women and men. Men's patterns also find their roots in early infancy. Compared with girls, who have a same-sex identification figure from the earliest months, boys are subjected to pressures to refrain from identifying with their primary, opposite-sex caretaker and with the caretaking functions she represents. Instead, they are encouraged to identify with the *image* more than the *reality* of a paternal presence. This identification, because of the relative distance of the father, is likely to be fragile, partially developed, and vulnerable to distortion. Furthermore, boys learn that self-knowledge and identity formation come from moving *away* from relationship, not toward it. Being in a close and caring relationship, which in early years would typically be with an opposite-sex person, is experienced at least in part as a threat to the core self-structure. This dynamic is consistent with Gilligan's (1982) findings from adults' responses to Thematic Apperception Test (TAT) cards, that men were most threatened by intimacy and women by isolation.

Boys continue through childhood and adulthood along this developmental pathway that stresses individualistic qualities of independence, isolated achievement, and the inhibition of affect, especially within close relationships. Self-enhancement takes precedence over the enhancement of the self/other matrix, as is posited for women. The qualities that foster psychological development are seen as unidirectional, moving from the "other" to the individual, rather than as enhancing a mutually empathic process. While it is true that most men are in relationships, often intimate ones, their own capacity to foster connection and contribute to the growth of others is not a central part of their relational experience or their sense of self.

Illustrations of these broad developmental patterns appear frequently in the writings on male development by Levinson (1978), Vaillant (1977), and White (1966). What emerges in these writings is a much more focused self—a self whose primary conscious preoccupation and locus of self-image lie within the world of "work." As Vaillant (1977, 9) stated, "A man's work is the primary basis for his life in society." There is little sense of the dialectic between work and love found in the women's patterns. While many of the men may be uncertain about what career they want or may question their future success in the world of work, the centrality of their identity within that world is invariant. In the men studied by Levinson, White, and Vaillant, relationships are definitely present, though their roles vary from individual to individual. But in no case do relational identities override vocational identities: no men find themselves fathers who happen to be working. In fact, relationships more often are strongly subordinated to the needs and demands of the work world, or close relationships foster the professional aspirations of the men.

In Levinson's work, the main theme of early adulthood for men is situating themselves professionally. As Levinson (1978, 45) states: "Occupation has important sources within the self and important consequences for the self. It is often the primary medium in which a young man's dreams for the future are defined, and the vehicle he uses to pursue those dreams." Marriage and family, in turn, become subordinated within this primary thrust: "Marriage ordinarily creates a new home base for the young man. It is a center on which he establishes his place in the community and his changing relationships. . . it provides a vehicle for traveling a particular path in early adulthood."

This subordination of the relational sphere to the occupational sphere is rather dramatically illustrated in White's portrayal of Hartley Hale, a Harvard graduate who went on to a successful surgical career. White (1966, 73) suggests that Hale's choice of a mate was fueled in part by his felt need to "select a girl who would make him a blithe, happy, sympathetic companion while not being bothered by erratic hours nor demanding of his time and attention." Indeed, these characteristics became very much called for. During his internship and residency, Hale worked most of the day and part of the night, so that, in his words, "you can imagine, I didn't see much of my wife or my child. As a matter of fact, I never saw the child when it was awake until it was a year old." What is striking here is not just the temporal consideration, but the absence of regret or longing. In fact, the affect fits the behavior. The child, as White points out, had become an "it," and Hale evinces no signs of conflict or distress about the course of events. There is no conscious "relational paralysis" to parallel, for example, Ruddick's experience of a "work paralysis." The relational world is externalized on hold.

There is also, for men in early adulthood, less sense that the occupational world is enriched by relational connection. According to Levinson, a number of key relationships play a formative role in men's occupational development, but they serve an instrumental function in advancing the occupational self rather then being a dynamic of connection that mutually empowers both participants. The first relationship is with a mentor and is defined by its occupational function. It is not the *process* of *being in a relationship* that is at issue, but the services that the mentor can provide for the protégé, which include acting as host and guide, sponsor, role model, influence, and counsel. The mentor's purpose is unambivalently to help the protégé realize his occupational dream; to foster the young man's development by believing in him.

In addition, the goal of the mentor relationship is not to enhance the capacity to work *relationally* within the occupational world but clearly, according to Levinson, to develop the protégé's sense of his own authority and his capacity for autonomous, responsible action. That is, the relationship becomes a temporary position on the trajectory toward independence, not a model for learning through connection and collaboration. In fact the mentor relationship not only always ends, but often ends with strong conflict and bad feelings on both sides. Thus the striving and achievement that are the underlying purposes of the relationship ultimately turn back on the relationship itself. Again, rather than being a dialectical process, relationship becomes one of the dimensions on which the occupational world is nurtured.

The other primary way relationship enhances men in early adulthood, according to Levinson, is through the "special woman" described in fact as like the "true mentor." "The special woman helps him to shape and live out the Dream. She shares it, believes in him as its hero, joins him on the journey and creates a boundary space within which his aspirations can be imagined and his hopes nourished" (p. 109). Here, despite the suggestion of intimacy, the primary purpose of the relationship becomes fostering the needs and ambitions of one of the members, along lines that are external to their relational process.

In the accounts of older men, portrayed most clearly by Levinson, the merger of work and love seen in the women seems much less in evidence. Some of the men interviewed, regardless of the course of their lives, still gather their self-esteem and their self-identity from the world of work. Competition and the wish for fame or success remain the major motivating forces, though by no means always successfully. Caring about the effect one's behavior has on others emerges for this group of men as a sign of weakness. One of Levinson's subjects states: "I think I'm not hard driving enough. I have a guilt complex about being too easy on people. . . . Instinctively, I'm soft and compassionate toward people, to a fault" (p. 307).

Other men show signs of struggling to blend competitive and relational needs, with moderate success. For some the family remains in the background until they have sufficiently established their career. For others, the home life becomes incorporated into their competitive mode, as was true for the man whose abiding dream, which he fulfilled, was to build a large and impressive home. Others drew relational strength from their families. For example, a writer in Levinson's study acknowledged that his marriage had moved into a more viable stage "because of Sara's strengths: she was adaptable in ways that I am not" (p. 298). Many of these men, then, moved toward some integration of love and work, but often with a tinge of sadness and a sense of personal failure.

The implication that for men the relational life is inconsistent with the world of work is further borne out by Meyerhoff's portrayal of the men at the senior center. In general, she found the men to be "quieter, vaguer, more sad and angry compared with the vitality and assertiveness of the women" (Meyerhoff 1980, 242). She attempts to explain her observation that the "men seemed more demoralized and worn out than the woman" (p. 248) by recognizing that the primary task in the "career of aging" (referred to earlier) lies within the realm of expressive functions—a realm for which men are generally not well prepared. Thus older men find themselves in a career for which they have not trained, and not having trained, they lack the social support that is the "payment" for such a career and is so sustaining at this time. Further, bodily and mental changes have limited their capacity to act within their familiar "instrumental" realm.

Male-Female Development and Abuser-Victim Status

From these general outlines of the trajectories of adult development for women and men, we can begin to identify some of the dimensions on which the normal contains the seeds of the pathological. This search is somewhat different for women and men. Men constitute the majority of abusers, and further, a moderate proportion of men in American society are abusive or capable of being so. Surveys by Koss et al. (1981), Russell (1983), Finkelhor (1979), and others suggest that from 10 to 20 percent of American men acknowledge that they have been abusive or have been identified as such. Malamuth (1981), interviewing college men, found that 25 percent said they would be willing to use force to get sex, and a full 51 percent said they would be willing to attempt rape if they knew they could get away with it. One might reasonably conclude that these prevalence figures suggest we are deal-

ing with a basic social problem, not simply with individual disturbances. The issue, then, is to explain not the individual situation but
rather the collective behavior as it derives from normative patterns of
male development.

With women, the task is not to find the developmental roots of
women as victims, because multiple sources of data demonstrate that
while some women are more likely to be abused than others, all women
are vulnerable to becoming victims. However, once abused, there are
ways women behave that make their continued safety less likely or that
compound the negative impact of that abuse. This behavior, we believe, can be traced back to its roots in patterns of normal development
for women.

The prevalence of violence in men seems to be anchored in men's
internalization of cultural prescriptions. In a patriarchal society, men
are given permission to expect gratification of individual needs and to
use their dominant status to seek such gratification (Miller 1976). As
seen in the studies by Levinson and others, men are encouraged to
believe that others (mentors, special women), are legitimately there to
further men's purposes in a unidirectional relationship. This view is
consistent with the developmental line for men that I have described,
in which emphasis is placed not on participating in a *process* of connection, but rather on continued striving for achievement and advance-
ment, with the relational world subordinated to this broader goal.
Relationship itself becomes defined not as a mutual endeavor but
rather as a unidirectional source of support for one's achievements.
Affect is subordinated to action, and the needs of others are experienced in terms of the needs of the self.

One can speculate that this combination of factors can, if taken to a
destructive extreme, become the pattern out of which abusive behavior
emerges. If men assume that others are there to meet the men's own
needs at the expense of their own, and that men have the right to
exercise their socially granted power to make this happen, then there
are no built-in constraints against the use of force to effect these aims.
Further, if men develop along a line that fosters individualized motivations rather than the betterment of the relational matrix, then they
have little motivation to take in and empathize with the emotional
impact their behavior has on others. There is little sense that their
own well-being and the well-being of the other are an intrinsic whole;
rather, they feel that their own well-being should take precedence or
be enhanced even at the expense of the other. Most men do not take
this developmental pattern to the extreme described. But what is
important is that the normative developmental pattern seems to contain no constraints sufficient to protect against abuse. In addition,

powerful and increasingly frequent societal messages specifically linking sexuality with violence against women and condoning physical and sexual abuse serve as constant reinforcers of this developmentally grounded permission.

For women, the issue for which we seek developmental roots is their reaction to abusive situations. Self-in-relation theory suggests one possible explanation for the common observation that abused women do not always act in health-preserving ways: it is not unusual for battered women to stay in the battering relationship, and it is not unusual for rape victims, especially if they know their abuser, to protect him more than themselves. In our understanding of women's development, self-identity and self-esteem lie with the capacity to take care of the relational process—to attend to the needs of the self/other matrix. If this is true, then, despite the dangers, women may feel more threatened by the loss of their capacity to preserve the relationship than by the physical and emotional harm they are risking. Or they may feel responsible for causing the abuse and remain in connection with the abuser in hopes of rectifying the relationship. Ending the relationship closes one possible avenue to increased self-esteem through relational change.

In remaining within an abusive relationship, women may be acting in what feels to them like a self-preserving manner, despite the real dangers they are facing. There is a sense in which their well-being feels tied to the well-being of the other and in which to act against the other, even if he is abusive, is hostile and destructive to both the abuser and the abused. In working with battered women, one repeatedly hears their sympathetic accounts of why their partners could not help themselves or of how unfair it would be to take definitive action against them. One of the tasks of counselors working with these women is to help them recognize both the positive attributes of their capacity for attending to their connection with others and also the need to acknowledge their right to protect themselves against the dangers this particular connection has for them.

There is also a strong tendency for abused women to take responsibility for their abuse, to assume that they must have caused it themselves. Cultural paradigms have long supported this position and are echoed in popular media and in the mental health literature. In fact, the assumption that women are responsible for their abuse is frequently taken one step further, to suggest that they have desired it. Women as well as men have in many cases come to accept this position, partly because until recently few voices have been heard in opposition. In addition, many women are explicitly told that they themselves are responsible for their victimization.

Self-in-relation theory suggests an additional reason that women have been susceptible to this cultural message. Because women experience self-enhancement through actively promoting a relationship, they take responsibility for furthering the relationship that preserves their context for growth. But they must thus also take responsibility for relational failure, even in abusive conditions. This in no way means that women enjoy or want the abuse, but avoiding abuse may be secondary to preserving relational connection—their central source of self-esteem.

By locating the roots of abusive behavior and victim behavior in normative developmental paradigms, I do not mean to imply that current patterns are inevitable. But I am suggesting that significant changes in the patterns and extent of violence against women will require attending to their developmental origins and sorting out positive developmental characteristics from culturally grounded distortions. For women this means separating the positive wish to promote connection from the dangers of taking responsibility for relational dynamics that are beyond their control. For men the implications are more basic, because they suggest a need to foster an empathic connection with others so as to lessen the felt distance between the needs of self and of others. This is not only an individual endeavor; it also requires collective support that is then reflected in changes in the normal social structure.

References

Finkelhor, D. 1979. *Sexually victimized children.* New York: Free Press.

Gilligan, C. 1982. *In a different voice.* Cambridge: Harvard University Press.

Jordan, J. 1984. Empathy and self-boundaries. In *Work in progress*, no. 16. Working Paper series. Wellesley, Mass.: Stone Center, Wellesley College.

Kaplan, A. G. 1984. The self-in-relation; Implications for depression in women. In *Work in progress*, no. 14. Working Papers series. Wellesley, Mass.: Stone Center, Wellesley College.

Koss, P., et al. 1981. Personality and attitudinal characteristics of sexually aggressive men. Paper presented to the American Psychological Association, Los Angeles.

Levinson, D. 1978. *The seasons of man's life.* New York: Ballantine.

Malamuth, N. M. 1981. Rape proclivity among men. *Journal of Social Issues* 37:4.

Meyerhoff, B. 1980. *Number our days.* New York: Simon and Schuster.

Miller, J. B. 1976. *Toward a new psychology of women.* Boston: Beacon Press.

————. 1984. The development of women's sense of self. In *Work in progress,*, no. 12. Working Papers series. Wellesley, Mass.: Stone Center, Wellesley College.

Ruddick, S., and Daniels, P. 1977. *Working it out.* New York: Pantheon Books.

Russell, C. 1983. The prevalence and incidence of forcible rape and attempted rape of females. *Victimology: An International Journal* 7:1 4.

Stiver, I. P. 1985. The meanings of care: Reframing treatment models. In *Work in progress*, no. 20. Working Papers series. Wellesley, Mass.: Stone Center, Wellesley College.

Vaillant, G. 1977. *Adaptation to life.* Boston: Little, Brown.

White, R. W. 1966. *Lives in progress.* New York: Holt, Rinehart, and Winston.

7 Rape in Marriage

DAVID FINKELHOR AND
KERSTI YLLO

Marital rape is the one form of family violence that remains legal in much of the United States. Although many lawyers and legislators debate this issue, the researchers, counselors, therapists, and doctors who could best help victims have paid little attention to the problem. Even feminist recognition of marital rape is coming well after other types of violence against women have become national concerns. Nonetheless, public and professional awareness about marital rape is slowly growing. Rape in marriage is not a rare crime that may blossom into a headline-grabbing trial, but a persistent problem in a large number of marriages.

The Prevalence of Marital Rape

Evidence about violence in general against wives leads to a suspicion that forced sex in marriage is fairly commonplace. For a long time, any type of wife abuse was considered rather unusual, but results of

---

An earlier version of this chapter appeared in Finkelhor et al. 1983.

recent large-scale surveys have reversed this notion. For example, Straus, Gelles, and Steinmetz (1980) found that 16 percent of all American couples admitted to a violent episode in the course of the previous year, and for 4 percent the violence was severe enough to qualify as wife battering.

Similarly, testimony from battered women confirms their high vunerability to marital rape. Spektor (1980) surveyed 304 battered women in ten shelters in the state of Minnesota and found that 36 percent said they had been raped by their husbands or cohabiting partners. Giles-Sims (1979) found a similar proportion of women in shelters reporting a forced sex experience, and Pagelow (1980) reported that 39 percent of the 119 battered women she studied in California had also been victims of marital rape. Forced sex is clearly a common element in wife battering.

Diana Russell's ground-breaking study *Rape in Marriage* (1982) presented the first direct evidence about the prevalence of marital rape in the population at large. Russell surveyed a random sample of 930 female residents of San Francisco, eighteen years old or older, about any incident of sexual assault at any time throughout their lives. Of the 644 married women in the sample, 14 percent reported sexual assaults by husbands: 12 percent had been forced to have intercourse, and 2 percent had experienced other types of forced sex. Sexual assaults by husbands were the most common kind of sexual assault reported, occurring over twice as often as sexual assault by a stranger.

In evaluating Russell's findings it is important to realize that she did not ask any of her respondents whether they had been "raped"— a stigmatizing term that many women are reluctant to use to describe sexual assaults. Instead, she asked women to describe any kind of unwanted sexual experience with a husband or ex-husband, and then she included in her tally only those women who described encounters that met the legal definition of rape: "forced intercourse, or intercourse obtained by physical threat(s) or intercourse completed when the woman was drugged, unconscious, asleep, or otherwise totally helpless and hence unable to consent." Russell's finding that marital rape is the most common kind cannot thus be ascribed to semantics. She used the same definition of sexual assault in tabulating the experiences with husbands as for those with strangers.

The findings from Russell's study are bolstered by a survey we recently completed in Boston. In a study on the related subject of childhood sexual abuse, we also asked a representative sample of 326 women whether a spouse or a person they were living with as a couple had ever used physical force or threats to try to have sex with them. Of the women who had been married (or coupled), 10 percent answered yes. These women too reported more sexual assaults by husbands than by strangers (10 percent versus 3 percent). Forced sex in marriage is a frequent—perhaps the most frequent—type of sexual assault.

Wives Avoid the Label of Rape

Few women whose husbands have forced them to have sex define themselves as having been raped (Gelles 1979). Most women see rape as something that happens primarily between strangers. They share the cultural and legal assumption that there is no such thing as rape between husband and wife. Violent and unpleasant as a husband's assault might have been, most wives would resist calling it rape. No doubt raped wives, like battered wives, use many self-deceptions to avoid facing the realities of an intolerable marriage because the alternatives—loneliness, loss of financial security, admitting failure—are equally untenable (Gelles 1979). For these reasons, women do not say they have been raped by their husbands. More victims identify such an experience as "forced sex" than as "marital rape."

Varieties of Coercion

Another definitional problem concerns the question of when sex is forced. It has been argued that given the power inequality in the institution of marriage, all marital sex is coerced (Brogger 1976). It may be that when sex is not explicitly desired it should be considered forced. However, we can make some important distinctions among different types of coercion.

Four basic types of coercion can be identified. Some women submit to sex in the absence of desire because of social pressure—because they believe it is their wifely duty. This can be considered *social coercion.* Other wives comply because they fear their husbands will leave them if they do not or because their husbands have threatened to cut off their source of money or humiliate them in some way. In these cases husbands use their resource and power advantage to force their wives. This second type of coercion, *interpersonal coercion,* refers to threats by husbands that are not violent in nature. The third type involves the threat of physical force. *Threatened force* can range from an implied threat that a woman might be hurt if she does not give in to an explicit threat that she will be killed unless she complies. For many women, the memory of previous beatings is enough to ensure cooperation. The fourth kind of coercion, *physical coercion,* requires little explanation. Instances of physical coercion range from holding a woman down to striking her, choking her, tying her up, or knocking her out to force sex on her.

Focus on Physical Force

The varieties of sexual coercion in marriage could be the subject of an intriguing study, but that is beyond the scope of this research. We have limited our study to physical force for two main reasons. First, such force is most life and health threatening, and in that sense is most extreme. Second, the presence or absence of physical threats and actual violent coercion is somewhat easier to determine empirically than is the presence or absence of more subtle forms of coercion. This is not meant to imply that other forms of coercion cannot be brutal or that "marital rape" can occur only when physical force is involved.

In-Depth Interviews

The following sections represent an overview of our exploratory study of marital rape from the victim's perspective. Our findings are based on fifty in-depth interviews with women whose husbands or partners had used force or threat of force to try to have sex with them. Our interviewees were recruited from a number of sources. The majority (56 percent) were clients of family planning agencies in northern New England. These clinics routinely take a limited sexual history from each client. For the purposes of this study an additional question was added to the form: "Has your current partner (or a previous partner) ever used force or threat of force to try to have sex with you?" If the answer indicated that the client had had such an experience with a spouse or cohabitant, she was asked to participate in an additional interview for research purposes, for which she would be paid ten dollars.

Other interviewees were recruited through area shelters for battered wives. When it was determined that a woman's violent experiences included forced sex, she was asked to participate in the research if shelter staff felt she could tolerate an interview. Additional interviewees (28 percent) were self-referrals. These women heard of our research in the media or through our public speaking and approached us offering to discuss their experiences. Finally, a few interviews (10 percent) were arranged as a result of an advertisement placed in *Ms.* magazine.

Although the sample is not representative, we do not regard this as a serious drawback because of the nature of this research. Our goal in this exploratory study was not to determine incidence rates or demographic data (our Boston survey provides such information). Rather, our purpose was to talk at length with women who were willing to discuss their forced sex experiences so that we could gain a qualitative understanding of marital rape and begin to outline issues for further research. The clinics and shelters were sites where these intimate subjects could be raised fairly easily and where intervention services could be made available to women needing them.

Three Types of Marital Rape

The forced sex experiences of the women we interviewed can be divided roughly into three types. One group can be described as typical "battered women." These women were subjected to extensive physical and verbal abuse, much of which was unrelated to sex. Their husbands were frequently angry and belligerent toward them and often had alcohol and drug problems. The sexual violence in these relationships appeared to be just another aspect of the general abuse. Along with the other kinds of anger and physical pain these men heaped on their wives, they also used violent sex.

Let us quote briefly from a case study of one of these "battering rapes":

> The interviewee was a twenty-four-year-old woman from an affluent background. Her husband was a big man, over six feet tall, compared with her five feet two. He drank heavily and often attacked her physically. The most frequent beatings occurred at night after they had had a fight and she had gone to bed. She would awaken to find him physically abusing her. Such attacks, at their worst, occurred every couple of weeks. After one incident her face was so bruised that she could not attend class for a full week.
>
> Their sexual activities had violent aspects, too. Although they shared the initiative for sex and had no disagreements about its timing or frequency, she often felt he was brutal in his lovemaking. She said, "I would often end up crying during intercourse, but it never seemed to bother him. He probably enjoyed my pain in some way."
>
> The most violent sexual episode occurred at the very end of their relationship. Things had been getting worse between them for some time. They had not talked to each other in two weeks. One afternoon she came

home from school, changed into a housecoat, and started toward the bathroom. He got up from the couch where he had been lying, grabbed her, and pushed her down on the floor. With her face pressed into a pillow and his hand clamped over her mouth, he proceeded to have anal intercourse with her. She screamed and struggled to no avail. Afterward she was hateful and furious. "It was very violent," she said; "if I had had a gun there, I would have killed him." Her injuries were painful and extensive. She had a torn muscle in her rectum so that for three months she had to go to the bathroom standing up. The assault left her with hemorrhoids and a susceptibility to aneurysms that took five years to heal.

Women in the second group have somewhat different relationships. These relationships are by no means conflict free, but on the whole there is little physical violence. In this group the forced sex grew out of more specifically sexual conflicts. There were long-standing disagreements over some sexual issue, such as how often to have sex or what sexual activities were appropriate. The following is an excerpt from a case study of the woman who experienced what we term a "force-only" rape.

The interviewee was a thirty-three-year-old woman with a young son. Both she and her husband of ten years are college graduates and professionals. She is a teacher and he is a guidance counselor. Their marriage, from her report, seems to be of a modern sort in most respects. There have been one or two violent episodes in their relationship, but in those instances the violence appears to have been mutual.

There is a long-standing tension in the relationship about sex. She prefers sex about three times a week but feels under considerable pressure to have more. She says she is afraid that if she refuses he will leave her or that he will force her.

He did force her about two years ago. Their lovemaking on this occasion started out pleasantly enough, but he tried to get her to have anal intercourse with him. She refused. He persisted. She kicked and pushed him away. Still he persisted. They ended up having vaginal intercourse. The force he used was mostly his weight on top of her. At 220 pounds, he weighs twice as much as she. "It was horrible," she said. She was sick to her stomach afterward. She cried and felt angry and disgusted. He showed little guilt. "He felt like he'd won something."

In addition to the sexual assaults we classified as battering and force-only, there were a handful that defied such categorization. These rapes were sometimes connected to battering and sometimes not. All, however, involved bizarre sexual obsessions in the husbands that were not evident in other cases. Husbands who made up this group were heavily involved with pornography. They tried to get their wives to participate in making it or imitating it. They sometimes had a history of sexual problems, such as difficulty in becoming aroused or guilt about earlier homosexual experiences. Sometimes these men needed force or highly structured rituals of sexual behavior to become aroused. A case study of one of these "obsessive rapes" is illustrative:

> The interviewee was a thirty-one-year-old marketing analyst for a large corporation. She met her husband in high school and was attracted by his intelligence. They were married right after graduation because she was pregnant. After the baby was born he grew more and more demanding sexually. "I was really just his masturbating machine," she recalls. He was very rough sexually and would hold a pillow over her face to stifle her screams. He would also tie her up and insert objects into her vagina and take pictures that he would share with his friends. There were also brutal "blitz" attacks. One night, for example, they were in bed having sex when they heard a commotion outside. They went out in their bathrobes to investigate and discovered it was only a cat fight. She was heading back to the house when her husband told her to wait. She was standing in the darkness wondering what he was up to when suddenly he attacked her from behind. "He grabbed my arms behind me and tied them together. He pushed me over the log pile and raped me." she said. As in similar previous assaults, he penetrated her anally. The interviewee later discovered a file card in her husband's desk that sickened her. On the card he had written a list of dates that corresponded to the forced sex episodes of the past months. Next to each date was a complicated coding system that seemed to indicate the type of sex act and a ranking of how much he had enjoyed it.

Force and Resistance

The incidents uncovered in our study varied in both the force the men used and the resistance the women offered. In some cases the man applied massive force, dragging the woman somewhere, tearing off her clothes, and physically beating her. In other situations, particularly where the two were already in bed, the force was more moderate. In several cases women mentioned the men's weight and their persistent attempts to penetrate them as the main elements of force.

Many women said they did not put up much of a fight, however. They felt that it was no use or was not worth it. This is an important point to understand, because so many victims of sexual force have been ridiculed for not meeting the masculine stereotype of how vigorously a threatened person should resist. Lack of violent resistance is often interpreted as a sign that the victims really "wanted" sex on some level or that it was not so traumatic.

There appear to be three main factors that inhibited the women's attempts to defend themselves from sexual aggression by their partners. First, many of the women felt they could not ward off the attack no matter how hard they tried. They perceived their partners as very strong. Indeed, we were struck by the large size disparity between our subjects and their partners. Women who are much smaller than their husbands may be a particularly vulnerable group, not only because they are weak in comparison but because they feel weak as well.

Second, many of the women feared that if they resisted they would be hurt even worse, especially those who had been beaten before. They expected that they would be punched, bruised, and manhandled and that the sexual act itself would be even more painful and damaging.

Third, many of the women believed that they themselves were in the wrong. In several cases their husbands had convinced them that they were frigid. They believed they were at fault for whatever marital dispute was in process and felt responsible for their husbands' mood or frustration. Although they did not want the sexual act, they were not armed with the conviction that they were justified in not wanting it, which made it difficult for them to put up a fight.

In general it appeared that certain kinds of ultimate resistance tactics seemed out of the question for these women. Most did not run out of the house or physically resist by gouging at their partners' eyes or kicking them in the groin. No doubt they were hampered by their socialization to not even consider such actions. Moreover, unless they were prepared to leave, they knew they would have to face the men later on, in the morning or later the next day. Since most were not prepared to make it on their own, a central goal was "keeping the peace." They were not willing to bring out the ultimate weapons because they had to continue living with these men, and they wanted to make things more tolerable for themselves. Appeasement rather than massive resistance appeared to be the preferable approach from their immediate point of view.

The Trauma of Marital Rape

Many people fail to become alarmed about the problem of marital rape because they think it is a rather less traumatic form of rape. Being attacked by a stranger in the street, they imagine, must be much more damaging than having sex with someone one has had sex with before.

This misconception is based on a failure to understand the real violation involved in rape. Those who see rape primarily in sexual terms think the degradation comes from the womans' having been robbed of her reputation. Although this element can be present, what is salient for rape victims is most often the violence, the loss of control, and the fear.

Women raped by strangers often go through a long period of being afraid, especially about their physical safety. They become very cautious about being alone, about where they go, and about who they go with (Burgess and Holmstrom 1974). Women raped by their husbands, however, are often traumatized at an even more basic level: in their ability to trust. The kind of violation they have experienced is much harder to guard against, short of a refusal to trust any man. It touches a woman's basic confidence in forming relationships and trusting intimates. It can leave her feeling much more powerless and isolated than if she were raped by a stranger.

Moreover, a woman raped by her husband has to live with her rapist, not just with a frightening memory of a stranger's attack. Being trapped in an abusive marriage leaves many women vulnerable to repeated sexual assaults by their husbands. Most of the women we interviewed were raped on multiple occasions. These women do not feel they have the option of obtaining police protection (as do other rape victims).

The research bears out the traumatic impact of marital rape. Russell found that marital rape victims in her study rated their experience as having a more serious impact on their lives than did the victims of stranger rape (Russell 1982). Other studies, too, have shown that rape by intimates in general is more, not less, traumatic than rape by strangers.

Public Attitudes about Marital Rape

It is only within the past decade that marital rape has been criminalized in most states in the United States (National Center on Women and Family Law 1987). However, it would be naive to think that simply removing the spousal exemption will dramatically reduce the occurrence of marital rape. Evidence suggests that even where such laws exist, they are infrequently used (Geis 1978). Even the minority of women who may recognize that their husbands have committed a crime against them are for various reasons—loyalty, fear, unwillingness to go through a grueling public exposure—still extremely reluctant to press charges. The lesson of spouse abuse is that laws alone have relatively little effect (Field and Field 1973). Physical spouse abuse is a crime and has been for many years; yet in spite of such laws, all evidence suggests that such abuse is epidemic.

The spousal exemption is merely one manifestation of a complex set of social attitudes surrounding the physical and sexual abuse of wives. Until these attitudes also change, the problem will remain critical with or without a law. These social attitudes portray marital rape as acceptable behavior, at least in some circumstances, and even if it is sometimes considered objectionable, it is not seen as very seriously so.

For insight on these attitudes, we asked groups of undergraduate students for their opinions about marital rape, and some of their replies are revealing. Some denied entirely that it could occur: "No. When you get married, you are supposedly in love, and you shouldn't even think of lovemaking as rape under any circumstances," one student responded.

Others expressed the view that implicit in the marriage contract is an acceptance of the use of force. "Sexual relations are a part of marriage, and both members realize this before they make a commitment," said another in explaining why there was no such thing as marital rape.

A number of students believed that forced sex was a reasonable solution to marital conflict. "If the wife did not want to have sex after many months the husband may go crazy. [Rape] would be an alternative to seeking sexual pleasure with someone else." Or, "If she doesn't want sex for a long amount of time, and has no reason for it—Let the old man go for it!"

Besides expressing the opinion that force is an acceptable way of trying to salvage a marriage, such statements reveal other attitudes that work to justify marital rape—for example, the belief in a man's overpowering need for sex and the belief that women withhold sex from their husbands for no good reason. Note also the myth, discussed earlier, that forced sex is primarily a response to a woman who is denying satisfaction to her husband.

The refusal by politicians and the public to see marital rape as a crime is also based on the belief that it is not a very serious offense. Peter Rossi presented a random sample of people living in Baltimore with descriptions of 140 offenses ranging from planned killing of a policeman to being drunk in a public place. Although the respondents ranked "forcible rape after breaking into a home" as the fourth most serious of all 140 offenses, just above the "impulsive killing of a policeman," they ranked "forcible rape of a former spouse" sixty-second, just above "driving while drunk" (Rossi et al. 1974). While many people consider that some types of rape constitute serious offenses, rape of a former spouse is not seen as a very serious crime. Imagine how low the ranking would have been had Rossi asked about rape of a "current" rather than a "former" spouse. This corresponds with what we know about attitudes toward violence: the more intimate the victim and rapist, the less serious the assault is considered to be.

This can be read as rather sobering evidence that the "marriage license is a raping license." Not only is it true that by marrying a man feels immunity to the charge of rape (a form of license), but it also appears true that people are much less likely to disapprove of his sexually violent behavior if he directs it against the woman to whom he is married rather than some other woman. If people do not think that spousal rape is a serious offense, it certainly contributes to a climate where husbands feel they can commit it with impunity. The climate also affects the victims, who conclude from social attitudes that they are wrong to be so upset and that few people will sympathize with them. They then consciously decide not to raise the topic with anyone.

Although the change in the spousal exemption law is unlikely to bring many offenders to court for their offenses, it may have some effect on the general climate of acceptance of marital rape. In particular, the political debate should alert the community, the criminal justice system, and mental health professionals to the problem. The change in the law may also put some potential husband rapists on notice that their behavior is not generally acceptable and, in fact, is a crime. Finally, the change may give vulnerable women a tool for protecting themselves. Attitudes must also change so that we, as a society, no longer condone this form of violence.

Implications for Professionals

The list of professionals who have the potential to help marital rape victims is long. It includes doctors, especially family physicians who know the patient and the family, gynecologists, who deal with women's sexual functioning, and emergency-room physicians and nurses, who treat a great number of traumatic injuries and rapes (many of which they may not be aware of). It includes lawyers, who now handle a large volume of divorces, and marriage counselors, social workers, psychologists, and psychiatrists, who treat people's troubled relationships. It includes clergy, who are the first people many Americans consult when faced with a personal problem. All of these professionals could be crucial links in providing help; yet the vast majority have not considered the problem of marital rape at all.

Probably the single most important service these professionals could perform for victims of marital rape is to ask about it. Women who have suffered this kind of abuse almost never bring it up spontaneously. They have never heard it discussed and usually feel ashamed to mention it themselves. Professionals who are unaware of the problem or are too embarrassed to discuss it collude in the silence. By initiating discussion, professionals give marital-rape victims the permission they need to talk about it.

There are numerous situations in which a question about forced sex ought to be routine. Doctors, especially gynecologists, take routine sexual histories designed to identify any problems. Psychiatrists, psychologists, marriage counselors, social workers, and clergy should also consider marital rape in their assessment of individuals coming to them for marital problems. Unfortunately, though they often ask about sex as a way of assessing the health of the relationship, the subject of force rarely comes up. Lawyers too should inquire about physical and sexual abuse in every initial conference with a client seeking divorce.

In sum, professionals in a wide range of areas must ask about forced sex in marriage, and then they must be willing to hear about it and begin providing help. In order to offer effective services to victims of marital rape, professionals must first take responsibility for educating themselves on this subject.

Conclusion

This review of current information about marital rape and our findings regarding wives' forced sex experiences are a first step toward a full understanding of this social problem. Our research shows that "marital rape" is not a contradiction in terms, but rather a form of violence against wives that is not rare, just rarely discussed.

The case studies and typologies developed here are intended to encourage the generation of hypotheses about and further analysis of forced sex in marriage, its antecedents, consequences, and implications. As a whole, our research is intended to add to the ground swell of concern about violence against women, to signal that the time has arrived for concerted investigation and discussion of the problem of rape in marriage and for action in political, legal, academic, and clinical arenas.

References

Bart, P. 1975. Rape doesn't end with a kiss. *Viva* 40–42:101–7.
Brogger, S. 1976. *Deliver us from love.* New York: Delacorte.

Burgess, A., and Holmstrom, L. 1974. *Rape: Victims of crisis.* Bowie, Md.: Brady.

Celarier, M. 1979. I kept thinking I could help him. *In These Times,* January, 10–16.

Croft, G. 1976. Three years in rape of wife. *Boston Globe,* 15 September.

Doron, J. 1980. Conflict and violence in intimate relationships: Focus on marital rape. Paper presented at the annual meeting of the American Sociological Association, New York.

Field, M., and Field, H. 1973. Marital violence and the criminal process: Neither justice nor peace. *Social Service Review* 47(2): 221–240.

Finkelhor, D.; Gelles, R.; Hotaling, G.; and Straus, M. 1983. *The dark side of families.* Beverly Hills, Calif.: Sage.

Geis, G. 1978. Rape-in-marriage: Law and law reform in England, the U.S. and Sweden. *Adelaide law Review* 6:284–302.

Giles-Sims, J. 1979. Stability and change in patterns of wife-beating: A systems theory approach. Ph.D. diss., University of New Hampshire.

Hunt, M. 1974. *Sexual behavior in the 1970's.* Chicago: Playboy Press.

National Center on Women and Family Law. 1987. Marital rape exemption packet (Fall).

Pagelow, M. D. 1980. *Does the law help battered wives? Some research notes.* Madison, Wis.: Law and Society Association.

Rossi, P.; Waite, E.; Bose, C.; and Berk, R. 1974. The seriousness of crimes: Normative structures and individual differences. *American Sociological Review* 39:224–37.

Russell, D. 1980. The prevalence and impact of marital rape in San Francisco. Paper presented at the annual meeting of the American Sociological Association, New York.

———. 1982. *Rape in marriage.* New York: Macmillan.

Schulman, J. 1980a. The marital rape exemption. *National Center on Women and Family Law Newsletter* 1(1): 6–8.

———. 1980b. Expansion of the marital rape exemption. *National Center on Women and Family Law Newsletter* 1(2):3–4.

Spektor, P. 1980. Testimony delivered to the Law Enforcement Subcommittee of the Minnesota House of Representatives, 29 February 1980.

Straus, M.; Gelles, R.; and Steinmetz, S. 1980. *Behind closed doors: Violence in the American family.* Garden City, N.Y.: Doubleday.

Wolfe, L. 1980. The sexual profile of the Cosmopolitan girl. *Cosmopolitan* 189(3): 254–57, 263–65.

X, Laura. The Rideout trial. Women's History Research Center, mimeographed.

8   Surviving: Women's Strength through Connection

CAROLYN F. SWIFT

Men's physical victimization of women through the ages is well documented. What is new in this century is the collective effort by women to deliver themselves from their attackers and to protest the values and practices associated with such institutionalized violence. Feminist scholarship has established that women and men relate differently to their worlds and to each other. Failure to recognize these differences is reflected in traditional scholarship that includes women in generalizations drawn from studies based on men. New theories projecting women's development and behavior from studies of women themselves challenge conventional wisdom in the field of human behavior and cast new light on heterosexual relationships in which violence occurs.

Norms Supporting Violence against Women

Two major cultural norms support violence against women. The first is the unequal distribution of power between the sexes, which is associated with traditional sex roles. The second norm condones the use of physical force to resolve disputes. These norms create institutional stresses for each sex, reflected in discriminatory policies and practices.

In addition, they differentially alter the quantity and quality of resources available to women and men in coping with the stresses of
their daily lives, including problems in relationships.

The Unequal Distribution of Power

One constant in all forms of violence between males and females is the
misuse of power. The bigger, the stronger, and those with greater
access to valued resources impose their will on those who are smaller,
are physically weaker, and have less access to resources. Finkelhor
(1983, 18), in describing family violence, puts the principle succinctly:
"The most common patterns in family abuse are not merely for the
more powerful to abuse the less powerful but for the most powerful to
abuse the least powerful. Abuse tends to gravitate to the relationship
of *greatest power differential.*" The most powerless victims, children
under six, suffer the highest incidence of physical abuse. The abuser
in most cases is the more powerful parent, the father (Finkelhor 1983).

In our culture, major power differentials are sorted by age; by sex,
with males in general commanding more social, economic, political,
and physical power than females; and by ethnicity, with the white
majority commanding more power than other ethnic groups. When
these differences are compounded, abuse increases. For example, Berk
et al. (1983) found that the incidence of abuse was higher among white
males married to Hispanic females than in couples where both partners
were white. Martin (1976) has noted a similar effect for white males
married to Asian women.

The traditional power imbalance between female and male heads of
household sets up conditions for economic, social, or physical abuse in
the marital relationship. Both sexes are burdened by discriminatory
traditions that dictate the "appropriate" role of each in family life and
in the world outside the family. In the context of these roles, the male
partner is seen as the breadwinner. His area of expertise and action is
the public world, which encompasses societal institutions and the commerce between them. The female partner is assigned primary responsibility for maintaining the home and bearing and raising children.
Women are not expected, according to the traditional worldview, to
seek fulfillment through lifetime careers outside the home, and men
are not expected to contribute any major effort to what have become
known as homemaking activities or to daily child care. These role
restrictions and prescriptions create situations that increase the probability of abuse. Sex-role socialization sets up a power imbalance, with
males in dominant roles and females in submissive roles.

Evidence from cross-cultural studies supports the finding that where both male dominance and interpersonal violence are accepted, females are at high risk for victimization. For example, in a study of ninety-five societies, Sanday (1981) classified 47 percent as rape free and 18 percent as rape prone. A common feature in the rape-free societies is the relatively equal balance between the sexes. The contributions of women in these societies are respected and valued, particularly their functions associated with reproduction, growth, and social continuity. Sanday found that the incidence of rape in a society was positively correlated with the ideology of machismo as well as the intensity of interpersonal violence. Interpersonal violence is rarely found in rape-free societies.

Male aggression against females, then, is neither biologically determined nor inevitable. According to Sanday, it results from social learning and from the balance between population needs and environmental resources.

> In tribal societies women are often equated with fertility and growth, men with aggression and destruction. More often than not, the characteristics associated with maleness and femaleness are equally valued. When people perceive an imbalance between the food supply and population needs, or when populations are in competition for diminishing resources, the male role is accorded greater prestige. Sexual violence is one of the ways in which men remind themselves that they are superior. As such, rape is part of a broader struggle for control in the face of difficult circumstances. Where men are in harmony with their environment, rape is usually absent. (Sanday 1981, 25)

As Sanday writes, "The correlates of rape strongly suggest that rape is the playing out of a socio-cultural script in which the expression of personhood for males is directed by, among other things, interpersonal violence and an ideology of toughness" (1981, 24).

The cultural profile Sanday identifies as destructive to women is consistent with findings in our own culture. For example, Burt (1980) conducted a study of rape myths, defined as "prejudicial, stereotyped, or false beliefs about rape, rape victims and rapists" (p. 217). Rape myths condemn victims as lacking in virtue, resistance, or credibility while viewing rapists as overcome by lust, insanity, or both. The prevalence of rape myths, evident in both public and professional attitudes, contributes to a culture in which rape is common, victims are denigrated, and rapists are rarely apprehended or convicted. Surveying a random sample of adults in a midwestern state, Burt found that acceptance of rape myths could be predicted from attitudes of sex-role stereotyping and adversarial sexual beliefs (e.g., the belief that sexual relationships involve exploitation and acceptance of interpersonal violence).

The Use of Physical Force

The second factor that contributes to the prevalence of physical attacks on women is the cultural acceptance of violence to enforce compliance. Our culture has a long tradition of using physical force to resolve interpersonal conflicts. Physical discipline and punishment are commonly accepted ways for parents to control their children, and corporal punishment is still legal in most states. Accepted practices for controlling children are readily adapted to use against women and reflect a social tolerance of interpersonal violence by the strong against the weak. (See parts 1 and 2 of this volume for a more complete discussion of the use of physical force against children.)

Social Network Response

The value of supportive relationships for healthy functioning and their role in buffering the destructive effects of stress have been extensively documented (Gottlieb 1981, 1983; Mitchell and Trickett 1980). Social supports constitute a critical variable in Albee's (1981) formula for calculating the incidence of mental and emotional dysfunction. Along with coping skills and self-esteem, social supports reduce dysfunction caused by environmental stress. When the source of stress is human rather than environmental, as in male violence against women, the customary function of social supports in our society is reversed.

Confronted with stressful life changes, most people turn for help to their spouses, other family members, friends, and neighbors. For the battered woman it is the spouse or partner who inflicts pain. She not only suffers the pain of the attack but loses the support of her primary relationship as well. Relatives and friends often side with the attacker. In these cases close network ties can perpetuate the violence.

> The assumption that the kin network will be opposed to violence is not necessarily correct. For example, a number of women indicated that when they left their husbands because of a violent attack, their mothers responded with urgings for the wife to deal with the situation by being a better housekeeper, by being a better sex partner, or just by avoiding him, etc. In some cases, the advice was "you have to put up with it for the sake of the kids—that's what I did!" (Straus 1980, 246)

Instead of countering the stress of victimization, the woman's personal and institutional support systems are likely to add to her burden. The support network reflects, through attitudes, policies, and practices, the cultural norms that denigrate a woman's roles and contributions and condone interpersonal violence against her. Whether by actively blaming her for provoking the attack or by simply withdrawing customary emotional and material resources, persons and institutions in the woman's social network often have a negative impact on her capacity to survive attack.

Beyond immediate family and friends, the professional community can usually be counted on to provide assistance in most life crises. Here too women attacked by their male partners not only find little support but often encounter blame and hostile judgment instead. The church, through its clergy, is the institutional resource most frequently approached by battered women (Pagelow 1982). In a recent survey of Protestant clergy in the United States and Canada (Alsdurf 1985), investigators confirmed that pastors have patriarchal attitudes toward women that lead them to distrust women's accounts of family violence and to discount violence as grounds for dissolving the marriage.

> One-third of the respondents felt that the abuse would have to be severe in order to justify a Christian wife leaving her husband, while 21 percent felt that no amount of abuse would justify a separation. Twenty-six percent of the pastors agreed that a wife should submit to her husband and trust that God would honor her action by either stopping the abuse or giving her the strength to endure it. (Alsdurf 1985, 10)

Another survey of helping professionals—physicians, psychiatrists, psychologists, social workers, and clergy—found that social workers identified the largest number of abused women while physicians and clergy identified the fewest (Burris 1984). That most social workers are female and most physicians and members of the clergy are male suggests that the traditional male denial of the scope of the problem and its effect on victims may account for this difference.

Physicians are generally held to underestimate abuse by not identifying cases in their practice. It seems, however, that at some level they differentiate battered women from other injured women: battered women are more likely than others to leave the emergency room with a prescription for pain medication (cited in Stark, Flitcraft, and Frazier 1979). Semmelman (1982) found that four times as many battered women as nonbattered women in shelters were taking psychotropic medication (21 percent versus 5 percent). Although the medication may blunt pain, it also blunts the woman's alertness to imminent danger and reduces her ability to defend herself from attack in the short run. Over the long run, it undermines her capacity for problem solving. Stark (1984, 307) notes that "despite its failure to 'see,' medicine responds in distinct and punitive ways to battered women. . . . By decontextualizing emergent social problems and treating the psychosocial consequences of abuse as an occasion for family maintenance, medicine helps stabilize families in which escalating violence is inevitable."

The legal system, through its codification of crimes and social norms, supports the rights of citizens against attack. However, the legal system has usually failed to protect women from their male partners' violence. The laws dealing with partner abuse and the enforcement of these laws reflect the patriarchal values of the traditionally male prosecutors, judges, and police officers who staff the legal system. Lerman (1986), in a recent review, amassed evidence that from the battered woman's first contact with the system through final disposition of the case, she is routinely discouraged from effectively registering her protest of the crime committed against her and from seeking redress. Police file reports in fewer than 20 percent of the domestic abuse cases for which they are called, and they arrest the abuser in fewer than 5 percent of these cases. Even when the abuser is arrested, he has roughly a fifty-fifty chance that the prosecutor will dismiss the charges. Convictions in family violence cases are rare, and when they do occur, penalties are relatively light. Lerman concludes, "This pattern suggests that in most places prosecution is seldom an available remedy for battered women" (1986, 265).

In the field of penology it has been established that it is the certainty of punishment, not its severity, that serves as an effective deterrent to crime (Andanaes 1975; Erickson and Gibbs 1973; Tittle 1969). In cases of violence against women the certainty principle effectively rewards the attacker and punishes the victim. He can count on not being arrested, prosecuted, convicted, or punished. She can count on not being protected against assault. A Canadian study found that in a one-year period, out of ten thousand men who assault their wives, only eight hundred are arrested and only two end up going to jail (Dunwoody 1982).

The new visibility of rape and battering has had two important consequences. First, though progress toward changing discriminatory institutional practices is slow, it is nevertheless occurring, as is reflected in rape-law reform (Geis and Geis 1978; Loh 1981) and in a greater readiness to arrest and convict rapists and batterers (Smith 1981). Second, the increased visibility of woman-targeted violence has helped women find resources and support from each other and to create alternatives outside the system of violence.

Gender Differences with Implications for Intimate Relationships

A major contributor to the perpetuation of violence against women is the invisibility of women's experience.[1] This invisibility is effectively enforced by patriarchal custom and practice. In the context of violence toward women there are three major areas in which women's experiences differ from men's: ethics, epistemology, and the use of power. There is evidence that males and females resolve moral problems differently, evaluate information differently, and use power differently.

Ethics

Carl Gilligan (1982) outlined two major approaches to resolving ethical dilemmas. It is clear that both males and females have access to both approaches. It is also clear that in Western patriarchal culture males tend to use one approach predominantly, while females tend to use both. The first approach sees ethical problems as occasions for creating or enforcing rules that spell out the rights of those involved. Rules and rights are seen as necessary to define the limits of autonomy and to ensure its exercise. Autonomy in this view is a highly desired state or goal—the end of a process that begins with *separation* from the mother in childhood. An ethic that emphasizes rights and rules and is grounded in autonomy as the organizing principle is the predominant ethic in Western patriarchal culture.

The second approach to the resolution of ethical problems sees these problems in the context of the relationships in which they are embedded. In this approach there is an attempt to identify and assign the responsibilities of those involved in a way that maintains caring and connectedness. In our culture the ethic of responsibility, caring, and connectedness is most likely to be implemented by women. When faced with an ethical dilemma men are more likely to resolve it by asserting their rights, invoking rules, and more often than not preserving their autonomy. Women, on the other hand, are likely to consider the impact of various solutions on the relationship involved and to opt for assigning responsibility in such a way as to preserve these connections—in as caring a way as possible. Women tend to value relationships more highly than autonomy, whereas the opposite is true for men. This difference is extremely important for understanding the

---

1. An earlier version of this section appears in Swift 1987.

topic of family violence, since it means that women will be more devoted to preserving the relationship even through the stress of violence.

Epistemology

The second area of difference between the sexes that has implications for violence toward women is epistemology. A number of feminist scholars have explored the ways gender roles generate alternative thought paradigms for women and men. Clinchy and Zimmerman (1985) and Belenky et al. (1986) have described several approaches to knowing, two of which are especially pertinent to this topic. One approach, based on Ferry's work (1970, 1981), emphasizes a method of thinking that uses objective criteria to analyze new information. The analysis compares the information with what is already known, notes differences, and tests the new knowledge against established standards. Clinchy and Zimmerman (1985) called this type of knowing "separate" in reference to the autonomous nature of the self in making comparisons and seeing differences. Another approach to knowing involves not separating the self from what is to be known, but entering into the new frame of reference in order to understand it. It is this type of knowing, called "connected" knowing, that leads to empathy. Clinchy and Zimmerman gave the example of students studying a poem. Those using the method of "separate" knowing "ask themselves: 'What standards are being used to evaluate my analysis of this poem? What techniques can I use to analyze it?' The orientation is toward impersonal rules and procedures." Those using the method of "connected" knowing ask "'What is this poet trying to say to me?'" (1985, 3). The orientation here is to place the self in the poem to understand the author's meaning.

It is the thesis of these scholars that connected knowing is more often found in women, although both sexes use both separate and connected knowing. The significance of this difference in understanding situations in which women are attacked is that the woman is more likely to feel and relate to the pain of the other (the male partner). This capacity for feeling the other's pain may contribute to the woman's lesser readiness to initiate or return violence—a position that places her at a disadvantage in protecting herself against her partner's violence.

Ruddick's (1984) illuminating account of what she calls "maternal thinking" focuses on the ways maternal practices have shaped the thought process. While both sexes have the capacity to engage in maternal thinking, it is found more often in women because of their more intimate connection with children and their greater responsibility for bearing and rearing them. The demands of both the child and the culture are reflected in maternal practice, and they determine the priorities of maternal thinking. These priorities are to preserve life, to foster development, and to shape growth into forms acceptable to the culture at large. Confronted with responsibility for the life of another human being, the maternal parent develops an attitude Ruddick calls "holding." This attitude values keeping over acquiring. Its aims are to conserve and maintain resources to sustain fragile life. "It is an attitude elicited by the work of 'world *protection*, world *preservation*, world *repair* . . . the invisible weaving of a frayed and threadbare family life'" (Ruddick 1984, 217).

The foundation of maternal thought lies in the capacity to attend to and love the other—prototypically, the child. This capacity for attention and love is expressed in the question "What are you going through?" (Ruddick 1984, 224) and in the empathy required to hear the response. Although maternal thinking has its roots in the mother-child relationship, the bonding of self-interest with the interests of the cared-for other is a characteristic of an intimate relationship for women.

Because maternal thinking centers on the experience of the other, because its priorities are to preserve the safety and foster the growth of the other, the maternal thinker is singularly unprepared to defend against attack from a significant other. Defense against physical attack requires an understanding of personal risk as separate from the attacker's risk. Habituated to feeling what the other is going through, the maternal thinker is psychologically unequipped to make the abrupt and sudden shift of attention from other to self needed to mobilize energy for self-defense.

Many women subjected to battering do not make this shift. Mills (1985), in a series of interviews with women who had been battered, noted that a loss of self occurs over time. She saw this loss as taking two forms, a loss of identity and a loss of what she called the observing self. Many of the women interviewed described an incapacity to act, "like: 'being in a shell,' 'like a zombie,' 'a mechanical robot,' 'being numb,' and 'like being dead'" (1985, 113). Finding their judgments and perceptions about the relationship shattered, suffering the pain and shock of attack, they have few resources—either within themselves or in the world outside—to stop the violence or restore their sense of self.

Other women victimized by battering partners react by consciously choosing not to defend themselves. For many this strategy is calculated to heal some past wound perceived in the batterer and to create the opportunity for growth in the relationship. The following first-person accounts of battered women illustrate this strategy:

> *Deb:* I feel he can be helped with treatment. I know he feels rejected because of all his brothers and sisters, he was the only one they gave away. So, I thought that he was trying to make me give him away just like everybody else. So, I thought if I didn't play his game, if I don't reject him, he would get over it. (Mills 1985, 110)

> *Maggie:* I think a reason I got a master's in social work was to see what could be done. That's what I wrote my thesis on—how to help the men. I spent the first year trying to find out how to make it different so we could have a good marriage. (Mills 1985, 110)

> *Woman:* I had the idea that I'm doing this for him. I'm coping. I'm controlling the amount of abuse I'm taking. I must be a good person. The importance I got was what I was doing for him. (Schechter 1982, 13)

Although the maternal thinking Ruddick describes has clear evolutionary benefits, it contributes to the physical and psychological destruction of adherents who are paired with violent partners.

The Use of Power

The third area of difference between men and women involves the use of power. The discussion here is based on the work of Jean Baker Miller (1976, 1982). Issues of power, like issues of morality and knowing, are viewed differently by the sexes. Males tend to define power in terms of the capacity to effect their will, with or without the consent of those involved. Domination is a key concept in the male definition and exercise of power. Miller's definition—and one that more accurately represents women's experience of exercising power—is that power is the capacity to effect change, to move something from point A to point B.

In our patriarchal society, women have not been viewed as needing to exercise power. In fact, women do exercise power. However, they are more likely than men to do this in the service of others. One primary way women "empower" others is by promoting the growth and development of children in psychological, social, and intellectual spheres. Another way is by promoting their mates' growth and development. Women have traditionally provided psychological and material support to further their husbands' goals—autonomy and success in the world outside the home. For women to use their power to effect change—to move something from point A to point B—*in their own self-interest* threatens patriarchal values and may invoke frightening images in the women themselves.

Miller (1982) identified three fears women associate with exercising power in their own self-interest: fear of being selfish, fear of being destructive, and fear of being abandoned by those they care about. Enhancing one's own power in our culture is often connected with reducing the power of another. Women fear that to act in their own self-interest risks putting down others; such action is seen as selfish. To act in one's own self-interest, when one is a member of a subordinate group, is often to act in ways inimical to the interests of the dominant group; such actions may in fact alter or even destroy the arrangements perpetuated by the dominant group:

> Women have lived as subordinates and, as subordinates, have been led by the culture to believe that their own self-determined action is wrong and evil. Many women have incorporated deeply the inner notion that such actions must be destructive. . . . In most institutions it is still true that if women do act from their own perceptions and motivations, directly and honestly, they indeed may be disrupting a context which has not been built out of women's experience. Thus, one is confronted with feeling like one must do something very powerful that also feels destructive. (Miller 1982, 4)

The fear of being abandoned is related to the other two fears. If women do act in their own self-interest, and if these actions disrupt existing relationships, then women may suffer attack or abandonment as a consequence. Miller pointed out, "All of us exist only as we need others for that existence." Men tend to deny this view; women have incorporated it in an extreme form. "Along with it we women have incorporated the troubling notion that, as much as we need others, we also have powers and the motivations to use those powers, but if we use them, we will destroy the relationships we need for our existence" (1982, 4).

Women, then, are at an immense psychological as well as physical disadvantage in resolving conflicts with their male partners. First, they place the highest priority on preserving the relationship—on staying connected—when disputes arise. Second, their capacity to "know" the other in connected, empathic ways, rather than in the critical, objective ways characterized by "separate" knowing, makes them the partner more likely to feel the pain of the other, even in the midst of their own suffering. And third, in abuse situations women are in a double bind in attempting to use their power in their own interest. If they save their physical selves by leaving to avoid the battering, they risk

destroying their primary relationship and their psychological and economic security. If they act to preserve the primary relationship and
their psychological and economic security, they put themselves at risk
of physical destruction. Women in battering situations are forced to
choose which parts of themselves they will save—their physical safety
and well being or their psychological and economic safety and well-
being. It is not surprising that many women find this a difficult choice.

Empowerment through Healthy Connections

Why do women stay with battering partners? The question implies a
freedom of choice and a multiplicity of options that do not exist for
many battered women. Beyond this, it is the wrong question, even
though it is the one most often asked by those dealing with domestic
abuse. The more appropriate question is, "Why do men batter their
intimate partners?" It is not a priority in Western patriarchal culture
to find an answer to this question. Roughly nine out of every ten
studies of battering focus on the victimized woman, with little or no
attention to the batterer.[2] When issues concerning the batterer are
addressed, the method often involves eliciting information about him
from his victim rather than from the abuser himself (e.g., see Walker
1984).

In the absence of significant efforts to identify the causes of battering and to prevent such behavior in men, victimized women are in
need of shelter and resources to help them lead abuse-free lives. The
information in studies on battered women sheds light on factors that
strengthen women's abilities to help each other and to help themselves
avoid male-initiated violence.

A frequent comparison made in the research literature is between
women who stay with battering partners and women who leave them.
Although many women leave and return more than once, those whose
economic situation gives them the option of independence are more
likely to leave the batterer and not return. The women who leave
battering partners are more likely to be employed and have generally
achieved a higher level of education than women who stay (Hilbert
and Hilbert 1984; Strube 1984). Of the employed women who find
themselves in battering relationships, those with higher salaries are
more likely to leave. Women who suffered child abuse are less likely

---

2. This ratio is based on a literature review covering psychological, sociological, family,
and dissertation abstracts for the years 1982 to 1985.

to leave their battering partners than women without this history (Dalto 1983). Early exposure to physical abuse may contribute to learned helplessness (Walker 1984) or to an increased tolerance of abuse in intimate relationships.

Psychological differences have also been examined. Feldman (1983) found that "leavers" had significantly higher self-esteem, had a more internalized locus of control, and subscribed to less traditional sex-role ideology. Walker's (1984) study, based on interviews with over four hundred battered women, shows conflicting results. Contrary to her prediction, she found that both stayers and leavers scored significantly higher than the norm on internal locus of control measures, and both groups were more depressed than the norm.

How the woman herself perceives the relationship is a key factor. If she believes the battering is unavoidable, that she has no control over it, that the batterer does not love her or will not change, she is more likely to leave. If, on the other hand, she believes she can avoid the battering, that she is in part to blame for it, that her partner loves her or will change his battering behavior, she is more likely to stay (Butehorn 1985; Dalto 1983; Porter 1983; Strube 1984). The frequency and severity of battering also affect whether the woman stays or leaves (Gelles and Cornell 1985; Hilbert and Hilbert 1984; Kremen 1985). Daily violence has been associated with leaving and weekly violence with staying (Butehorn 1985).

The responses of those in the woman's personal network, as well as institutional response, also affect whether the woman stays with the batterer. When those in her personal network are seen as favoring a reconciliation, the woman is more likely to return to the batterer (Dalto 1983). In one study, stayers were more likely to receive feedback that their networks would not help them if they left (Butehorn 1985). Several investigators have found that leaving is associated with the responsiveness of community agencies and social institutions (Hodson 1982; Lidkea 1982). In general, helpful responses are negatively related to the length of the battering relationship. Unfortunately, as described earlier, social institutions and agencies not only have historically not been helpful to women victimized by violence but have, by their discriminatory policies and practices, added to the women's stress.

Leaving the batterer is often preceded by a transformative experience in which another person, one who stands outside the battering relationship, reflects the woman's reality in a way that enables her to acknowledge and assess her risk more objectively. The responses of therapists and counselors are critical, as described by two women in Mills's study. The first told how she decided to leave her husband after talking with a therapist: "She convinced me that my life was in danger. I realize now that it was. I was ignoring a lot of signs even though I was in the middle of it" (Mills 1985, 116).

The second woman described the beginnings of the restoration of her sense of self after meeting with a therapist: "One weekend I took an overdose of pills and had to go to the hospital. So, they said since I took an overdose I had to see a psychiatrist. And the funny thing about it, he said the problem was my husband and not me. He said that if I got away from him, I'd be a lot better off. I thought that was pretty good because I thought maybe I was the one that was crazy" (Mills 1985, 115).

The availability of women's shelters and their value as islands of security and support outside the victim's battering system have proved to be critical way stations in the woman's exodus from her violent home. Research supports the conclusion that battered women use shelters to practice living on their own, apart from the battering partner. The greater the number of previous separations (Snyder and Scheer 1981), the more times the woman has returned to the shelter (Okun 1983), and the longer the duration of the shelter visit(s) (Dalto 1983; Hilbert and Hilbert 1984; Snyder and Scheer 1981), the more likely it is that the woman will leave the batterer. It is important for this information to reach the field, since shelter workers tend to count the women who make multiple visits as failures and may treat them punitively—that is, may refuse them entry on subsequent visits (Martin 1976). If return visits are seen as rehearsals rather than recidivism, it should be easier for shelter workers to welcome returnees and support their efforts to practice the skills needed to live independently from the batterer.

What are the features of the shelter experience that promote the decision to leave the batterer? Data are not available to assess the relative value of the shelter's material versus psychological resources. But it is clear from the literature that one of the most important features of the shelter experience is the opportunity it provides for women to develop healthy connections with others. Fleeing an unhealthy relationship, the battered woman finds in the shelter other women like herself who offer her understanding, who believe her story, who are committed to her safety and well-being, and who value her. A common finding is that women who form close relationships with other battered women in the shelter, or who identify with a shelter role model, are less likely to return to the abuser (Dalto 1983; Okun 1983).

Battered women receive valuable psychological resources from relationships formed in shelters. They are listened to and believed. They participate in problem solving with other women who share similar experiences. They form a more accurate picture of themselves and of the batterer. And they gain increasing confidence in their ability to live violence-free lives (Swift 1987). In sum, the research indicates that women who leave battering relationships are aided in doing so by making healthy connections with persons outside the battering system. The shelter movement and the women who have left shelters to live violence-free lives demonstrate that one of the ways women survive male violence is by creating alternative ways of living, both collectively and individually.

References

Albee, G. 1981. Primary prevention in the community mental health centers. In *The health care system and drug abuse prevention: Toward cooperation and health promotion*, 38–44. DHHS Publication (ADM) 81–1105. Washington, D.C.: U.S. Government Printing Office.

Alsdurf, J. 1985. Wife abuse and the church: The response of pastors. *Response to the Victimization of Women and Children* 8:9–11.

Andenaes, J. 1975. General preventions revisited: Research and policy implications. *Journal of Criminal Law and Criminology* 66:338–65.

Belenky, M.; Clinchy, B.; Goldberger, N.; and Tarule, J. 1986. *Women's ways of knowing: The development of self, voice and mind*. New York: Basic Books.

Berk, R.; Berk, S. F.; Loeske, D.; and Rauma, D. 1983. Mutual combat and other family violence myths. In *The dark side of families*, ed. D. Finkelhor, R. Gelles, G. Hotaling, and M. Straus, 97–212. Beverly Hills, Calif.: Sage.

Burris, C. A. 1984. Wife battering: A well-kept secret. *Canadian Journal of Criminology* 26:171–77.

Burt, M. R. 1980. Cultural myths and supports for rape. *Journal of Personality and Social Psychology* 38:217–30.

Butehorn, L. 1985. Social networks and the battered woman's decision to stay or leave (wife battering, women, morality, family violence). *Dissertation Abstracts International* 46105-B, 1741.

Clinchy, B., and Zimmerman, C. 1985. Growing up intellectually: Issues for college women. In *Work in progress*, no. 19. Working Papers series. Wellesley, Mass.: Stone Center, Wellesley College.

Dalto, C. 1983. Battered women: Factors influencing whether or not former shelter residents return to the abusive situation. *Dissertation Abstracts International* 44/04-B, 1277.

Dunwoody, E. 1982. Sexual abuse of children: A serious widespread problem. *Response* 5:1–2, 13–14.

Erickson, M., and Gibbs, J. 1973. The deterrence question: Some alternative methods of analysis. *Social Science Quarterly* 54:534–55.

Feldman, S. 1983. Battered women: Psychological correlates of the victimization process. *Dissertation Abstracts International* 44/04-B, 1221.

Finkelhor, D. 1983. Common features of family abuse. In *The dark side of families,* ed. D. Finkelhor, R. Gelles, G. Hotaling, and M. Straus, 17–28. Beverly Hills, Calif.: Sage.

Geis, G., and Geis, R. 1978. Rape reform: An appreciative-critical review. *Bulletin of the American Academy of Psychiatry and the Law* 6:301–12.

Gelles, R., and Cornell, C. 1985. *Intimate violence in families.* Beverly Hills, Calif.: Sage.

Gilligan, C. 1982. *In a different voice: Psychological theory and women's development.* Cambridge: Harvard University Press.

Gottlieb, B. H., ed. 1981. *Social networks and social support.* Sage studies in Community Mental Health. Beverly Hills, Calif.: Sage.

———. 1983. Opportunities for collaboration with informal support systems. In *The mental health consultation field,* ed. S. Cooper and W. Hodges, 181–203. New York: Human Services Press.

Hilbert, J. C., and Hilbert, H. C. 1984. Battered women leaving shelter: Which way to they go? A discriminant function analysis. *Journal of Applied Social Sciences* 8:291–97.

Hodson, C. 1982. Length of stay in a battering relationship: Test of a model. *Dissertation Abstracts International* 43/06-B, 1983.

Kremen, E. 1985. Battered women in counseling and shelter programs: A descriptive and follow-up study. *Dissertation Abstracts International* 45/10-A, 3211–12.

Lerman, L. 1982. Court decisions on wife abuse laws: Recent developments. *Response* 5:3–4, 21–22.

———. 1986. Prosecution of wife beaters: Institutional obstacles and innovations. In *Violence in the home: Interdisciplinary perspectives,* ed. M. Lystad, 250–95. New York: Brunner/Mazel.

Lidkea, M. 1982. Counseling as a factor in the later incidence of wife abuse: A follow up study of the clients of Brevard Family Aid Society, Inc. *Dissertation Abstracts International* 43/12-B, 4153.

Loh, W. D. 1981. What has reform of rape legislation wrought? *Journal of Social Issues* 37:28–52.

Martin, H., ed. 1976. *The abused child: A multidisciplinary approach to development issues and treatment.* Cambridge, Mass.: Ballinger.

Miller, J. B. 1976. *Toward a new psychology of women.* Boston: Beacon Press.

———. 1982. Women and power. In *Work in progress,* no. 1. Working Paper series. Wellesley, Mass.: Stone Center, Wellesley College.

Mills, T. 1985. The assault on the self: Stages in coping with battering husbands. *Qualitative Sociology* 8:103–23.

Mitchell, R., and Trickett, E. 1980. Social network research and psychosocial adaptations: Implications for community mental health practice. In *Environmental variables and the prevention of mental illness,* ed. P. Insel, 43–68. Lexington, Mass.: D. C. Heath.

Okun, L. 1983. A study of woman abuse: Three hundred batterers in counseling. *Dissertation Abstracts International* 44/06-8, 1972.

Pagelow, M. 1982. *Woman battering.* Beverly Hills, Calif.: Sage.

Perry, W. 1970. *Forms of intellectual and ethical development in the college years.* New York: Holt, Rinehart and Winston.

———. 1981. Cognitive and ethical growth: The making of meaning. In *The modern American college,* ed. A. Chickering. San Francisco: Jossey-Bass.

Porter, C. 1983. Blame and coping in battered women. *Dissertation Abstracts International* 44/05-B, 1641.

Ruddick, S. 1984. Maternal thinking. In *Mothering: Essays in feminist theory,* ed. J. Trebilcot, 213–32. Totowa, N.J.: Rowman and Allanheld.

Sanday, P. R. 1981. The socio-cultural context of a rape: a cross-cultural study. *Journal of Social Issues* 37:5–27.

Schechter, S. 1982. *Women and male violence.* Boston: South End Press.

Semmelman, P. 1982. Battered and nonbattered women: A comparison. *Dissertation Abstracts International* 43/08-B, 2716.

Smith, B. 1981. *Non-stranger violence: The criminal court's response.* Washington, D.C.: National Institute of Justice, U.S. Department of Justice.

Snyder, D., and Scheer, N. 1981. Predicting disposition following brief residence at a shelter for battered women. *American Journal of Community Psychology* 9:559–66.

Stark, E. 1984. The battering syndrome: Social knowledge, social therapy and the abuse of women. *Dissertation Abstracts International* 45/01-A, 307.

Stark, E.; Flitcraft, A.; and Frazier, W. 1979. Medicine and patriarchal violence: The social construction of a private event. *International Journal of Health Services* 9:461–93.

Straus, M. 1980. Social stress and marital violence in a national sample of American families. *Annals of the New York Academy of Sciences* 347:229–50.

Strube, M. J. 1984. Factors related to the decision to leave an abusive relationship. *Journal of Marriage and the Family* 46:837–44.

Swift, C. 1987. Women and violence: Breaking the connection. In *Work in Progress,* no. 27. Working Paper series. Wellesley, Mass.: Stone Center, Wellesley College.

Tittle, C. 1976. Crime rates and legal sanction. *Social Problems* 16:409–23.

Walker, L. E. 1984. *The battered woman syndrome.* New York: Springer.

9   Trauma in Men: Effects on Family Life

BESSEL A. VAN DER KOLK

In the past decade, much attention has been focused on the effects of psychological trauma on children and on women: there is a burgeoning understanding of the causes and long-term effects of child abuse (e.g., Cicchetti 1984; Cicchetti and Rizley 1981; Cicchetti and Rosen 1984; Green 1980; Green 1984; Finkelhor 1984; Greensbauer and Sands 1979); rape (e.g., Burgess and Holmstrom 1974; Kilpatrick, Veronen, and Best 1985; Kilpatrick, Veronen, and Resnick 1979; Schucker 1979; Notman and Nadelson 1976); incest (e.g., Herman 1981; Gelinas 1983); and wife battering (e.g., Hilberman 1980; Hilberman and Munson 1978; Gayford 1980). In a largely separate area of study, the effect of trauma on men has received attention in the context of understanding the psychological consequences of the Vietnam War for combat veterans (Figley 1978; Kolb 1984). While it is now generally recognized that the human response to overwhelming, uncontrollable life experiences is quite constant regardless of the nature of the trauma (American Psychiatric Association 1980), this recognition has not always received sufficient attention, since the debate on violence and traumatization in society often is colored by political considerations and a search for someone to blame. In studies on family violence and abuse, the effects of trauma on men all too often are minimized because the perpetrators of sexual abuse and violence are overwhelmingly men.

Hence there has been a temptation to reduce the role of men in abuse and family violence merely to that of the victimizer who is responsible for much of the origin and continuation of trauma.

Relatively little attention has been paid to the fact that most victimizers once were victims themselves and that their current behavior must be understood and treated with that perspective in mind (Kempe and Kempe 1978). Although many males who started life as victims later are violent toward others, many other traumatized males respond with emotional withdrawal and constriction, leaving different emotional responses and scars on both themselves and their surroundings (Finkelhor 1984).

The Trauma Response

To gain a greater understanding of the effect the traumatized male has on the family, one first needs to understand the universal human response to severe psychological trauma. Trauma can be defined as an event that overwhelms both psychological and biological coping mechanisms. Depending on the age of the victim, the severity of the trauma, the social support system, and the history of prior traumatization, psychological trauma may cause lasting alterations in the ways victims react to subsequent stress. Many people with a history of trauma continue to respond to even minor stress with an intensity that is appropriate only to emergency situations (van der Kolk 1986). This continued intensity of arousal interferes with their ability to make calm and rational assessments of later stressful situations; they continue to react with the somatic responses of fight, flight, or freeze. As a result, many traumatized people go immediately from stimulus to response, relying on action rather than thought to meet new challenges. Any degree of emotional arousal may precipitate fear and emergency responses.

The immediacy with which trauma victims react to stress is familiar to all clinicians who deal with that population: rape victims experience intense anxiety in any situation reminiscent of the trauma (Kilpatrick, Veronen, and Best 1985); Vietnam veterans may misinterpret the movements of a sleeping bed partner as a Viet Cong attack and react accordingly; mild noises played into the rooms of sleepers suffering from post-traumatic stress may precipitate nightmares in which old traumatic occurrences are recreated in exact detail (van der Kolk and Greenberg 1986).

Kardiner (1941) described the five principal features of post-traumatic stress disorder (PTSD) as persistence of startle response and irritability; proclivity to explosive outbursts of aggression; fixation on the trauma; constriction of the general level of personality functioning; and atypical dream life. Almost forty years later, the *DSM III* (American Psychiatric Association 1980) adopted most of these criteria in its definition of PTSD, emphasizing the biphasic nature of the trauma response, with coexistence of, and alternations between, intrusive and numbing responses. Major stress events tend to be followed by involuntary intrusion of elements of the original trauma into thought, emotion, and behavior. Such responses tend to occur in phases and to alternate with periods when the person is relatively successful at warding off repetitions, manifested by ideational denial and emotional numbness (Horowitz 1976).

Thus the symptoms of PTSD can be divided into intrusive and numbing responses. The intrusive symptoms consist of hyperactivity, anxiety, explosive aggressive outbursts, startle responses, nightmares, flashbacks, and reenactments. The numbing symptoms of PTSD consist of constriction, depression, social isolation, retreat from family obligations, anhedonia, and a sense of estrangement. It often is difficult to determine whether a person has integrated the long-term effects of psychological trauma: many victims make a successful adaptation during periods of life stability and social and physical well-being, only to have a recurrence of symptoms when faced with major life stresses. These stresses include object losses, decline in physical health, or decrease in security of the social matrix. In adults, 30 to 95 percent of people who have been exposed to overwhelming psychological trauma such as rape, combat, and concentration camps have been found to have long-term residual sequelae and to continue to live, to a greater or lesser degree, in the emotional environment of the traumatic event, with enduring vigilance for and sensitivity to environmental threat (Kardiner 1941; Burgess and Holmstrom 1974; Horowitz 1976; Hilberman 1980; Kilpatrick, Veronen, and Best 1985; van der Kolk 1986).

Moreover, psychological trauma also causes a number of other psychological defects that profoundly affect a person's social functioning, including learned helplessness, poor tolerance for physiological arousal, loss of ability to articulate specific and differentiated emotions, tendency to experience emotions as physical states, and fixation (addiction) on the trauma.

Learned Helplessness

Trauma victims often lose the sense that they can actively influence their lives, particularly in interpersonal spheres. This leads them to position themselves at either extreme of the dependence-independence spectrum; that is, they lose their capacity to modulate intimacy and dependency (van der Kolk 1986). In practice this means that many trauma victims either become intensely dependent on their caregivers, which is accompanied by a loss of personal initiative, or take a counterdependent stance, with lack of involvement with others—a retreat from family obligations, usually accompanied by excessive involvement in work (Flannery 1986). Traumatized people often have difficulty in modulating intimacy: they develop a disorder of hope (van der Kolk 1986). They expect either too much or too little and have difficulty discriminating between appropriate and inappropriate demands. They may blame themselves for obvious physical or emotional abuse by a partner, but they are enraged about minor disappointments coming from others. Unable to appropriately assess their own and others' contributions to interpersonal tension, they often continue to experience most interpersonal transactions as further victimization (Notman and Nadelson 1976).

Our research with traumatized men has shown that though many trauma victims are able to return to a semblance of normal functioning, they may in fact be suffering from profound constriction in their involvement with others and may experience a substantial alteration in their capacity to modulate feelings (van der Kolk and Ducey 1984). This numbing response to trauma can be understood as a way of dealing with the fear of its recurrence. By shunning all situations, or even all emotions, associated with the trauma, many traumatized people seem to gain some sense of control. Thus many of them avoid intimate relationships with others out of fear of another violation of an attachment. This avoidance of emotional involvement in actual relationships diminishes the significance of life since the trauma and thus perpetuates the central role the trauma plays in their lives (van der Kolk and Ducey 1984).

Poor Tolerance for Physiological Arousal

Regardless of the precipitating event, traumatized people continue to have a poor tolerance for physiological arousal. They have a tendency to react to stress with an all-or-nothing response—either with unmodulated anxiety, which is often accompanied by motoric discharge, including acts of aggression against the self or others, or with social and emotional withdrawal (Kolb 1984; Kardiner 1941). They have difficulty modulating affect: they often respond to emotional stimulation with an intensity appropriate to the original trauma, or they may barely react at all. Sounds, smells, or situations may easily stimulate a traumatic memory or, in a dissociated way, the overwhelming feelings associated with earlier traumatic events.

Loss of Ability to Articulate Specific and Differentiated Emotions

In our work with Vietnam veterans with PTSD (van der Kolk and Ducey 1984), Rorschach tests demonstrated further that our patients were incapable of modulated affective experience. The men with chronic PTSD had lost their capacity to resolve victimization through symbols, fantasies, or sublimation. Hence they were deprived of exactly those psychological mechanisms that allow people to cope with the small injuries of daily life and to accumulate restitutive gratifying experiences (Krystal 1984). We later replicated these findings in children with a history of severe physical or sexual abuse (Fish-Murray, Koby, and van der Kolk 1986).

Tendency to Experience Emotions as Physical States

The decreased capacity to modulate physiological arousal, combined with the reduced ability to use symbols and fantasy to cope with stress leaves traumatized individuals vulnerable to experiencing subsequent stresses primarily as somatic states rather than as discrete historical events that require specific solutions. The somatic experiencing of stressful life events may take the form of psychosomatic symptoms, panic attacks, rage reactions, or other physical activity. Lacking the proper historical reference (i.e., conscious understanding about the reason for the intensity of these reactions that are out of proportion to the severity of the current life stressors), these patients lack verbal or symbolic control over their responses and frequently need psychopharmacological agents or biofeedback to help them modulate the intensity of their somatic reactions (Krystal 1978; van der Kolk and Greenberg 1986). Patients frequently medicate themselves with alcohol and drugs in an ill-fated effort to gain control over inexplicable somatic expressions of emotional events (Lacoursiere, Godfrey, and Rubey 1980).

Fixation on (Addiction to) the Trauma

A certain proportion of traumatized patients remain centrally preoccupied with their trauma at the expense of other life experiences. This may take the socially and psychologically useful form of sublimated preoccupation by being of assistance to other victims or "bearing witness." However, other trauma victims continue to recreate the trauma in some form for themselves or for others. War veterans may enlist as mercenaries; incest victims may become prostitutes; some victims of childhood physical abuse may provoke subsequent abuse in foster families and others may grow up to become self-mutilators. Still others recreate the trauma by identifying with the aggressor and perpetrating the same heinous acts on others that were once inflicted upon them (Lewis, Shanok, and Pincus 1979; Lewis and Balla 1976; Ross 1980; van der Kolk et al. 1985). The clinical impression is that these people have in common a vague sense of apprehension, emptiness, boredom, and anxiety when not involved in activities reminiscent (often unconsciously) of the trauma. Much of our current research work is centrally concerned with this issue, which Freud called the repetition compulsion. However, to date we are pessimistic about Freud's expectation that repeating the trauma will eventually lead to mastery and resolution.

Sex Differences in Response to Trauma

While our knowledge about differential responses to trauma between the sexes is incomplete and probably highly dependent on cultural factors, such differences between males and females are consistently found not only in humans, but in nonhuman primates as well (for a review, see van der Kolk 1986). Trauma consistently seems to be followed by increased rage, but men tend to vent this rage on their social surroundings, while women are more prone to turn it upon themselves in the form of self-destructive behavior and a decreased capacity to set limits on the expression of aggression in others (Jaffe, Wolfe, and Wilson 1986). In a study of psychiatric inpatients, Carmen, Reiker and Mills (1984) found marked sex differences in the expression of aggression in victims of childhood physical or sexual abuse: 33 percent of abused males coped with anger by turning aggression outward, compared with 14 percent of the females; 66 percent of females directed anger inward with self-destructive behavior, compared with 20 percent of the male patients. Children who have been exposed to early separation, abuse, or neglect have been found to develop extreme reactivity to internal and external stimulation; that is, they overreact to subsequent situations and frustrations and have trouble tolerating anxiety. Boys in particular display a constant high level of motor activity, while girls more frequently show a depressed picture of anxious withdrawal, dependent clinging, and passivity (Green 1980; Pynoos and Eth 1985; Garmezy and Rutter 1983). Traumatized children have trouble modulating aggression and tend to be destructive toward others or themselves (Cicchetti 1984). Moreover, there is a strong correlation between childhood abuse and subsequent adult criminal behavior, particularly in men (Kempe and Kempe 1978; Lewis and Balla 1976).

The Social Context of Traumatization

Transmission of Trauma to Children

People develop a sense of meaning and control over their lives in the context of secure social attachments. The necessity for secure affiliative bonds makes children and adolescents particularly vulnerable to the long-term effects of trauma. Following psychological trauma, both in children and in adults, interpersonal attachments are characterized either by anxious and clinging ties to others, accompanied by idealization and an abandonment of psychological autonomy, or by interpersonal numbness: "a giving up of hope for satisfactory human contact, which is the result of the destruction of basic trust" (Krystal 1978). Either way, trauma results in a temporary or lasting undervaluation or overvaluation of others' capacity to provide emotional gratification and security.

The most powerful influence in overcoming the impact of psychological trauma is the availability of a caregiver who can be blindly trusted when one's own resources are inadequate. If that caregiver responds with rejection and abuse, children are likely to blame themselves rather than the caregiver for this rejection. When those who are supposed to be the child's sources of safety and nurture are simultaneously the sources of danger against which protection is needed, a child maneuvers psychologically to reestablish some sense of safety, often becoming fearfully and hungrily attached, unwillingly or anxiously obedient, and apprehensive lest the caregiver be unavailable when needed (Cicchetti 1984). In an essay on the long-term consequences of child abuse and neglect, Bowlby (1973b, 22) suggested that expression of anger between members of a family can serve to maintain attachment bonds. He points out that family violence is often a distorted or exaggerated version of behavior that is potentially functional. An infant seeks increased attachment in the face of any external danger, even when a parent is the source of this danger. Thus, paradoxically, abused infants cling more strongly to their abusing parents than children raised in secure surroundings: "The immediate consequence of parental rejection is the accentuation of proximity seeking on the part of the child" (1973b, 22).

The immediacy with which abused boys repeat aggressive interactions has suggested to Green (1980) a linkage between the compulsion to repeat trauma and identification with the aggressor. Since Freud, students of child abuse have been struck by this identification with the aggressor, which seems to allow fear and helplessness to be replaced with feelings of omnipotence and power. It seems that such identification is more likely to occur in boys, who then repeat abuse in the next generation on their spouses and children, whereas women are more likely to identify with the victim: linking up with violent and abusive men, but taking an either actively or passively abusive stance toward their own children (Carmen, Reiker, and Mills 1984). Parents who batter each other are likely to abuse their children as well, and many people who batter their children are thought to have been victims of parental abuse in their own childhood (Lewis, Shanok, and Pincus 1979). Thus the compulsion to repeat the trauma is transmitted through both men and women.

Adolescence

In adolescence, peer relationships allow for the affirmation of self-worth that is essential to breaking dependent ties with parents. Although the peer group already plays a central role in children's lives before adolescence, the family generally still functions as the safe base from which a child can explore other interpersonal ties. Adolescence has been described as the great second chance (Blos 1979): even if the family failed to provide sufficient safety and proper role models, adolescent experiences of intimacy and competence within the peer group can to some degree compensate for earlier deficiencies. Aichorn (1948) first made it clear that adolescent males often cover up underlying feelings of emptiness, loneliness, and fear with acts of bravado, including antisocial behavior, which serve the need for acceptance by and dependence on the peer group. A girl often deals with her dependency needs by taking care of a male who is troubled and by trying to exert a restitutive influence that was not possible in her family of origin (Offer and Offer 1975; Sharp 1980). Some girls who have had incestuous experiences tend to vacillate between complete avoidance of involvement with men and overinvolvement, including prostitution (Sharfman and Clark 1967; Gelinas 1983; Ferenczi 1955).

Erikson (1956, 56) marked the resolution of adolescence with the final dimension of identity: "Man, to take his place in society, must acquire a conflict free habitual use of a dominant faculty, to be elaborated in an occupation; a limitless resource, a feedback, as it were, from the immediate exercise of this occupation, from the companionship it provides, and from its tradition; and finally, an intelligible theory of the processes of life." For men, positive identification with their fathers greatly facilitates their committing themselves to a positive role identification. For young men with ambivalent or negative relationships with their fathers, the military has traditionally served as an avenue to such an identity. Ambivalent feelings toward weak or rejecting fathers can be dealt with in the armed services, which provide total security based on total subjugation (Elder 1986). Young men with secure affiliations with their fathers are less likely to find gratification in such a setup than those whose paternal relationships are dominated by disappointment. Those with disrupted early family relationships are likely to form more intensely dependent relationships in the military and thus are more vulnerable to further disappointment and loss. In a study of Vietnam veterans with persistent PTSD ten years and more after combat, I found (van der Kolk 1985) that the subjects with PTSD displayed an extreme avoidance of expressing aggression and, regardless of the level of social adjustment, experienced a profound sense that they could not control their destinies. I found that those who developed PTSD were much younger when in combat than those who did not. In contrast to the control group, the younger men had developed intense attachments to other men in their combat units that had been disrupted by the death of the buddy, a loss often followed by retaliation and subsequent profound feelings of helplessness. Vietnam veterans with PTSD had felt particularly close to their combat units, and most had wanted revenge and had committed atrocities after a buddy was killed in action: they reacted to the death of a friend as a narcissistic injury rather than as an object loss. In other words, they had experienced their friends as extensions of themselves rather than as separate individuals. Like Fox, I found that the subjects developed a need to avenge their friends' deaths that persisted "despite the passage of time and even after specific acts of revenge had been committed against the enemy" (Fox 1974). They had become fixated on the trauma and continued to respond to subsequent slights with intense rage.

Despite apparently good social adjustment, all men with PTSD appeared to just go through the motions of a normal life. Regardless of personality predisposition, the affective experience connected with intimacy and accomplishment was lacking. All subjects with PTSD stated that they had lost a sense of controlling their destinies and complained that they had difficulty feeling emotionally close to their families. One former Vietnam marine sergeant, who had become a lawyer, had severe and recurrent nightmares marking the anniversaries of the deaths of his many comrades who had died in the field. The patient sabotaged any attempt to control these nightmares psychopharmacologically, because he felt he needed his nightmares as a memorial to his dead comrades "lest they have died in vain." This concern did not extend to his wife and children; emotional demands such as childbirth or sickness were followed by an increase in emotional withdrawal and preoccupation with the death of his comrades.

Trauma and the Family

Although the family is the most likely source of support to help individual members cope with trauma, and though many families in all likelihood fulfill that function day to day, research shows that families often disintegrate in the face of overwhelming trauma to one or more members (Erikson 1976; Bromet, Schulberg, and Dunn 1982). Since the emotional life of trauma victims is organized around avoiding traumatic memories and experiences, shunning intimacy is one way to prevent rupture of attachment bonds. Conversely, once a commitment to a relationship has been made, controlling all aspects of the partner's life could protect against feelings of helplessness. Either way, trauma victims maneuver even more intensely than nontraumatized individuals to remain in optimal control over their surroundings: there are to be no surprises, since these are apt to be experienced as a recurrence of the trauma. The fear of recurrence leads to anxious relationships organized around the anticipation of abandonment. Autonomy of spouse or children often is experienced as an emergency and accompanied by feelings of rage and helplessness (Danielli 1985; Krugman 1986). Anger about loss of dominance over the spouse may lead to diminished role functioning, accompanied by hypochondriacal complaints, insistent demands for attention, and critical and self-righteous behavior. In many families with a traumatized husband, the fear of aggravating a physical illness or of precipitating verbal abuse is sufficient to ensure compliance in spouse and children at least until the crises of adolescence, when conflicts over autonomy either precipitate more overt psychopathology in the husband or touch off antisocial acts (including acting out, unwanted pregnancies, and drug abuse) or depression in the children. When this happens, traumatized men are prone to resort to physical violence against others or themselves to regain control over the behavior of other family members. Thus family violence serves to prevent family members from becoming autonomous and keeps them in a constant state of alertness to satisfy the needs of the traumatized member. At the same time, violence allows for intense emotional engagement and dramatic scenes of forgiveness, reconciliation, and physical contact (Krugman 1986). Such scenes often end with sexual intercourse, which restores the fantasy of fusion and symbiosis.

Traumatization often begins in the family with wife battering and is transmitted to the next generation through the physical and sexual abuse of children. Many victims of violence compensate for their loss of power by victimizing those weaker than themselves (Krugman 1986). Parents who themselves were abused as children often have the fantasy that their own children will ensure them a constant supply of love and affection. If the child is ungratifying or does not meet developmentally inappropriate demands, parental rage is unleashed, with little or no remorse (Boszormeny-Nagy and Spark 1973). Traumatized individuals almost invariably lack empathy with other people's needs. Steel (1970) pointed out that traumatized parents under stress give priority to their own needs "as if responding to the need to ward off traumatic anxiety." Traumatized parents, particularly those who were abused as children, often have a diminshed capacity to be affected by a child's suffering because they lack the empathy necessary to put themselves in the child's position (Belsky 1980).

Marriages always change after the birth of a child, but marriages in which one or both partners have been traumatized are particularly likely to become severely disrupted. Mothers who receive inadequate mothering themselves are prone to overreact to the ordinary frustrations of raising an infant with extremes of depression, hopelessness, and anger. Even when parenting is generally a joyful and fulfilling experience for the mother, traumatized males will tend to react to the ordinary frustration of sharing the spouse's attention with a baby with a revival of fears of abandonment and rage at the now less available wife. In general the newborn child is either seen as the new savior who will compensate for past injustice and fear, if female, or scapegoated and treated as a threat if male. Thus the typical pattern is that girls are pushed into a parental role as the only people in the family capable of providing happiness for the traumatized father, while sons are actively rejected and made into projection figures for the father's sense of failure, anger, and inadequacy. The lack of paternal attention and respect leaves the next generation of males with a lifelong search for acceptance and, often, revenge.

Implications

The chronic sense of helplessness that follows unresolved trauma leads the victim to excessive dependence on current surroundings for the basic emotional necessities of life. When the family fails to provide for his needs, he is reduced to a state of helpless rage that may be expressed either in outbursts of anger—which may or may not be accompanied by physical violence—or by withdrawal into physical illness or drug and alcohol abuse. Either way the family will react with loss of autonomy and cooperation: different members will take on roles that express the sense of helplessness, guilt, and rage engendered by the frustrations of the traumatized parent. Boys will be affected by the lack of proper identification figures and may grow up with a pervasive sense of inadequacy, which they will compensate for with acts of bravado, preoccupation with acceptance, excessive competition, and a chronic sense of failure. Daughters often grow up as parent-children who, while competently taking care of their elders, do not experience the personal satisfaction that accompanies a job well done.

The lack of affect tolerance in traumatized fathers leads to a family environment in which plans, feelings, and conflicts are not negotiated between members but instead are acted out. Reliance on action rather than verbal communication leads to a lack of clarity about the causes of emotional outbursts in the family. Children in such families invariably grow up with distorted ideas about their roles in family conflicts: they are likely to blame themselves and carry around a core of self-hatred that is difficult to undo in later life. These children often develop difficulties in emotional involvement with others; their object relations frequently are characterized by withdrawal and caution lest the wounds of emotional betrayal once again be opened, or by intense involvements and repeated disappointments as nobody is found who can compensate for the sense of loss and betrayal they have carried since childhood.

Reliance on action rather than verbal communication in families also impairs the children's development of linguistic/symbolic representations of feeling states. Such representations are necessary if a person is to gain distance from external stimuli and plan for a proper response to emotional arousal (Greenberg and van der Kolk 1986). Inability to verbally comprehend stimuli and put them in perspective leads to a propensity to experience affects as physical states (Krystal 1978). Thus, strong feelings can be experienced as panic attacks or physical pain without reference to the emotional stimulus that preceded these somatic sensations (van der Kolk and Greenberg 1986). These incomprehensible physical states frequently lead people to medicate themselves with drugs or alcohol. Such individuals frequently grow up to become "action junkies": as long as they are involved in strenuous physical activity, preferably of a somewhat dangerous nature, they are able to keep anxiety at bay. When prevented from engaging in these activities, they often become irritable, anxious, and hypochondriacal.

Fixation on the trauma keeps the victim in a lifelong state of alertness against its return, often including an unconscious preoccupation with making sure that the next time he will be prepared to meet the challenge. Thus a victim remains centrally preoccupied with the return of the trauma—either through immunizing himself against recurrence by withdrawal from intimacy or through seeking to repeat the trauma in order to defeat its impact. Similarly, daughters of violent men may avoid intimate involvement with men altogether, or they may get actively involved with violent men in the unconscious hope of resolving and mastering the pain their fathers caused during their childhood. Either way, the unconscious preoccupation with undoing or mastering the past causes the trauma to remain central in these people's lives and detracts from the accumulation of restitutive life experiences (van der Kolk and Ducey 1984). It interferes with their capacity for empathy with others, including spouse and children, who tend to be viewed through the trauma prism rather than as separate and distinct individuals who are not resurrections of the ghosts of the past.

Once the trauma is in actual fact repeated in the next generation, life without traumatic reenactment becomes difficult to conceive, and the predominant affects are depression and rage, without hope of restitution. Shame becomes a central motivating factor: such victims feel defeated and unequal to the challenge of undoing the past. Their contacts with the surrounding world are characterized by secrecy and by their struggle to disguise their violent feelings and their fear that they are out of control. Shame, hopelessness, and lack of trust combine to make these individuals resist treatment, which implicitly invites a reexamination of the helplessness and the obvious defeat they carry with them (Krugman 1986).

Therapy can help by directing an examination of the past that rekindles longings and feelings of disappointment, failure, and hatred. But these feelings almost invariably are acted out either by termination of treatment or by destructive behavior against self or others. Therapy of the traumatized individual or family needs to include first of all reempowerment—regaining a sense of control over one's life. Before a therapist unearths all the miserable events and feelings that led to contact with mental health professionals, control must be established. This may involve the cessation of alcohol or drug abuse; physical separation of members of the family, if necessary by hospitalization; and the administration of psychopharmacological agents—hypnotics to allow sleep, antidepressants to relieve depression, and a variety of drugs to curb impulsivity (van der Kolk and Greenberg 1986). Violence must cease: psychotherapy cannot proceed under terror.

Reempowerment also involves action: actively experiencing the effects of saying no to violence; actively taking control over small chunks of one's life and experiencing the relation between cause and effect. Reempowerment means actively taking control of one's own body in terms of diet, sleep patterns, and exercise (Flannery 1986) and attempting to control one's own actions rather than those of others. Reempowerment also involves using words to express feeling states and understanding the relation between emotionally upsetting events and response patterns. Trauma victims who can mediate between stimulus and response, and who can spare their loved ones from the spillover of emotionally upsetting events by withdrawing into thoughtful evaluation, experience true empowerment.

The question whether understanding the past is absolutely necessary to overcome the effects of trauma has not yet been settled. Many professionals have assumed that unless a connection is made between past events and current feeling states, the trauma is bound to be reenacted (Freud 1954; van der Kolk and Kadish 1986). But many others, particularly clinicians, have discovered that for most traumatized individuals reliving the trauma merely becomes a reexperience of the nightmare rather than the resolution of it (Spitz 1947; Krystal 1978). This issue requires much study. Current evidence favors the view that the principal treatment issue for traumatized men is helping them reexperience a sense of order and meaning by gaining control over intrusive affects related to the trauma in everyday life. This self-control depends on whether they can transcend the pervasive sense of helplessness that always follows psychological trauma.

References

Aichorn, A. 1948. *Wayward youth*. New York: Viking.

American Psychiatric Association. 1980. *Diagnostic and statistical manual III (DSM III)*. Washington, D.C.: American Psychiatric Association Press.

Belsky, J. 1980. Child maltreatment: An ecological integration. *American Psychologist* 35:320–35.

Blos, P. 1979. *The adolescent passage*. New York: International University Press.

Boszormeny-Nagy, I., and Spark, S. 1973. *Invisible loyalties*. New York: Harper and Row.

Bowlby, J. 1969. *Attachment and loss, vol. 1. Attachment.* New York: Basic Books.

———. 1973. *Attachment and loss, vol. 2. Separation.* New York: Basic Books.

———. 1973b. Violence in the family as a disorder of the attachment and caregiving systems. *American Journal of Psychoanalysis* 44:9–27.

Bromet, E.; Schulberg, H. C.; and Dunn, L. 1982. Reactions of psychiatric patients to the Three Mile Island nuclear accident. *Archives of General Psychiatry* 39:725–30.

Burgess, A. W., and Holmstrom, L. 1974. Rape trauma syndrome. *American Journal of Psychiatry* 131:981–86.

Carmen, E. H.; Reiker, P. P.; and Mills, T. 1984. Victims of violence and psychiatric illness. *American Journal of Psychiatry* 141:378–79.

Cicchetti. D. 1984. The emergence of developmental psychopathology. *Child Development* 55:1–7.

Cicchetti, D., and Rizley, A. 1981. Developmental perspectives on the etiology, intergenerational transmission, and sequelae of child maltreatment. *New Directions for Child Development* 11:31–55.

Cicchetti, D., and Rosen, K. S. 1984. Theoretical and empirical considerations in the investigation of the relationship between affect and cognition in an atypical population of infants. In *Emotions, cognition and behavior*, ed. C. Izard, J. Kagan, and R. Zajanc. New York: Cambridge University Press.

Danielli, Y. 1985. The treatment and prevention of long-term effects and intergenerational transmission of victimization: A lesson from Holocaust survivors and their children. In *Trauma and its wake*, vol. 1, ed. C. R. Figley. New York: Brunner/Mazel.

Elder, G. H. 1986. Military times and turning points in men's lives. *Developmental Psychology* 22(2):233–45.

Erikson, E. H. 1956. The problem of ego identity. *Journal of the American Psychoanalytic Association* 4:56–121.

Erikson, K. T. 1976. *Everything in its path: Destruction of community in the Buffalo Creek Flood.* New York: Simon and Schuster.

Ferenczi, S. 1955. Confusion of tongues between adults and the child: The language of tenderness and passion. In *Problems and methods of psychoanalysis*, ed. S. Ferenczi. London: Hogarth Press.

Figley, C. M. 1978. *Stress disorders among Vietnam veterans: Theory, research and treatment implications.* New York: Brunner/Mazel.

Finkelhor, D. 1984. *Child sexual abuse: New theory and research.* New York: Free Press.

Fish-Murray, C.; Koby, E.; and van der Kolk, B. A. 1986. The effects of abuse on children's thought. In *Psychological trauma*, ed. B. A. van der Kolk. Washington, D.C.: American Psychiatric Association Press.

Flannery, R. B. 1986. A stress reduction model in the treatment of learned helplessness. In *Psychological trauma*, ed. B. A. van der Kolk. Washington, D.C.: American Psychiatric Association Press.

Fox, R. P. 1974. Narcissistic rage and the problem of combat aggression. *Archives of General Psychiatry* 31:807–11.

Freud, S. 1954. Inhibitions, symptoms and anxiety. In *Standard edition,* vol. 20. London: Hogarth Press. Originally published 1926.

Garmezy, N., and Rutter, M., eds. 1983. *Stress, coping, and development in children.* New York: McGraw-Hill.

Gayford, J. J. 1980. Wife battering: A preliminary survey of 100 cases. *British Medical Journal* 1:194–98.

Gelinas, D. J. 1983. The persistent negative effects of incest. *Psychiatry* 46:312–32.

Green, A. 1980. *Child maltreatment.* New York: Jason Aronson.

Green, A. H. 1984. Dimensions of psychological trauma in abused children. *Bulletin of the Association for the Psychoanalytic Medium* 23:64–70.

Greenberg, M. S., and van der Kolk, B. A. 1986. Resolution of the trauma using the "painting cure." In *Psychological trauma,* ed. B. A. van der Kolk. Washington, D.C.: American Psychiatric Association Press.

Greensbauer, T. J., and Sands, K. 1979. Disturbed affective communications in abused/neglected infants and their potential impact on caretakers. *Journal of the American Academy of Child Psychiatry* 18:236–50.

Herman, J. L. 1981. *Father-daughter incest.* Cambridge: Harvard University Press.

Hilberman, E. 1980. Overview: The wife-beater's wife reconsidered. *American Journal of Psychiatry* 137:974–75.

Hilberman, E., and Munson, M. 1978. Sixty battered women. *Victimology,* 2:460–71.

Horowitz, M. J. 1976. *Stress response syndromes.* New York: Jason Aronson.

Jaffe, P.; Wolfe, D.; Wilson, S. K., et al. 1986. Family violence and child adjustment: A comparative analysis of girls' and boys' behavioral symptoms. *American Journal of Psychiatry* 143:74–77.

Kardiner, A. 1941. *The traumatic neuroses of war.* New York: P. Hoeber.

Kempe, R., and Kempe, C. 1978. *Child abuse.* Cambridge: Harvard University Press.

Kilpatrick, D. G.; Resick, P. A.; and Veronen, L. J. (1981). Effects of the rape experience: A longitudinal study. *Journal of Social Issues* 37:105–22.

Kilpatrick, D. G.; Veronen, L. J.; and Best, C. L. 1985. Factors predicting psychological distress in rape victims. In *Trauma and its wake,* ed. C. Figley, 113–41. New York: Brunner/Mazel.

Kilpatrick, D. G.; Veronen, L. J.; and Resick, P. A. 1979. The aftermath of rape: Recent empirical findings. *American Journal of Orthopsychiatry* 49:658–69.

Kolb, L. 1984. The posttraumatic stress disorders of combat: A subgroup with a conditional emotional response. *Military Medicine* 140:237–43.

Krugman, S. 1986. Trauma and the family: Perspectives on the intergenerational transmission of violence. In *Psychological trauma,* ed. B. A. van der Kolk. Washington, D.C.: American Psychiatric Association Press.

Krystal, H. 1984. Psychoanalytic views on human emotional damages. In *Posttraumatic stress disorder: Psychological and biological sequelae,* ed. B. A. van der Kolk. Washington, D.C.: American Psychiatric Association Press.

——. 1978. Trauma and affects. *Psychoanalytic Study of the Child* 33:81 116.

Lacoursiere, R.; Godfrey, K.; and Rubey, L. 1980. Traumatic neurosis in the etiology of alcoholism. *American Journal of Psychiatry* 137:966–68.

Lewis, D., and Balla, D. 1976. *Delinquency and psychopathology.* New York: Grune and Stratton.

Lewis, D.; Shanok, S. S.; Pincus, J. H.; et al. 1979. Violent juvenile delinquents: Psychiatric, neurological, psychological and abuse factors. *Journal of Child Psychiatry* 18:307–19.

Notman, M., and Nadelson, C. 1976. The rape victim: Psychodynamic considerations. *American Journal of Psychiatry* 133:408–12.

Offer, D., and Offer, J. 1975. Three developmental routes through normal male adolescence. In *Adolescent psychiatry,* vol. 4, ed. S. C. Feinstein and P. L. Giovacchini. New York: Jason Aronson.

Pynoos, R. S., and Eth, S. 1985. Developmental perspective on psychic trauma in childhood. In *Trauma and its wake,* ed. C. R. Figley. New York: Brunner/ Mazel.

Ross, R. R. 1980. Violence in violence out: Child abuse and self-mutilation in adolescent offenders. *Juvenile and Family Court Journal* 31:33–44.

Schucker, E. 1979. Psychodynamics and treatment of the sexual assault victim. *Journal of the American Academy of Psychoanalysis* 7:553–73.

Sharfman, M. A., and Clark, R. W. 1967. Delinquent adolescent girls: Residential treatment in a municipal hospital setting. *Archives of General Psychiatry* 17:441–47.

Sharp, V. 1980. Adolescence. In *Child development in normality and psychopathology,* ed. J. Bemporad, 175–218. New York: Brunner/Mazel.

Spritz, R. 1945. Hospitalism: An inquiry into the genesis of psychiatric conditions in early childhood. *Psychoanalytic Study of the Child* 1:53–74.

Steele, B. F. 1970. Parental abuse of infants and small children. In *Parenthood: Its psychology and psychopathology,* ed. R. J. Anthony and T. Benedict. Boston: Little, Brown.

Titchener, J. L., and Kapp, F. 1976. Family and character change in Buffalo Creek. *American Journal of Psychiatry* 133:295–99.

van der Kolk, B. A. 1985. Adolescent vulnerability to traumatic stress disorder. *Psychiatry* 48:365–70

———. 1986. The long term effects of psychological trauma. In *Psychological trauma,* ed. B. A. van der Kolk. Washington, D.C.: American Psychiatric Association Press.

van der Kolk, B. A., and Ducey, C. P. 1984. Clinical implications of the Rorschach in post-traumatic stress. In *Post-traumatic stress disorder: Psychological and biological sequelae,* ed. B. A. van der Kolk. Washington, D.C.: American Psychiatric Association Press.

van der Kolk, B. A., and Greenberg, M. S. 1986. The psychology of the trauma response. In *Psychological trauma,* ed. B. A. van der Kolk. Washington, D.C.: American Psychiatric Association Press.

van der Kolk, B. A.; Greenberg, M. S.; Boyd, H.; and Krystal, J. 1985. Inescapable shock, neurotransmitters and addition to trauma: Towards a psychobiology of post traumatic stress. *Biological Psychiatry* 20:314–25.

van der Kolk, B. A., and Kadish, W. 1986. Amnesia, dissociation, and the return of the repressed revisited. In *Psychological trauma,* ed. B. A. van der Kolk. Washington, D.C.: American Psychiatric Association Press.

Zetzel, E. 1949. Anxiety and the capacity to bear it. *International Journal of Psychoanalysis* 30:371–85.

10   *Elder Abuse*

TERRY FULMER

Overview of Elder Abuse

Current estimates suggest that between 500,000 and 1,400,000 American elders are victims of abuse, neglect, exploitation, or abandonment each year (U.S. Senate 1980). Most authors believe elder abuse occurs with approximately the same frequency as child abuse, at about 4 percent of the general elderly population. Although abuse of children is the focus of well-organized legal and social welfare programs, abuse of the elderly has received little attention and accounts for only 7 percent of all preventive services provided to United States citizens.

The number of elderly people in America increases dramatically each year. Every day one-thousand people join the ranks of those over sixty-five, at present constituting about 11 percent of the United States population. With advances in medical technology and pharmaceutical sophistication, we are noting a rapid growth in the segment of the aged over seventy-five, the "old old" or "frail elderly." Innovative medical advances such as pacemakers, renal dialysis procedures, and the many antibiotic therapies have brought about "death control."

We can estimate that by the year 2020 fully 20 percent of the American population will be "elderly," that is, over sixty-five years of age. This population will present new and difficult demands for our society. Today more than ever before, a middle-aged adult is likely to have one or both parents still living, a trend that will continue. The average life expectancy is now sixty-nine years for males and seventy-seven years for females. As the post–World War II baby boom generation approaches the sixty-five-year mark, we can expect an elderly majority. Modern advances in family planning will have left us with fewer adult children to act as caretakers for our elderly.

Changing Family Dynamics

Traditionally, daughters have cared for aged parents. They may have brought aging parents into their homes or arranged for living quarters nearby. Today, with approximately fifty percent of all married women in the labor force (out of inclination or economic necessity), it is less clear who is the logical choice for providing supportive care to elderly family members. Hickey and Douglass (1981) believed that the sudden or unwanted dependency of a parent is a key factor in understanding neglect or abuse. They suggested that "in the absence of the personal resources and family support necessary to maintain autonomy and independence in late-life, the dependency of rising numbers of old people seems inevitable."

Since World War II, ours has been a society of the nuclear family: mother, father, and children. The increased mobility of the family unit has helped shape our current structure, with the father's employment determining the family's place of residence. It has not been the practice to bring grandparents along for the frequent geographical transfers careers may impose on a family. It is not clear at this time how rising housing costs, increasing taxes, and economic changes will affect future housing trends for our elderly. A return to reliance upon the extended family unit may be one alternative.

Profile of the Victim of Elder Abuse

In the studies conducted to date, the typical abused elder is a very old (over seventy-five), frail, multiply dependent female who usually presents with health care needs concerning hygiene, nutrition, safety, toileting, and orientation. Since females have a longer life expectancy than males, it is not surprising that they are more frequently cited as elder abuse cases. Further, most individuals over sixty-five have an average of 3.5 chronic health disorders which, in most cases, become more numerous over time. When care providers cannot meet the needs of these individuals, symptoms of abuse, neglect, or mistreatment may ensue. It is common to receive a referral that describes an elder as confused, incontinent, dehydrated, or malnourished, and there may also be evidence of skin breakdown, fractured bones from falls, and drug toxicity from improper prescriptions. The person reporting elder abuse must determine abuse or neglect based upon many factors, including the nature and extent of the trauma, the likelihood of abuse or neglect given the care provider's resources, and the level of account-ability the care provider can be held to. In cases of intentional physical abuse that results in trauma to the elderly, few professionals would argue against the validity of the label "elder abuse." However, many responsible adults are not educated to prevent or detect risk factors for subsequent neglect. When an elderly individual, cared for at home by well-intentioned family members, presents with symptoms of neglect such as urine burns and decubitus ulcers, the determination of abuse is not so clear. Table 10-1 lists common indicators of abuse and neglect that serve as a basis for initial screening.

Profile of the Abuser

Similar studies depict elder abusers as usually under some situational stress such as unemployment or divorce. They may be substance abus-ers, coping with alcoholism or drug addiction, or they may have a known psychiatric history. Usually some life crisis has preceded the alleged abuse. To date it is not clear whether a relative or a nonrelative is more likely to be an abuser, but some studies, such as the one done by Block and Sinnott (1979), have indicated that family members are more likely to be abusers. Regardless of the relationship, all abusers are overwhelmed by their elders' many needs and cannot provide adequate care.

Definitions of Abuse, Neglect, and Mistreatment

When an elderly person is said to have been abused, neglected, or mistreated, it is important that the terms be defined and understood

Table 10.1 Physical Indications of Abuse and Neglect

Type of Abuse/Neglect	Physical Indications

Physical	Unexplained bruises and welts
	    on torso, back, buttocks, thighs
	    in various stages of healing
	    clustered, forming regular patterns
	    reflecting shape of article used to inflict (e.g., electric cord, belt buckle)
	    regularly appearing after absence, weekend, or vacation

	Unexplained burns
	    cigar, cigarette burns, especially on soles, palms, back, or buttocks
	    immersion burns (socklike, glovelike, doughnut shaped on buttocks or genitalia)
	    patterned like electric burner, iron, etc.
	    rope burns on arms, legs, neck, or torso

	Unexplained fractures
	    to skull, nose, facial structure
	    in various stages of healing
	    multiple or spiral fractures

	Unexplained lacerations or abrasions
	    to mouth, lips, gums, eyes
	    to external genitalia

Physical neglect	Constant hunger, poor hygiene, inappropriate dress
	Consistent lack of supervision, especially in dangerous activities or for long periods
	Constant fatigue or listlessness
	Unattended physical problems or medical needs
	Abandonment
Sexual abuse	Difficulty in walking or sitting
	Torn, stained, or bloody underclothing
	Pain or itching in genital area
	Bruises or bleeding of external genitalia, vaginal or anal area Venereal disease
Emotional maltreatment	Habit disorder (sucking, biting, rocking, etc.)
	Conduct disorders (antisocial, destructive, etc.)
	Neurotic traits (sleep disorder, speech disorders, inhibition of play)
	Psychoneurotic reaction (hysteria, obsession, compulsion, phobias, hypochondria)

as clearly as possible. *Abuse* refers to "physical contact which harms or is likely to harm the person." *Neglect* is defined as "the failure to provide treatment and services necessary to maintain the health and safety of the person." And *mistreatment* is defined as "the use of medications, isolation or use of physical or chemical restraints which harms or is likely to harm the person" (Massachusetts General Laws, chap. 3, sec. 72F–72L, 1980).

Examples of physical abuse include overt injuries such as broken bones, lacerations, welts, sprains, and abrasions. Neglect includes symptoms of malnutrition, dehydration, lack of appropriate medical attention, or inadequate clothing and shelter. Mistreatment can be reflected in inappropriate drug regimens, skin damage (secondary to immobility in a long-term care setting), or undue withholding of an appointment to obtain false teeth, glasses, or a hearing aid. Because the definitions above are necessarily broad and open to interpretation, it is imperative that charges of abuse, neglect, or mistreatment be extremely well documented.

Theories of Causation

To date there are five major theories about the cause of elder abuse, and each adds a quantitative dimension to an overall theory of causation. It is extremely difficult to separate one theory from another because so often more than one seems applicable in any given case. However, to provide a theoretical background, I shall present each separately.

The Impairment Theory

The impairment theory advances the idea that elderly persons who have a severe physical or mental impairment are most likely to be abused (Block and Sinnott 1979). Because of their impairment, they are likely to be dependent and therefore highly vulnerable to abuse and neglect. Since only 5 percent of the nation's elderly are in long-term care institutions but 45 percent of the population over sixty-two years of age experience some limitation of activity owing to chronic conditions (Rowe and Besdine 1982), there is reason to believe that a higher proportion of the elderly have dependency needs as they advance in age.

The Theory of Psychopathology of the Abuser

The theory of psychopathology of the abuser focuses on abusers, contending that they have personality traits or character disorders that cause them to be abusive. Most researchers working with the elderly would hold that this theory is simplistic, but there is evidence that individuals with drug dependencies, alcoholism, mental retardation, or mental illness are far more likely to be abusive than those without these impairments.

Lau and Kosberg (1979) used the term "nonnormal" caregiver to describe elements of this theory. They cite the examples of mentally retarded or alcoholic offspring who may not have the decision-making capacity to make appropriate judgments regarding the needs of their elderly parents.

The Transgenerational Violence Theory

The transgenerational violence theory holds that violence is a learned, normative behavior pattern in some families. While growing up, a child observes violence as an accepted reaction to stress and internalizes it as a behavior. This leads to a cyclical family pattern in which the abused child becomes an elder abuser. It has been postulated that retribution may also be a factor in these situations.

The Stressed Caregiver Theory

The stressed caregiver theory examines the perceived burden an elderly dependent places on the family, focusing on both the caregiver's somatic and psychosomatic complaints and general environmental stressors (O'Malley, Segal, and Perez 1979). Complaints such as anxiety, headaches, insomnia, and depression among caregivers have been described. Similarly, Block and Sinnott (1979) discuss how adult children exhibit frustration and resentment toward elderly parents who are dependent for a long time. This theory contends that as internal stresses mount, abuse is likely to result. This theory further postulates that such factors as income, employment, status, and marital state may have an impact on the incidence of abuse. O'Malley, Segal, and Perez (1979) reported that abusers are likely to be experiencing some form of external stress at the time of abuse. Douglass, Hickey, and Noel (1980) also suggested that life crises such as loss of a job, divorce, change in residence, or decrease in income can have a detrimental effect on family members' ability to care for their elders and may trigger abuse.

The Exchange Theory

The exchange theory is relatively new (Pillemer 1984) and examines the impact of external influences upon the relationship between the victim and abuser. This theory holds that people outside the violent relationship can decrease and even prevent the abuse. The watchful eyes of others can break the isolation of victims and deter potential abusers from acting violently.

Hypotheses about Causal Factors

Douglass, Hickey, and Noell (1980) proposed the following hypotheses about the causes of elder abuse, based on current theories:

Hypothesis 1: Dependence incurred in old age increases the risk of abuse or neglect.

Hypothesis 2: A child who is abused or who witnesses abuse grows up to be an abusive adult.

Hypothesis 3: Life crises in either the abused or the abuser trigger abusive behavior.

Hypothesis 4: Environmental stresses can bring about neglectful and abusive behaviors.

Theories of abuse provide important background for successful assessment and a clearer understanding of causal relationships. However, acute-care settings vary in their resources and systems for following cases of suspected elder abuse, neglect, or mistreatment. Availability of qualified workers, funds, and follow-up procedures greatly aids case review. To discuss the acute care setting, I shall describe the program at Beth Israel Hospital in Boston, as an institutional response to evaluation of elder abuse.

Boston's Beth Israel Hospital

Once elder abuse is identified, intervention is based on the nature of the alleged abuse, neglect, or mistreatment, the setting the elder has come from, and the sources of information available. When a problem is recognized, hospital staff members choose among three possible actions. They may decide not to pursue the question of abuse, they may intervene on their own to correct the situation, or they may refer the case to the Elder Assessment Team.

Problem Identification

Star (1980) suggested that the three community agencies most likely to encounter incidents of elder abuse are police departments, social service agencies, and emergency units. The Beth Israel Hospital emergency unit records show that approximately 16 percent of patients registered each year are over seventy years of age. Of these elders, the admission rate is about 51 percent (15 percent of all hospital admissions each year). The hospital does not have a pediatric department and therefore sees a higher proportion of elderly patients than do other city hospitals. The department of medicine accounts for most of these admissions, followed by the department of surgery and the department of orthopedics (table 10-2).

Other factors may also increase the number of geriatric patients in the Beth Israel emergency department: the neighborhood around the hospital is known to have a high proportion of elderly citizens, and the Harvard Division on Aging has a strong base at Beth Israel Hospital.

The emergency unit nurses have all had special training in elder abuse screening and detection as part of their orientation to the unit. In January 1981, after the first state law on reporting elder abuse was

Table 10.2 Emergency Unit Population at Beth Israel Hospital, 22 December 1981 to 24 January 1983

Total patients registered	**N = 39,036 (100%)**
Total patients over seventy years old	*N* = 6,363 (16.3%)
Female	*N* = 3,942 (62%)
Male	*N* = 2,421 (38%)
Patients over seventy admitted	*N* = 3,300 (51%)
Services admitted to	
Medicine	*N* = 2,515 (76%)
Surgery	*N* = 282 (8%)
Orthopedics	*N* = 261 (7%)
Other	*N* = 242 (7%)

Average number of admissions to Beth Israel Hospital per year = 22,000
Average number of admissions via emergency unit per year = 6,500

passed in December 1980, the department of nursing initiated plans to respond to the intent of the law. In-service training sessions were held, and each nurse received a training packet that included a summary of the law, a screening protocol for assessing elder abuse, and copies of journal articles to help educate them to the signs and symptoms of abuse, neglect, and mistreatment. Guest lecturers were invited, and frequent sessions were held to clarify the screening process. All new emergency nurses are now trained in assessing elder abuse as part of their orientation to the unit by the staff project coordinator.

Initially, there were many false-positive referrals as the nurses began their screening. Over the years, however, screening techniques have been refined, and cases referred to the Elder Assessment Team are usually appropriate. When elders enter the emergency unit, a nurse evaluates them for high-risk signs and symptoms of abuse, neglect, or mistreatment. A nurse who feels there is evidence of any of these fills out an elder assessment form (Fulmer, Street, and Carr 1984), which is then sent to the Elder Abuse Team. Usually the patient in question is admitted to the hospital for a medical problem, and follow-up is done during admission. In cases where the patient has no problems that require hospitalization, necessary information is collected to provide follow-up by the team. This information includes place of residence, primary-care provider, and family contacts. Should the patient be in jeopardy for further abuse in the absence of a medical problem requiring hospitalization, a protective service admission can be made and is authorized by the hospital administration. This last option is rarely used but is important for the patient's safety.

Referrals to the Team

Once the case is referred to the Elder Assessment Team, a multidisciplinary evaluation is conducted by medicine, nursing, and social services. The nature of the problem is explored in light of the patient's medical history, functional abilities, and social support systems. If the assessment indicates that abuse, neglect, or mistreatment has in fact occurred, a report is sent to the hospital administration, which makes the formal report to the designated state agency. If the assessment reveals no abuse, neglect, or mistreatment, the information and surrounding circumstances are documented and reported to the referring department or individual. Although most referrals are from the emergency unit, they may also come from primary-care providers, inpatient units, consultation services, or family and friends of the patient.

Since the nature of the referral varies from case to case depending on the point of entry into the hospital system and the time of day, it is important to have an intake mechanism for each situation. An alternative method, not used at Beth Israel Hospital, is the beeper-call system where someone is on call each day for elder abuse referrals. Although this method may simplify the process, it is not preferred in this institution. Individuals on the team are easily accessible, and the additional cost of keeping someone on call has not been found necessary. Urgent life-threatening cases are immediately admitted for medical treatment, which is the first priority. Less obvious cases benefit instead from a multidisciplinary team assessment.

The Team Process

There are twelve members on the Elder Assessment Team: five nurses, three social workers, three physicians, and one social policy/ethical specialist. The team meets weekly to discuss referred cases, questions of policy, educational programming, and research. Each case is assigned a nurse, physician, and social worker from the team, who examine the nature of the event that triggered referral. The assignment is based on familiarity with the case and the unit the referral came from. Since patients have commonly had previous admissions to the hospital owing to advancing age and chronic health problems, they are frequently known to one or more members of the team. If they are new to the system, case assignment is based on workload and area of expertise. If the chief complaint is predominantly a nursing issue, the nurses on the team initiate the follow-up, with social services and medicine as consultant back-up services. Medicine and social work follow the same pattern. Once all information is gathered, the case is presented and a decision is made on whether it should be reported to the hospital administration or labeled a DNP (do not pursue). DNPs are entered into the hospital admitting records in case the patients return for another admission. If so, they are immediately referred back to the team for further evaluation, and any emergency patterns are noted.

Because most elderly patients have three or more chronic medical problems, it is likely that recidivism will be high, since their delicate balance between health and illness is easily upset. Every effort is made to teach family, nursing home staff, and other primary-care providers about the early warning signals of disease and about treatment to avoid acute illness. In reality, many of the referrals are elders who are very close to dying, and the care required is difficult, with a low chance of cure or recovery. The mortality rate of patients referred to the Elder

Abuse Team is 50 percent within six to twelve months of the referral. Unlike cases of child abuse, it is almost impossible to sort out cause and effect for these patients. Given an elderly patient with a history of chronic renal failure or cancer, one must consider evidence of malnutrition, dehydration, and skin deterioration within the context of the case. Yet historically it has been this ageism that prevents professionals from asking questions about abuse even if the presentation suggests it. Health care providers have come to expect all old people to be badly deteriorated, and they often view decubitus ulcers, urine burns from incontinence, and hips broken during episodes of confusion as "inevitable." It is the premise of most state reporting laws that these situations are avoidable and could result from neglect or mistreatment by care providers. Therefore the laws mandate that such cases be examined and diagnosed individually.

The Beth Israel system places the burden of peer review on care providers designated to screen for elder abuse. Although the state requires that cases of "suspected" abuse, neglect, and mistreatment be reported, the vague connotation of suspicion lends itself to a variety of responses. The ramifications of the report, such as disruption of family care systems, alienation of nursing homes, and paternalistic actions on behalf of the elder, can cause more difficulty than was initially present. Often the care providers are devoted to the elder and are unaware that certain actions may be detrimental to health. Aggressive perineal care may dislocate a hip; force-feeding may cause aspiration pneumonia. The multiplicity of the elder's health problems creates a situation where the lesser of two evils may be viewed as neglect.

Additionally, the hospital professional may feel there is a conflict of interest when the nursing home in question is housing several other patients known to them. To report a case places that relationship in jeopardy. Although reporting laws preserve anonymity the source of the report is apparent if the patient has never been anywhere but the nursing home and the hospital. The shortage of nursing home beds poses additional problems for hospital staff, and placement is complicated when one home is not used. Any increase in the number of days a patient is kept waiting for nursing home care is very expensive for the hospital and the patient. Good relationships with long-term care facilities and practical considerations must be weighed against patient care and safety.

Family members react in various ways to the report of elder abuse. Once they are alerted that abuse is suspected in the nursing home where their relative is placed, they may refuse to permit a return, even if abuse is not substantiated. The mere suspicion may cause them alarm, and rightly so. The patient may then suffer the disruption of an unnecessary transfer. If family members are suspected of abusing the elder, they may gladly resign any obligation and insist the person is too difficult to care for at home. They may also react with indignation and consider such a report libelous.

Identifying and reporting elder abuse is a sensitive process with many arenas for conflict and a limited number of viable options for care. However, as the number of frail elderly increases, so does the need for creative and compassionate solutions to the problems of their abuse, neglect, and mistreatment.

References

Block, J. M., and Sinnott, J., eds. 1979. *The battered elder syndrome: An exploratory study.* College Park: Center on Aging, University of Maryland.

Douglass, R. L.; Hickey, T.; and Noell, C. 1980. *A study of maltreatment of the elderly and other vulnerable adults.* Ann Arbor: Institute of Gerontology, University of Michigan.

Fulmer, T.; Street, S.; and Carr, K. 1984. Abuse of the elderly: Screening and detection. *Journal of Emergency Nursing* 10(3): 131–40.

Hickey, T., and Douglass, R. C. 1981. Neglect and abuse of older family members: Professional perspectives and case experiences. *Gerontologist* 21:171–76.

Lau, E., and Kosberg, J. I. 1979. Abuse of the elderly by informal caregivers. *Aging* 229(10): 15–15.

O'Malley, H. C.; Segal, H. D.; and Perez, R. 1979. *Elder abuse in Massachusetts: A survey of professionals and paraprofessionals.* Boston: Legal Research and Services for the Elderly.

Pillemer, C. A. 1984. The dangers of dependency: New findings on domestic violence against the elderly. Unpublished paper, Durham, N. H.

Rowe, J. W., and Besdine, R. W. 1982. *Health and disease in old age.* Boston: Little, Brown.

Star, B. 1980. Patterns in family violence. *Journal of Contemporary Social Work* 339–46.

U.S. Senate. 1980. Joint hearings before the Special Committee on Aging, U.S. Senate and Committee on Aging, U.S. House of Representatives, Ninety-sixth Congress, 11 June.

FOUR *Special Topics*

11 Physical Victimization across the Life Span: Recognition, Ethnicity, and Deterrence

ROBERT L. HAMPTON

Child abuse, spouse abuse, and elder abuse were once thought to be isolated events that happened only among a small segment of the population. Research conducted over the past two decades has shown that family violence is a widespread, pervasive social problem that occurs among families in every social and economic class.

In September 1984 the Attorney General's Task Force on Family Violence submitted its final report to the president. The task force was created to determine the nature, type, and prevalence of family violence and to articulate specific solutions. From its inception, the task force recognized that family violence is often much more complex in causes and solutions than are crimes committed by unknown attackers. Yet a victim of family violence is no less a victim than one set upon by strangers (Attorney General's Task Force 1984). A developmental approach to family violence has frequently focused on the transmission of abuse from generation to generation. Individuals who have experienced or witnessed violence in their families of origin are more likely to become child and spouse abusers in their families of procreation (Straus, Gelles, and Steinmetz 1980; Gelles 1985; Shirk, this volume). The task force report accepted the thesis of intergenerational transmission of violence and suggested that the ultimate task is to break the cycle and prevent family violence.

The task force recommended that solving the problem of family violence begin with the criminal justice system, adding that the legal responses to the problem must be guided primarily by the nature of the abusive acts, not the relationship between perpetrator and victim (Attorney General's Task Force 1984). Recommendations were also made for changes in the justice system, victim assistance programs, training programs, and data collection and reporting procedures.

Researchers and practitioners in the field of family violence see merit in many of the task force's recommendations. Any complete effort in this area must include programs for identification, intervention, prevention, referral, and follow-up. There remain, however, a number of vexing issues that must be addressed if we hope to reduce violence among intimates across the life span. This chapter will review three of these issues: recognition and reporting of family violence; racial and ethnic differences in the nature, type, and severity of family violence; and prevention versus deterrence as an approach to family violence. Although there are some obvious interrelations among these issues, I will discuss them separately.

Recognition and Reporting

Physical Child Abuse

Data on child abuse, wife abuse, and other forms of family violence come from a variety of sources, including clinical samples, official statistics, and survey samples. Each source has certain advantages and disadvantages that influence both the nature and the generalizability of the research findings (Gelles 1985). One major disadvantage of all three data sources is they do not let us assess the true prevalence of family violence. This can be illustrated by examining data gathered to estimate the prevalence of child abuse.

Nationally reported cases of child abuse have increased 158 percent since 1976. In that year, 416,033 child maltreatment cases were reported to the Child Protective Services system (CPS). The number of reported cases has grown annually to a total of 1,726,649 in 1984, the latest year for which data are available (American Humane Association 1986). This change can be attributed to a number of factors, but it is impossible to determine to what extent the increase in reports is directly associated with an increase in the number of maltreated children. It is likely that the increase in reports is due to greater public awareness and to improved accountability by state reporting systems.

The total number of reports is a general indicator of the level of activity by CPS. The number of reports is not equivalent to the number of children involved within families. In 1984, for example, the slightly more than a million reports represented more than 1.7 million children. The rate of reporting was estimated at 27.3 children per 1,000 in the United States (American Humane Association 1986).

Official statistics on child abuse do not show the full extent of abuse in families. The *National Study of the Incidence and Severity of Child Abuse and Neglect* (National Incidence Study 1981) was designed from a conceptual model based on the "iceberg" metaphor. This model assumed that although substantial numbers of abused and neglected children are recognized as such and are reported to CPS, the reported cases may represent only the tip of the iceberg.

The model assumes that additional abused children are known to other "investigatory" agencies such as police and public health departments, courts, and correctional agencies and to professionals in other major community institutions: schools, hospitals, and social service and mental health agencies. Even an unambiguous case of child abuse may go unreported and consequently may never be included in the official record.

The National Incidence Study collected data from a stratified random sample of twenty-six counties. CPS agencies received an estimated 718,200 reports of suspected abuse during the study year, 1 May 1979 to 30 April 1980. The estimated number of children involved in these reports totaled 1,101,500. Expressed as an incidence rate, 17.8 children per 1,000 were reported to CPS (National Incidence Study 1981). This study further estimated that another 600,000 abused children never become part of the official abuse statistics.

The tendency to operationalize child abuse as those cases that come to professional and official attention confounds the factors leading people to come forward or to be publicly labeled as abusers. In part to overcome this difficulty and provide additional estimates of the number of victimized children, random sample surveys in the general population have been constructed.

The survey by Straus, Gelles, and Steinmetz (1980) found that the yearly incidence of acts they defined as abusive violence (all acts that had the high probability of causing an injury—whether or not an injury occurred) was about 3.6 percent for all children three to seventeen years of age. The overall violence index based on responses to eight items in the Conflict Tactics Scale revealed that 63 percent of the parents used at least one of the eight forms of violence during the study year. Fourteen percent of these parents used severe violence on their children (i.e., kicking, biting, punching, hitting, or trying to hit with an object, beating, threatening with a gun or knife, or using a gun or knife).

In a resurvey conducted ten years after the original study, Straus and Gelles (1986) found that the rate for overall violent acts toward children in families remained virtually unchanged. The rate for severe violence declined from 14 percent in 1975 to 10.7 percent in 1985. The child abuse rate declined from 3.6 percent to 1.9 percent. An estimated 1.5 million children under age eighteen from two-parent families were subject to severe violence in 1985.

A major issue not only in the area of child abuse but for the entire family violence field is the process by which victims are identified and reported. One matter of particular concern is the way individuals outside the victim-perpetrator dyad come to recognize abuse in either a child or an adult.

In 1984 those who reported suspected cases of abuse to CPS agencies were evenly divided between professional sources and nonprofessionals. Friends, neighbors, and relatives were the single largest group of reporters (32.2 percent of cases). These individuals normally are not mandated reporters, and their reports tend to reflect a significant level of community concern (American Humane Association 1986). They may also see repeated signs of abuse, which would affect their desire for intervention in the objectionable treatment. By contrast, fewer than 2 percent of case reports were made by victims.

Although the distribution of reports between professional and nonprofessional sources is approximately even, there is some concern within the field about professional decision making in cases of child abuse and neglect. Before filing case reports, professionals must recognize maltreatment. A variety of personal and demographic factors affect judgments of parental acts and a professional's willingness to label an act abusive. Some frequently cited factors include the gender of the parent (Finkelhor 1984; Hampton and Newberger 1985; Herzberger and Tennen 1985); gender of the child (Finkelhor 1984); and race and socioeconomic status (Newberger et al. 1977; Turbett and O'Toole 1980; Gelles 1982; Hampton and Newberger 1985).

Once a professional determines that abuse has occurred, he or she may face the dilemma of whether to report the incident. The decision to report is supposed to be automatic for medical professionals, social workers, psychologists, the clergy, and teachers in most states (Herzberger 1986). Failure to report suspected cases is a violation of state law. In spite of this mandate, many labeled cases of abuse are not reported. For example, using a national sample of suspected abuse and neglect cases, Hampton and Newberger (1985) found that hospitals tend to underreport white families, more affluent families, and adolescent victims.

The true prevalence of child maltreatment is unknown. What we frequently see in official data is the outcome of several processes that include recognition, reporting, and case substantiation. Among the challenges we face are better detection, responsible reporting, and adequate funding of CPS agencies to meet the needs of families and children.

Adult Victims

One of the consequences of mandatory reporting laws for suspected cases of child maltreatment is that researchers often can obtain both case-level and aggregate-level data on victims and perpetrators. Although these data are limited to cases known to CPS agencies, they provide information on an extremely large number of children.

By contrast, there are at present no mandatory reporting statutes for other types of domestic violence. The most frequent sources of information are clinical studies, which, though important for collecting rich qualitative data, cannot be generalized to the larger population of domestic violence victims.

In an effort to estimate the actual incidence of marital violence, Straus, Gelles, and Steinmetz (1980) surveyed a representative sample of 2,143 couples. About 3.8 percent of wives in this sample were abused by their husbands in 1975. Applying this rate to all married couples, they estimated that 1.8 million wives had been victimized that year.

Stauss and Gelles (1986) reported that abuse by husbands declined from 3.8 percent in 1975 to 3 percent in 1985. Although this decline is not statistically significant, it is important. According to the authors:

> If the 1975 rate for husband-to-wife severe violence had remained in effect, the application of this rate to the 54 million couples in the US in 1985, would result in an estimate of at least 2,052,000 severely assaulted wives each year. However, if there has been a 21 percent decrease in the rate, that translates to 1,620,000 beaten wives, which is 432,000 fewer than would have been the case if the 1975 rate prevailed. (p. 470)

The 1975 and 1985 national surveys of family violence are the only source of epidemiological data for a large and representative sample of American families. They are conservative estimates of wife abuse. It is commonly assumed that most victims of interspousal violence, pre-marital violence, and elder violence underreport their victimization even in response to survey questions, much as victims of other crimes tend to refrain from reporting violence against them.

Not only are researchers concerned with obtaining accurate esti-mates of the prevalence of all forms of family violence, but they also suspect that policymakers have all too frequently ignored this social problem by claiming that it is rare. One consequence of the perception that family violence occurs among a very small segment of society is that legislators' often fail to appropriate sufficient resources for vic-tims' services.

It is clear to most why perpetrators do not report their involvement in family violence. The problems of victim recognition and reporting and third-party recognition and reporting are less clear. Why is family violence underreported?

Self-Reports by Victims of Family Violence

Broadly defined, the victim has four options: report the abuse (to friends, police, or helping professionals); seek a private solution; cog-nitively reevaluate the situation; or do nothing (Ruback, Greenberg, and Westcott 1984). If one assumes that victims of domestic violence are similar to victims of other crimes, then the results from the 1979 National Crime Survey are of interest. This survey not only measured the incidence of nonreporting by victims but also assessed victims' reasons for not reporting the crime. This study found that

> the single most frequent reason for not reporting was they felt the offense was not important enough to warrant police attention (Gottfredson & Gottfredson, 1980). The second most prominent reason was that "nothing could be done." Add to these feelings of helplessness, a threat of further trouble, police insensitivity, and the strong fear engendered by the experi-ence and the reluctance to report crime is understandable. (Kidd and Chayet 1984, 40)

Reporting a crime or seeking help from the criminal justice system is far from simple for victims. Most victims want to reduce their distress. They struggle to lose the sense that they have been treated inequitably and may be vulnerable in the future (Ruback, Greenberg, and Westcott 1984). Some victims prefer to seek private solutions, which in some cases include retaliation against the offender (Walker 1984; Straus 1986; Mann 1986; Saunders 1986; Browne 1985). Other victims cope by cognitively redefining the situation. They reduce their level of distress by blaming themselves for the incident, lowering their judgments about the inequity of the events, or altering their beliefs about whether battering will recur.

Although the context and severity of the victimization may vary, three interrelated factors are commonly believed to inhibit reporting: fear, thoughts of personal and police powerlessness, and threats of further victimization from authorities (Kidd and Chayet 1984). Support from significant others, police, and helping professionals can significantly increase the likelihood that a victim will decide to report her abuse (Ruback, Greenberg, and Westcott 1984).

Hospitals and Victims of Domestic Violence

Hospitals and medical personnel have played important roles in the diagnosis, reporting, and treatment of child abuse and neglect, and they are important in recognizing, reporting, and treating other forms of family violence as well (see Fulmer, this volume, for a discussion of hospitals and elder abuse). Despite the frequency with which health care professionals see cases of family violence, it is widely accepted that, especially for women, the abuse is often ignored or minimized and the victims are made scapegoats or disbelieved (Klingbeil 1986).

The available data suggest that health care professionals treat a large number of women for injuries that resulted from interpersonal violence. A study of a representative sample of 1,793 women in Kentucky (Shulman 1979) found that one out of ten had been physically assaulted by her partner during the year, and seventy-nine of the assaults were serious enough to require medical attention. Forty-three percent of the injured women required treatment, and 44 percent of those needed two or more treatments. Fifty-nine percent sought treatment in a hospital emergency room, and 38 percent went to a doctor's office. Seven percent of those injured required hospital admission. Taking these data to estimate the demand for medical resources deriving from spouse abuse, Straus (1986) calculated an annual incidence rate of 4.4 injuries requiring medical attention per 100 married women in Kentucky. This is significantly higher than the estimated 1 percent of married or cohabiting women in Texas who were injured seriously enough to require medical attention (Teske and Parker 1983).

Two hospital-based studies also concluded that battered women are seen frequently in emergency rooms. In a study conducted at a large general hospital emergency department in Detroit, 25 percent of the women examined were known to be victims of domestic violence (Goldberg and Tomlanovich 1984). Similar findings were reported by researchers in San Francisco, who concluded that 36 percent of admissions to the county trauma center resulted from interpersonal violence (Sumner, Mintz, and Brown 1986).

Physicians frequently ignore the initial signs of battering. Flitcraft, Frazier, and Stark (1980) found through their examination of emergency room records that many women seen initially for inflicted injuries returned to the emergency departments. Flitcraft et al. argued that, to some extent, emergency department staff helped to perpetuate the problem rather than to solve it. Similarly, Dobash and Dobash (1979) reported that most physicians in their study did not ask women about battering. They also found that only one-third of the doctors who were informed about beatings actually gave women any advice about how they might seek safety.

There is much variability in physicians' responses to victims, based on their medical specialty, their perception of the victim, and their training. It is clear that at the hospital and emergency service levels, staff must be trained to identify and document pertinent data on violence-related injuries of all types. The tendency to focus on the injury itself while ignoring the process and circumstances of the incident that produced it, precludes genuine understanding of the nature of such injuries, meaningful secondary intervention, and well-conceived prevention programs (Sumner, Mintz, and Brown 1986).

Comprehensive models are being developed to address the problems of family violence victims seen in hospital emergency rooms. One such model, developed by Harborview Medical Center in Seattle, seeks to deal with all aspects of interpersonal violence. The major aim of this program is to recognize, detect, assess, and treat all forms of violence (familial and extrafamilial). This model has a special focus on secondary and tertiary prevention in a hospital-based emergency room, but it appears to be applicable and replicable in other settings as well (Klingbeil 1986).

Hospitals are just one of the institutions that come into direct contact with victims of family violence. Victims seen in hospitals may reflect a subset of cases characterized by more severe injuries as well as those seeking assistance beyond bandaging a wound or setting a broken bone. Such institutions have the responsibility to train personnel to identify, assess, and treat family violence across the life span, as has been attempted for child maltreatment.

Race, Ethnicity, and Family Violence

Few studies thus far have attempted to examine racial and cultural differences in family violence, though it has been suggested that differences among ethnic populations must be taken into account in the delivery of optimal health and mental health service (Harwood 1981; McGoldrick 1983). Further, almost none of the existing compilations of incidence data present statistics on racial or ethnic groups unconfounded by social class. Garbarino and Ebata (1983, 774) argued:

> When class and ethnicity are confounded, we always run the risk of confusing legitimate ethnic differences in style with the deleterious effects of socioeconomic deprivation (at the lower end of the spectrum), and of elevating the values of the economically privileged to the status of universal standards (at the other end of the scale).

It is incorrect to assume that environments that are economically impoverished inevitably are socially impoverished (Garbarino and Crouter 1978). Groups generate legitimate culturally determined attitudes, values, and beliefs as a way of coping with their environments. Cultural differences are often ascribed to class rather than ethnicity. Class is a major aspect of family life experience, but not all differences can be attributed to it (McGoldrick 1983).

Several studies suggest that black families may have the highest rates of child abuse and neglect, followed by Hispanics and whites (Gil 1970; Lauderdale, Valiunas, and Anderson 1980; Jason et al. 1982; Spearly and Lauderdale 1983). In one such study of 4,132 cases of child abuse reported to the Los Angeles County Sheriff's Department from 1975 to 1982, Lindholm and Willey (1983) reported a number of significant differences they attributed to ethnic status. Physical abuse was highest in black families, with discipline most often given as the reason for abuse. The children also suffered different types of physical injuries. Black children were more likely to be whipped or beaten and to have lacerations or scars, whereas white children were more likely to have bruises. Although blacks constituted only 9.8 percent of the Los Angeles County population, they accounted for 23.8 percent of abuse victims. These data also showed that among whites and Hispanics, males (especially fathers) were the most frequent offenders. Among blacks, however, mothers were identified most frequently as abusers.

Similarly, Johnson and Showers (1985) found significant race effects for causes of injury to children in their sample of victims from Children's Hospital (Columbus, Ohio). They found that black children were more likely to be struck with a belt, a strap, or a cord than white children. Black children were also more commonly knifed or burned with an iron. By contrast, white children were more often struck with a board or paddle or hit with an open hand. These researchers felt that strong subcultural or racial differences might exist in approaches to discipline.

In my analysis of data from the National Incidence Study, I (Hampton 1987) showed further that in comparison with whites and Hispanics, black maltreatment occurred most frequently in families that were poor, were on public assistance, and had no father present. The analysis also showed that nonwhite children were younger than the white children; nonwhite parents had fewer years of formal education; nonwhite mothers were younger; and black mothers in particular were more likely to be unemployed. Additional differences were found in the nature, type, and severity of child maltreatment.

Ethnic variations in definitions of family violence and responses to it have also been found among residents of the rural Northwest (Long 1986). Similarly, substantial differences have been found in foster care placements and length of time in foster care among ethnic groups (Jenkins and Diamond 1985).

Although the studies cited above strongly support the concept of ethnic differences in child maltreatment, data from the National Survey of Family Violence (Straus, Gelles, and Steinmetz 1980) indicate little difference between black and white families in the rates of abusive violence toward children (15 percent in black families, 14 percent in white families). Although wife abuse was nearly four times as common in black as in white families and husband abuse was twice as common in black families, blacks in this sample were not more violent toward children.

In a more detailed examination of these data, Cazenave and Straus (1979) concluded that aid and support, especially child care, provided by the black extended family seemed to reduce the risk of abusive violence toward children. They found that when income and husband's occupation were controlled, blacks were *less* likely than other groups to engage in child abuse.

Ethnic differences in rates of family violence are most evident when one examines data on homicides in the United States. There is strong evidence that nonlethal violence is a frequent antecedent of homicide (Browne 1985) and that there are similar risk factors for lethal and nonlethal family violence (Hampton 1986). Several investigators have pointed out the importance of analyzing homicides categorized by victim-offender relationships or precipitating circumstances (Smith and Parker 1980; Jason, Flack, and Tyler 1983). When homicides have been so partitioned, they have almost always been dichotomized according to the relationship between the victim and the offender. Primary homicides are the most frequent type and generally involve family, friends, or acquaintances (Smith and Parker 1980). The precipitating factor is usually an argument. Secondary homicides generally involve offenders and victims who have no prior relationship and are generally committed in the course of another crime such as robbery or rape. Another way to view this dichotomy is that

> primary homicides can also be considered as interpersonally proximate events between a victim and offender whose relationship varies in degree of interpersonal intensity. By contrast, non-primary or secondary homicides can be regarded as more interpersonally distal events where the degree of intensity of relationships is variable, although often of lesser intensity. (Loya, Garcia, Sullivan, Vargas, Mercy, and Allen 1986, 118)

Between 1966 and 1970, 63 percent of all homicide victims died from assaults not related to another crime. The 1979 rate for black males was 7.3 times that for white males; the rate for black females was 5.8 times that for white females (Jason, Flack, and Tyler 1983). In that year 6,242 whites and 5,851 blacks were homicide victims.

The importance of ethnic/racial status as a demographic variable in the study of lethal interpersonal violence is best illustrated by Loya, Garcia, Sullivan, Vargas, Mercy, and Allen (1986) in their study of homicides in Los Angeles from 1970 to 1979. One of the starkest ethnic/race findings to emerge from this research was that Asians run the highest relative risk of being killed in a crime, even though there is an apparent absence of primary homicides among Los Angeles Asians. The authors suggest:

> Cultural mores that value group cooperation and resolution of conflict through compromise especially within the family are strong within traditional Asian ethnic groups, in addition, traditional Asian cultures are known to have stronger sanctions against homicide. The Asian racial group may represent a risk-free or very low risk population for primary homicide. (p. 123)

Both blacks and whites were more likely than Asians to be involved in fatal assaults within their families or other close relationships. Blacks had the highest rate of mate homicides. Although Hispanic mate homicides were proportionately lowest, Hispanic nonmate family homicides (e.g., parent-child, sibling, extended family) were among the most frequent.

Native Americans residing in the Los Angeles area were not as susceptible to fatal violence arising from interpersonally close relationships as the other major ethnic/racial groups (Loya, Garcia, Sullivan, Vargas, and Allen 1986). They were the only group, however, in which the female homicide rate was slightly higher than the male homicide rate.

Although blacks, Hispanics, and native Americans shared low socioeconomic status in the Los Angeles area, they had very dissimilar homicide rates and very dissimilar distributions within the primary homicide category. Loya, et al. suggested that we cannot ignore the importance of variations in culturally supported behaviors. These behaviors can be modified by socioeconomic status, acculturation level, and generational status, but their importance must be recognized (Loya, Garcia, Sullivan, Vargas, Mercy, and Allen 1986).

It is clear that ethnicity is associated with lethal family violence in a complex manner. Family violence occurs within a context of community, neighborhood, and sociocultural group. Each family is consequently exposed to group standards about what is acceptable or unacceptable in the way of impulse control, aggression, punishment, and violence. Among the important research needs in the area of domestic violence are well-designed, well-executed studies that can shed light on group differences in risk for violence and propose culturally sensitive interventions when violence occurs. These studies could point out special risk factors that may be present among ethnic or racial groups in a community and also highlight strengths of cultural and ethnic groups that may assist them in avoiding certain forms of interpersonal violence.

Deterrence versus Prevention

One of the recommendations that emerged from the study by the Attorney General's Task Force on Family Violence (1984) was that the criminal justice system should become more actively involved in punishing perpetrators of domestic violence. In its Law Enforcement Recommendation 2, the report states that "consistent with state law, the chief executive of every law enforcement agency should establish arrest as the preferred response in cases of family violence." The report further states:

> Intervention by the criminal justice system can effectively restrain assailants and make them responsible for their violence like any other perpetrator of crime. Arrest by law enforcement officers sends a clear signal to the assailant: abusive behavior is a serious criminal act and will not be condoned or tolerated. Prosecution policies that are not dependent upon a signed complaint from the victim reinforce that message. Courts confirm it by imposing sanctions commensurate with the crime. Such measures not only have a deterrent effect on the abuser but also provide protection for the victim. (p. 12)

Supporters of this statement in essence agree with the "deterrence model" for the control of antisocial behavior. This model is based on the assumption that deviant behavior is controlled when punishment is both certain and severe. Individuals are in effect coerced, threatened, and sanctioned into conformity.

Sherman and Berk (1984) conducted a natural experiment to assess the effect of police intervention in cases of wife abuse in Minneapolis. Of three randomly applied interventions—arrest, removing the husband from the home, and trying to cool down the situation—arrests resulted in fewer calls for help and fewer instances of repeated violence. In a related study that attempted to replicate the findings from the Minneapolis spouse abuse experiment, Berk and Newton (1985) found that, on the average, arrest deters new incidents of wife battering. They state that large deterrent effects were found for men whom police were inclined to arrest based on their perception of the likelihood of new violence. They caution, however, that there is no guarantee that if police were forced to arrest more frequently, the deterrent effects would be the same as in the study.

An important element in all the proposed "arrest the perpetrator" deterrent models is that the victim would not necessarily have to make a formal complaint. The police in most instances would be responsible for charging and arresting in cases of spouse abuse (Jaffe et al. 1986).

A major weakness of the deterrence model, and the research to date, is an overall failure to consider socioeconomic and demographic factors that could confound the results. For example, in a longitudinal study of criminal behavior, Piliavin et al. (1986) found little support for this model. Instead, they found evidence supporting an opportunity and reward model of rational choice frequently operating in criminal behavior. For example, people's perception of the opportunity, returns, and support for crime within a given situation are likely to influence their perception of risk. They found that for a person at high risk of formal punishment, perception of risk failed to influence the decision to violate the law. Rather, those decisions were influenced by his perception of his opportunities and his respect for criminal activities.

Similarly, Paternoster and Iovanni (1986) found that deterrence works primarily through informal processes, and that once these are controlled, perceptions of severity and certainty of punishment have no effect on deviant behavior. In general there is little evidence that raising the cost of violence by inflicting more punishment (or speedier or more severe or more certain punishment) results in less violence (Currie 1985).

In light of the seemingly contradictory evidence on the effectiveness of tougher criminal sanctions in reducing family violence, one can safely say there is a need for more empirical work in this area. Abusers may be deterred for a variety of reasons. Berk and Newton (1985, 262) stated:

> Perhaps offenders are responding to the fear of further criminal justice sanctions. Perhaps offenders are responding to the implications of arrest for relationships with friends, family and neighbors. Perhaps offenders are concerned about what an arrest will do to their employment prospects. Or perhaps arrest functions as a particularly pointed lesson about societal views on wife battery. Until these and other possible mechanisms are disentangled, theories of deterrence are little more than rhetoric.

Debates regarding deterrence should not impede efforts at the primary prevention of violence among intimates. At best, many deterrence approaches tested to date are attempts at tertiary prevention. That is, they are concerned with situations in which patterns of violence are already well established. These efforts are important, for they can in some cases prevent the escalation of interpersonal conflict into potentially lethal violence. However, tertiary prevention, which attempts to prevent the recurrence of violence, must be accompanied by efforts at primary prevention.

It is beyond the scope of this chapter to address the specifics of primary prevention across the life span. There are several excellent discussions of the topic in this volume and elsewhere (e.g., Newberger and Newberger 1982; Gelles 1984; Garbarino 1986). The goal of primary prevention is to reduce both the incidence and the severity of new cases of family violence by combating harmful forces that operate in the community and by strengthening the capacity of family members to withstand endemic and acute stress, whether caused by internal or external factors.

Primary prevention focuses on groups (not individuals) and the specific problems those groups experience (Klein and Goldston 1978). Prevention is proactive; that is, it builds new coping resources and adaptation skills and thus promotes emotional health (Albee and Gullotta 1986). Prevention programs are planned interventions that can be observed, recorded, and evaluated (Klein and Goldston 1977; Garbarino 1986). Prevention programming to date indicates that primary prevention is possible but that success does not come cheaply (Garbarino 1986).

Primary prevention efforts need to be directed at social, cultural, and legal aspects of the environment that perpetuate the nation's extraordinarily high rates of lethal and nonlethal violence. The technology of prevention uses four tools to fashion a healthier environment (Adams and Gullotta 1983). These tools are education, community or systems organization, promotion of competency, and natural caregiving. These tools have overlapping boundaries, and well-designed prevention programs include them all.

Education not only awakens our consciousness but informs us as well. As a tool for the primary prevention of violence it must be designed to enlist greater public and professional interest, concern, and involvement. There is a wealth of data to support the position that some violence is transmitted across generations (e.g., Straus, Gelles, and Steinmetz 1980). In such cases violence is learned from the experience of having been abused as a child. Parents model abusive parenting for their children. Parent education and reeducation programs can help many parents learn nonabusing techniques (Newberger and Newberger 1982).

For example, the National Institute of Mental Health recently funded a culturally sensitive parent education program for the primary prevention of violence toward children in black families. This project

> involved the adaptation of three standard parent training programs to the needs and circumstances of low-income black families. New instructional units were developed on traditional black discipline, modern black self-discipline, black pride, and single parenting. The purpose of the two units on discipline was to assist low-income black parents in developing more positive, affectionate parenting styles that could reduce and eliminate reliance on hitting as a means for child rearing. (Department of Health and Human Services 1986, 47)

The purpose of community organization and systems intervention is to ensure that societal inequities are stopped and not carried into the future (Gullotta, Adams, and Alexander 1986). It has been shown that poverty is one of the greatest contributors to family violence (Gil 1970; Straus, Gelles, and Steinmetz 1980). Impoverishment places heavy demands on families and tends to create situations of high need and low resources that threaten family life (Garbarino 1982). Until these inequities are resolved, misery and cruelty will prevail (Daniel, Hampton, and Newberger 1983). Social action directed toward a change in values about violence and inequities based on gender, race, and ethnicity are also important ingredients in a holistic approach to prevention. More specifically, a community organization or systems approach to prevention can work to modify or remove institutional barriers that limit access to life options or opportunities, develop community resources, and create needed legislative and judicial reforms (Gullotta, Adams, and Alexander 1986).

Social support systems are valuable in moderating life stresses. For example, health visitors can provide important family supports and have been used successfully with high-risk mothers (see discussion in

Garbarino 1986; Olds et al. 1986). One important aspect of health visitor programs is that they increase the participants' feelings of self-worth and self-esteem. The health visitor not only provides help and advice as needed, but also links families with the larger health care system. These programs also promote competency among participants by developing parenting skills and encouraging interpersonal and community relationships.

Nurturing environments further encourage nonviolent interpersonal relationships. Garbarino (1982) suggested that the most important aspect of the social environment is how far it encourages people to be "socially connected" and discourages them from becoming "socially isolated." In a socially rich environment, we can protect ourselves from the stresses and strains of daily life. Sharing knowledge and experiences, demonstrating compassion, and providing companionship and when necessary confrontation are all aspects of caregiving in the socially rich environment (Gullotta, Adams, and Alexander 1986). Professionals can encourage clients to become involved in natural caregiving networks. One example comes from Garbarino's (1982) analysis of ways physicians can help in treating and preventing child abuse. He suggests five prevention principles that emerge from the analysis of the social context of child abuse:

1. Treat the social network.
2. Support and create self-help groups.
3. Use "natural opportunities" to modify the social roles of parents.
4. Use the physician's authority as a bridge to connect isolated parents with formal support systems.
5. Encourage other medical personnel to be concerned with the social context of parent-child relations.

Each of these suggestions was made to help physicians prevent child maltreatment. It is clear, however, that with slight modifications they are applicable to other professionals in other settings. It is also clear that these suggestions speak to the importance of natural caregiving for families across the life span, in settings as varied as battered women's shelters, Parents Anonymous, and informal neighborhood, church, and volunteer groupings. We already have tools to prevent violence from being transmitted to the next generation. Now we must use them.

References

Adams, G. R., and Gullotta, T. P. 1983. *Adolescent life experiences*. Monterey, Calif.: Brooks/Cole.

Albee, G. W., and Gullotta, T. P. 1986. Fallacies and facts about primary prevention. *Journal of Primary Prevention* 6(4):207–18.

American Humane Association. 1986. *Highlights of official child abuse and neglect reporting*. Annual Report 1984. Denver: American Humane Association.

Attorney General's Task Force on Family Violence. 1984. *Final report*. Washington, D.C.: U.S. Government Printing Office.

Berk, R. A., and Newton, P. J. 1985. Does arrest really deter wife battery? An effort to replicate the findings of the Minneapolis Spouse Abuse Experiment. *American Sociological Review* 50:253–62.

Browne, A. 1985. Assault and homicide at home: When battered women kill. In *Advances in applied social psychology*, vol. 3, ed. M. J. Sakes and L. Saxe. Hillsdale, N.J.: Lawrence Erlbaum.

Cazenave, N., and Straus, M. A. 1979. Race, class, network embeddedness and family violence. *Journal of Comparative Family Studies* 10:281–300.

Currie, E. 1985. Crimes of violence and public policy: Changing directions. In *American violence and public policy*, ed. L. Curtis. New Haven: Yale University Press.

Daniel, J. H.; Hampton, R. L.; and Newberger, E. H. 1983. Child abuse and accidents in black families: A case controlled comparison. *American Journal of Orthopsychiatry* 53(4):645–53.

Department of Health and Human Services. 1986. *Homicide, suicide, and unintentional injuries*. Report of the Secretary's Task Force on Black and Minority Health, vol. 5. Washington, D.C.: U.S. Government Printing Office.

Dobash, R. E., and Dobash, R. P. 1979. *Violence against wives*. New York: Free Press.

Finkelhor, D. 1984. *Child sexual abuse*. New York: Free Press.

Flitcraft, A.; Frazier, W. D.; and Stark, E. 1980. Medical contexts and sequelae of domestic violence. Final report to National Institute of Mental Health.

Garbarino, J. 1982. Healing the wounds of social isolation. In *Child abuse*, ed. E. H. Newberger. Boston: Little, Brown.

———. 1986. Can we measure success in preventing child abuse? Issues in policy, programming and research. *Child Abuse and Neglect* 10(2):143–56.

Garbarino, J., and Crouter, A. 1978. Defining the community context of parent-child relations: The correlates of child maltreatment. *Child Development* 49:604–16.

Garbarino, J., and Ebata, A. 1983. The significance of ethnic and cultural difference in child maltreatment. *Journal of Marriage and the Family* 39:773–83.

Gelles, R. J. 1982. Child abuse and family violence: implications for medical professionals. In *Child abuse*, ed E. H. Newberger. Boston: Little, Brown.

————. 1984. Applying our knowledge of family violence to prevention and treatment: What difference does it make? Paper presented to the Second National Conference for Family Violence Researchers, Durham, N.H., 7–10 August.

————. 1985. Family violence. *Annual Review of Sociology* 11:347–67.

Gil, D. 1970. *Violence against children: Physical abuse in the United States.* Cambridge: Harvard University Press.

Goldberg, W., and Tomlanovich, M. C. 1984. Domestic violence victims in the emergency department. *Journal of the American Medical Association* 251(25): 3259–64.

Gottsfredson, M. R., and Gottfredson, D. M. 1980. *Decision making in criminal justice.* Cambridge, Mass.: Ballinger.

Gullotta, T. P.; Adams, G. R.; and Alexander, S. J. (1986). *Today's marriages and families: A wellness approach.* Monterey, Calif.: Brooks/Cole.

Hampton, R. L. 1986. Family violence and homicide in the black community: Are they linked? In *Homicide, suicide and unintentional injuries,* 69–93. Department of Health and Human Services, Report of the Secretary's Task Force on Black and Minority Health, vol. 5. Washington, D.C.: U.S. Government Printing Office.

————. 1987. Race, class and child maltreatment. *Journal of Comparative Family Studies* 18(1): 113–26.

Hampton, R. L., and Newberger, E. H. (1985). Child abuse incidence and reporting by hospitals: Significance of severity, class and race. *American Journal of Public Health* 75(1): 56–60.

Harwood, A. 1981. *Ethnicity and medical care.* Cambridge: Harvard University Press.

Herzberger, S. 1986. Labeling and abuse cases: Professional judgments and biases. In *Proceedings of symposium on professional ethics and child abuse.* Washington, D.C.: National Technical Information Service.

Herzberger, S., and Tennen, H. 1985. The effect of self-reliance on judgment of moderate and severe disciplinary encounters. *Journal of Marriage and the Family* 47(2): 311–18.

Jaffe, P.; Wolfe, D.; Telford, A.; and Austin, G. 1986. The impact of police charges in incidents of wife abuse. *Journal of Family Violence* 1(1): 37–49.

Jason, J.; Ambereuh, N.; Marks, J.; and Tyler, C. 1982. Child abuse in Georgia: A method to evaluate risk factors and reporting bias. *American Journal of Public Health* 72(12): 1353–58.

Jason, J.; Flack, M.; and Tyler, C. W., Jr. 1983. Epidemiologic characteristics of primary homicides in the United States. *American Journal of Epidemiology* 117(4): 419–28.

Jenkins, S., and Diamond, B. 1985. Ethnicity and foster care: Census data as predictors of placement. *American Journal of Orthopsychiatry* 55(2): 267–76.

Johnson, C. F., and Showers, J. 1985. Injury variables in child abuse. *Child Abuse and Neglect* 9(2): 207–16.

Kidd, R. F., and Chayet, E. F. 1984. Who do victims fail to report? The psychology of criminal victimization. *Journal of Social Issues* 40(1): 39–50.

Klein, D. C., and Goldston, S. E. 1978. *Primary prevention: An idea whose time has come.* NIHM, DHEW Publication (ADM) 77-447. Washington, D.C.: U.S. Government Printing Office.

Klingbeil, K. S. 1986. Interpersonal violence: A comprehensive model in a hospital setting from policy to program. In *Homicide, suicide and unintentional injuries*, 245-63. Department of Health and Human Services, Report of the Secretary's Task Force on Black and Minority Health, vol. 5. Washington, D.C.: U.S. Government Printing Office.

Lauderdale, M.; Valiunas, A.; and Anderson, R. 1980. Race, ethnicity, and child maltreatment: An empirical analysis. *Child Abuse and Neglect* 4: 163-69.

Lindholm, K. J., and Willey, R. 1983. *Child abuse and ethnicity: Patterns of similarities and differences.* Occasional Paper 19. Los Angeles: Spanish Speaking Mental Health Research Center, UCLA.

Long, K. A. 1986. Cultural considerations in the assessment and treatment of intrafamilial abuse. *American Journal of Orthopsychiatry* 56(1): 131-36.

Loya, F.; Garcia, P.; Sullivan, J. D.; Vargas, L. A.; Mercy, J.; and Allen, N. 1986. Conditional risks of homicide among Anglo, Hispanic, black, and Asian victims in Los Angeles, 1970-79. In *Homicide, suicide and unintentional injuries*, 117-36. Department of Health and Human Services, Report of the Secretary's Task Force on Black and Minority Health, vol. 5. Washington, D.C.: U.S. Government Printing Office.

Loya, F.; and Garcia, P.; Sullivan, J. D.; Vargas, L. A.; and Allen, N. 1986. Changes in the criminal homicide rate of American Indians for the city of Los Angeles, 1970-79: A research note. In *Homicide, suicide and unintentional injuries*, 137-43. Department of Health and Human Services, Report of the Secretary's Task Force on Black and Minority Health, vol 5. Washington, D.C.: U.S. Government Printing Office.

McGoldrick, M. 1983. Ethnicity and family therapy: An overview. In *Ethnicity and family therapy*, ed. M. McGoldrick, J. K. Pearce, and J. Giordano. New York: Guilford Press.

Mann, C. 1986. The black female criminal offender in the United States. In *Homicide, suicide and unintentional injuries*, 135-81. Department of Health and Human Services, Report of the Secretary's Task Force on Black and Minority Health, vol. 5. Washington, D.C: U.S. Government Printing Office.

National Incidence Study. *National study of the incidence and severity of child abuse and neglect.* Department of Health and Human Services·Publication (OHDS) 81-03026. Washington, D.C.: U.S. Government Printing Office.

Newberger, C. M., and Newberger, E. H. 1982. Prevention of child abuse: Theory, myth, practice. *Journal of Preventive Psychiatry* 1(4): 443-51.

Newberger, E. H.; Reed, R.; Daniel, J.; Hyde, J. N.; and Kotelchuck, M. 1977. Pediatric social illness: Toward an etiologic classification. *Pediatrics* 60:178-85.

Olds, D. L.; Henderson, C. R., Jr.; Chamberlain, R.; and Tatelbaum, R. 1986. Preventing child abuse and neglect: A randomized trial of nurse home visitation. *Pediatrics* 78(1): 65-78.

Paternoster, R., and Iovanni, L. 1986. The deterrent effect of perceived severity: A reexamination. *Social Forces* 64(3): 751-70.

Piliavin, I.; Gartner, R.; Thornton, C.; and Matsueda, R. 1986. Crime, deterrence, and rational choice. *American Sociological Review* 51:101–19.

Ruback, R. B.; Greenberg, M. S.; and Westcott, R. 1984. Social influence and crime-victim decision making. *Journal of Social Issues* 40(1): 51–76.

Saunders, D. G. 1986. When battered women use violence: Husband-abuse or self-defense? *Violence and Victims* 1(1): 47–60.

Sherman, L. W., and Berk, R. A. 1984. The specific deterrent effects of arrest for domestic violence assault. *American Sociological Review* 49:261–72.

Shulman, M. A. 1979. A survey of spousal violence against women in Kentucky. Law Enforcement Assistance Administration Study 792701. Washington, D.C.: U.S. Government Printing Office.

Smith, M.D., and Parker, R. N. 1980. Type of homicide and variation in regional rates. *Social Forces* 59:146–57.

Spearly, J. L., and Lauderdale, M. 1983. Community characteristics and ethnicity in the prediction of child maltreatment rates. *Child Abuse and Neglect* 7:91–105.

Straus, M. 1986. Medical care costs of intra-family assault and homicide to society. *Bulletin of the New York Academy of Medicine*, 62, 556–561.

Straus, M., and Gelles, R. J. 1986. Societal change and change in family violence from 1975 to 1985 as revealed by two national surveys. *Journal of Marriage and the Family* 48(3): 465–79.

Straus, M.; Gelles, R. J.; and Steinmetz, S. 1980. *Behind closed doors*. New York: Doubleday.

Sumner, B. B.; Mintz, E. R.; and Brown, P. L. 1986. Interviewing persons hospitalized with interpersonal violence-related injuries: A pilot study. In *Homicide, suicide, and unintentional injuries, 267–317.* Department of Health and Human Services, Report of the Secretary's Task Force on Black and Minority Health, vol. 5. Washington, D.C.: U.S. Government Printing Office.

Teske, R., and Parker, M. L. 1983. *Spouse abuse in Texas: A study of women's attitudes and experiences.* Huntsville, Tex.: Criminal Justice Center, Sam Houston State University.

Turbett, J. P., and O'Toole, R. 1980. Physicians' recognition of child abuse. Paper presented at the annual meeting of the American Sociological Association, New York.

Walker, L. 1984. *The battered woman syndrome*. New York: Springer.

12   *Special Groups at Risk of Abuse: The Disabled*

Nora E. Groce

The term "the disabled" includes persons with a number of physical and psychological conditions ranging from hyperactivity to mental retardation and including cerebral palsy, epilepsy, autism, deafness, blindness, paraplegia, quadriplegia, and many others. What the disabled in our society have most in common is not their specific physical or mental limitations, which may vary widely, but the fact that they must all deal with a larger nondisabled population that dictates the norms.

Although our definitions of what constitutes a disability and who is included within the disabled group are at times imprecise, nevertheless the literature on domestic violence indicates that disabled individuals appear statistically to be at a substantially greater risk for abuse and neglect than other members of society. Disabled children, disabled adults, and disabled adults who are themselves parents constitute three subgroups within this population.

Overview

The association between disability and abuse has long been noted by those who work in the field, and a great deal of research has been concentrated specifically on disabled children. Among the most prominent issues debated is whether children born disabled are at higher risk for being abused or whether abused children are at higher risk for becoming disabled through abuse. Of equal importance is whether neglected children are at higher risk of injury and subsequent disability than those who are not neglected. Finally, once the cycle of abuse and disability has begun, another topic of debate is whether disability or abuse does more damage to a child and how one or both might be prevented.

Children identified early as disabled are generally believed to be stressful to parents. Most publications and professionals discuss the way many parents react to the news that a child is disabled in terms of anger, guilt, fear, and denial. The stress placed on the parents is considered to be so great that they eventually may take it out directly on the child.

While disabled children are indeed stressful for parents, such stress may reflect the way we as a society perceive disabilities rather than the disability itself. As a nation, we expect all babies to be born healthy. Few people anticipate or plan for a disabled child. In fact most people are woefully unaware of and misinformed about the disabled. Unless we have an immediate family member or close friend who is disabled, many of us go through a lifetime with only the vaguest notions about what it is like to be disabled. Most of us are also unaware of what an important and welcome addition such a child might be to a family or of the contributions a disabled child can make to the larger society as an adult.

Unfortunately, the vast majority of parents with disabled children are initially no better informed than the rest of the population. When a disability is identified in a child, they are often forced into the untenable situation of being expected to accept the situation at once and become experts on the medical, social, and psychological aspects of the condition, as well as advocates for the child in these arenas. If all this is not overwhelming enough, they often must do so in isolation, for society assumes that the vast bulk of disabled individuals' care lies with the nuclear family. Friends and relatives frequently find themselves unable to "deal" with these situations, and support services in most communities are sparse if they exist at all.

Moreover, some children who are born disabled are very difficult to care for even with support and information. A specific disability might cause children to interact less effectively with parents, smile less, respond less to voices, make less eye contact with caretakers, and be fussier and harder to comfort than other children. Long before such children are diagnosed as disabled by medical professionals, they may already be a major stress on their parents.

Not only are those born with a disability at higher risk for abuse, it is now clear that abuse and neglect may themselves lead directly to disabling conditions. Developmental disability and neurological impairments are well-documented aftereffects of abuse and neglect; multiple signs of brain damage, seizures, mental retardation, cerebral palsy, sensory deficits such as impaired hearing and vision, and learning disorders have all been linked conclusively to trauma or neglect.

When a disabled child is also an abused child, the discussions in the literature of what came first, the disability or the abuse, often sound like the old chicken-and-egg riddle. Ultimately it is often unclear whether the developmental outcome reflects the original disability or the abuse the child has received.

Indeed, the abuse/disability cycle often precedes the birth of the child. Violence toward a child frequently is not an isolated event but an outgrowth of a violent household. In such households pregnant women are often the targets of beatings. When these beatings lead to premature delivery or injury to the fetus, the child has had early introduction to its family's methods of resolving differences. It is well established that when spouse abuse precedes the arrival of a demanding infant, the level of stress and potential violence within the family unit is likely to increase with its birth.

The problem of abuse and disability is not confined to children. While researchers have directed far less attention toward abuse of disabled adults, it is now certain that both physical and sexual abuse as well as neglect are ongoing problems for many disabled citizens. Some disabled persons are physically dependent on caretakers to fulfill many of their needs. Those who are residents of institutions or affiliated with them frequently have little contact with the outside world, and some are also unable to communicate their concerns and experience effectively. When those who staff such facilities are poorly trained, poorly paid, and poorly supervised, the disabled often find themselves at particular risk.

This is by no means a problem only in institutions. Most disabled citizens live and work in the community. When violence or neglect is part of their homelife, they often find themselves with few personal and community resources to rely on.

Finally, both disabled and normal children of disabled parents may have a unique set of problems that are rarely addressed. When disabled individuals choose to have children, we must recognize that some will have special concerns and difficulties as they seek to provide for their offspring in an environment that often appears hostile to their efforts.

Research on Disabilities and Child Abuse

The observation that the disabled are particularly "at risk" for abuse is cited so frequently that it is perhaps surprising that so little systematic research has been done on the subject. Statistics on this population are scanty at best (Camblin 1982). A number of the studies that have been undertaken have significant problems with research design, sample size, and control groups (see review articles by Toro 1982 and by Schilling et al. 1982 for a more thorough discussion of methodological issues in disability research). Few studies draw together data to address either the theoretical implications or the management concerns raised by the conclusions they do reach.

Several theories of child abuse state, in effect, that a disabled child faces increased risk as the result of child-produced stress. The appearance of a "special child" (or what parents *perceive* as a "special child") brings mounting psychological, economic, and physical stress, and parents may eventually pass their tolerance limits. As Friedrich and Boriskin (1976, 587) argued: "It is uncomfortable to think about a child playing a role in his own abuse, [but] the fact remains that a child is not always a benign stimulus on the parent."

This cycle of increasing tension can begin long before the child is diagnosed as having a disability. Pasamanic (1975), studying five hundred "at risk" children and five hundred control children over a span of twelve years, found that mothers whose premature children were later judged to be neurologically impaired were more tense ten months postpartum than mothers whose preterm babies were later found to be neurologically normal. (The mothers of neurologically normal premature infants were comparable to mothers of normal full-term babies.) Pasamanic concludes that "this seems to support the concept that those children, even when only slightly affected, are disorganized and unstable, with lower thresholds of stress" (1975, 550). Sandgrund, Gaines, and Green (1974) similarly showed that children with such cognitive and neurological deficits were more likely to display "unmanageable" behavior and to contribute to parent stress.

Disabilities such as deafness, blindness, and mental retardation, though often present at birth, may not be diagnosed for several years. Such types of undiagnosed disabilities can mute and distort the feedback cycles between parent and child. For example, deaf children are unresponsive to cooing parents. Not infrequently, long before a hearing loss is suspected, a child who is deaf will be thought to be deliberately provoking, refusing to come when called or to do as a parent orders. Ounstead, Oppenheimer, and Lindsay (1974, 450) cited an example of an abusive parent whose child had just been diagnosed as blind. The mother overwhelmed by guilt, explained her actions by saying the child "cried and cried and never looked at me."

A number of studies have shown a higher incidence of preexisting disabilities in children who have been abused or neglected. For example, in 1968, 70 percent of the ninety-seven abused children followed by the Denver Department of Welfare were found to have preexisting mental or physical disabilities (Johnson and Morse 1968). Birrell and Birrell (1968) reported that 25 percent of the forty-two children considered abused in their Australian hospital had some form of congenital anomaly, while Morse, Sahler, and Friedman (1970) found 43 percent of the children they studied had IQs below 80; all but one of these was thought to have been retarded before the abuse occurred. Similarly, Chotiner and Lehr (1976), in a national survey of Parents Anonymous members, found that 58 percent of the children reported as abused were listed as having "developmental" problems, and Gil (1970) also reported that in 29 percent of the six thousand confirmed cases of child abuse he studied the children had some sort of disability before abuse. In those instances where the burden of a disabled child adds stress to an already overtaxed or violence-prone household, the strain engendered by the immediate needs of the special child and the prospect of long-term care without relief may initially or eventually lead to violence.

Not only may the stress of caring for a disabled individual drive a parent or caregiver to the point of abuse or neglect, but abuse and neglect can in fact lead to disability in previously nondisabled children. This has long been suggested (Caffey 1964; Silverman 1953; Berenberg 1968), but it was first documented twenty years ago. Elmer and Gregg (1967) undertook a comprehensive follow-up of fifty-two children with multiple bone injuries five years after they were initially seen in the hospital. The findings were significant. Of Elmer and Gregg's original group, ten were either lost to follow-up or were judged to be from nonabusive homes. Of the remaining forty-two children, eight were dead and five were in institutions for the mentally retarded. Of the remaining thirty-three, 30 percent had signs of central nervous system damage and 57 percent had IQs below 80. The overall morbidity rate of this group of children, all of whom were assumed to be "normal" at the time of their initial reported injury, was an astonishing 88 percent.

Other studies have arrived at similar conclusions about the deleterious consequences of abuse upon the IQs of children. For example, Sandgrund, Gaines, and Green (1974), found that abused children were eight times as likely to have IQs below 70 as were children in a nonabused control group, as a direct consequence of permanent injury to the brain rather than psychosocial factors. If children considered neglected were added to this group, these traumatized children were *fifteen times* as likely to score in the retarded range as were the nontraumatized children from the control group.

In a retrospective study of mentally retarded individuals in Alaska, Eppler and Brown (1977) found that 14.9 percent of their sample of 436 individuals had been abused. In at least 37 percent of these cases there was strong evidence that abuse or neglect, or both, was the cause of the retardation. Indeed, evidence of abuse and neglect was so prevalent in their study that they concluded unequivocally that abuse and neglect are "preventable but underappreciated causes of mental retardation" (1977, 312).

This conclusion has been repeated many times in the research literature. For example, Martin (1972), in a three-year follow-up of forty-two abused children, found that 33 percent had IQs below 80, 43 percent were neurologically impaired, and fully a third were also below the third percentile in height and weight. The neurological impairments in these children were three times as frequent in those also considered mentally retarded as in those who had normal IQs. A history of skull fracture was four times as frequent in retarded children as in nonretarded ones, further indicating that actual damage had been done to the brain as a consequence of the abuse. These findings are supported by Oliver (1977), who studied children in a British "subnormality" hospital and found that in 3 percent of the total number of cases retardation was unquestionably linked to brain damage resulting from abuse by parent or caregiver. By adding those cases where abuse was strongly suspected but conclusive evidence was lacking, the proportion of cases strongly linked to abuse as a cause was increased to 11 percent.

Child abuse has also been associated with other disabilities. Dimond and Jaudis (1983), in an excellent study, closely examined the population of cerebral palsy patients at La Rabida Children's Hospital in Chicago and found that in 42 percent of their total patient population child abuse was an important feature in the child's history. In a *minimum* of 9 percent of the cases, cerebral palsy in the child was unquestionably the direct consequence of violent trauma to a previously healthy infant or toddler. An expanded follow-up study (Jaudis and Dimond 1985) of 162 children resulted in similar findings.

Most of these studies have looked at children who have been directly abused, but simple neglect may be as damaging as outright violence. A child who falls out an open window or, left unattended, continually eats lead paint chips, may suffer as severe and permanent damage as a child who is beaten or shaken. Neglected children tend to have language delays associated with cognitive deficits and mental retardation (Allen and Oliver 1982). Medical neglect is also associated with disability. For example, an ear infection left unattended or only partially treated can cause permanent hearing loss. Hearing-impaired children may be less responsive to parents and thus at increased risk for abuse. Similarly, diabetic children whose parents are inattentive or irregular in administering medication are also at risk for associated physical problems.

The connection between neglect and disability often boils down to economics: the parents' ability to pay for a doctor, safe housing, and someone to watch the children while they go to the store or across the street. Given the option, few parents would choose anything less than the best for their children. However, we live in a society that provides little protection to poor children. Perhaps it is more remarkable that so many parents, despite the limitations imposed by poverty and isolation, are able to watch their children carefully and keep them safe from harm. There are many reasons why poor parents are also sometimes neglectful, including their own life histories, depression, isolation, and exhaustion of resources. Whatever the reasons, neglected children can end up as disabled children.

In summary, the statistics on disability and child abuse indicate that between 3 percent and 10 percent of all noncongenital disabilities may in some way be linked to abuse or neglect and therefore are presumed to be preventable. The human toll is high. MacKeith (1974), discussing only Great Britain, estimated that there were four hundred new cases of chronic brain damage every year as a result of abuse. He further notes that of the sixteen hundred new cases of cerebral palsy and six hundred new cases of severe mental retardation that occur annually in children in the United Kingdom, fully half have no adequate explanation and may represent additional cases of abuse or neglect.

Even if only the lowest figure reported in these studies—3 percent—is an accurate estimate of the number of children disabled because of abuse and neglect, it would still have to be considered among the largest single (though unrecognized) causes of disabilities such as mental retardation and cerebral palsy. Again, the studies cited above involve relatively few patients. However, if the statistics obtained are even roughly representative of the population as a whole, by extrapolating we are talking about hundreds of thousands of children worldwide who are needlessly disabled annually.

We still know far less than we should about disabled abused children. Children with some types of disabilities may fare worse than others—for example, several studies have suggested that retarded children may be subjected to more serious abuse than those who are physically impaired. How parents respond to children with various types of disabilities may depend heavily on their own backgrounds. A highly educated parent may do very well with a child of superior intelligence who has cerebral palsy but react with anger and dismay to a severely retarded child. Conversely, a parent to whom education is less important, whose idea of being a parent involves playing ball and days at the beach, may do well with a retarded child but be at a loss with a child who uses a wheelchair.

Families familiar with a particular type of disability, such as an inherited disorder, may do well with a child born with a similar disability. Deaf children of deaf parents, for example, are at a distinct advantage over deaf children from hearing families, and their achievements in education, employment, marriage, family, and community involvement are notable compared with those of the rest of the deaf population (Groce 1985). By contrast, a disorder such as schizophrenia may be met with dread and rage as the disabled child calls to mind other family members with the same condition whose lives were fraught with worry, concern, and frustration. Having a disabled child might place stress on any marriage, but where a child's disorder is believed to be linked to one parent or one side of the family, this often proves to be an additional source of marital conflict.

Note also that child abuse researchers often describe the way one child in a family is singled out as a scapegoat. The strain of having and raising a disabled child is enormous, but resulting abuse is not necessarily directed at the disabled child. A "normal" sibling may well be targeted instead, and of this group we know virtually nothing. The effects of child abuse on nonabused siblings are often psychologically destructive (Friedman 1976); when a disabled sibling is a witness, the effects may be compounded for both children.

Although such information is still inconclusive and anecdotal, it also appears that the actual patterns of abuse and neglect may be different for disabled children. Much of the abusive behavior toward nondisabled children seems to begin in the first weeks or months of life, and it tends to decline after age three; infants and toddlers take the brunt of abuse in the nondisabled. In contrast, for the child born disabled, the abuse may begin later and may not disappear at age three, but rather continue unabated through childhood. For example, Glaser and Bentovim (1979), in their London study, found that over one-third (36 percent) of the nondisabled abused children had been abused by the age of six months, and the abuse decreased with age. In comparison, of those abused children whom they considered ill or disabled at birth, only 26 percent suffered some abuse in the early months. But once the abuse had begun, it persisted beyond age five.

Part of the explanation of this pattern may be that once past toddlerhood a nondisabled child may be physically adept and emotionally atuned enough to stay out of the way of an angry parent, hence avoiding injury, whereas a disabled one may not be aware enough, or mobile enough, to do so. Another explanation involves the consequences of a parent's "failure to bond" with a disabled infant, which leads to abuse later on. However, the data indicate that a serious disability noted at birth may in fact initially help to protect a child. The parent may be more protective and attempt to be more patient with the child than otherwise. Not only may prolonged hospitalization remove the child from the home for periods of time, but the involvement of health care workers and agencies may help parents cope with the new addition to their family. An important implication here is that potentially good parents may hang on for months or years under enormous stress before their self-control gives way and they become abusive. If this is the case, early and continuing professional assistance, including respite care and emotional support, may allow them to avoid becoming abusive.

A nondisabled child whose subsequent disability results from abuse is clearly at greatest risk of early and enduring problems. This child may show an early and continuing pattern of abuse from the first few months of life, through childhood and perhaps beyond.

For disabled children, the risk of neglect may be even greater than the risk of abuse. For example, Glaser and Bentovim (1979) found that while *abuse* was most common in their nonhandicapped patients, at 60 percent of the total, *neglect* was the most notable feature in the care of 71 percent of the disabled children they studied. A similar pattern was found by Jaudis and Dimond (1985). Moreover, correlating the severity of abuse with the degree of handicap and illness, Glaser and Bentovim found those in their sample who were considered more severely disabled were more apt to be neglected than actually abused. Again, the interpretation of these data suggests that a child who is active enough to interact with and possibly cause stress to parents is at greater risk for abuse, while a severe handicap may initially protect some children from direct abuse but increase the risk of neglect.

Whether a child is born disabled and then abused or disabled as a consequence of abuse, it is clear that continuing abuse of a handicapped child simply compounds problems. Although it is difficult for researchers to disentangle the intellectual, physical, and psychological consequences of abuse/neglect and disability for children, it is evident that continuing abuse further lowers their ability to function. In particular, long-term emotional problems have been described in a number of studies (e.g., Morse, Sahler, and Friedman 1970; National Center on Child Abuse and Neglect 1980). These studies have suggested that for any child, the enduring psychological effects of abuse and neglect will be low self-esteem, a sense of helplessness, and the feeling that others are in charge of one's destiny. Depression is cited most frequently and is associated with failure in school and with difficulties in employment and marriage. As Martin (1972, 110) cautioned, mistreatment may begin a "life of incompetence and failure." Such long-term psychological scars are also often reported for disabled individuals. Child abuse can only compound the problems disabled children will have to face as they grow toward adulthood.

Adults

Almost all the literature on violence and disability deals with the abuse or neglect of disabled children. In keeping with a general cultural perception of disabled individuals as being "childlike," issues such as sexuality, marriage, and childbearing, and parenting, and by extension domestic violence, and sexual abuse, are rarely addressed. But disabled adults, particularly those whose condition makes them dependent on others for some or all of their care, are also at risk for physical and sexual abuse in the home, in the hospital, in nursing homes, and in institutions. Again the body of carefully collected data is minimal, but all who have worked in the field, as well as many disabled individuals and groups in the disability rights movement, increasingly have called attention to this widespread and disturbing situation.

Violence is a very real presence in many American homes, and the homes of disabled adults are no exception. Violence in the deaf community, for example, has become an acknowledged "hot" topic in recent years (Melling 1984). Disabled spouses often find themselves in a situation where they not only are victims of violence in their homes, but are also unable to apply for even the few community programs designed for the nondisabled. Without a TTY (teletype machine) for example, a hotline is of little help to a deaf woman. A shelter without ramps is inaccessible to a wheelchair user who has been repeatedly beaten and needs to leave home. A general prejudice against the disabled that in part tells them they are "lucky to find anyone" further militates against their even considering a request for help.

Those who must relegate part or all of their physical care to others often rely on individuals or staff who are frequently undertrained, undersupervised, underpaid, and overworked. Staff members' anger may build, and often the victims are the very people they have been hired to care for. The most vulnerable are often the easiest targets. For example, abuse is known to be most widespread among elderly women with multiple physical and mental disabilities (Aiello and Capkin 1984; Fulmer, this volume).

Sexual abuse of the disabled is also known to exist, though it has rarely been discussed until recently. Again statistics are few, but they do suggest that victimization is as prevalent among the disabled as among others. Although the National Rape Information Center does not keep separate statistics on the disabled, Worthington (1984) estimated that between ten thousand and one hundred thousand disabled women were victims of rape in 1981. He notes that these figures do not include incest or other types of sexual assault by individuals well known to the victim, which are more prevalent than rape. Similarly, the Seattle Rape Relief and Sexual Assault Center provided services to nearly seven hundred rape victims who had some form of disability between 1977 and 1983 (Ryerson 1983), and project administrators estimate that this figure represents perhaps 20 percent of the total number of sexually abused disabled (Aiello and Capkin 1984). The high percentage of abuse by known assailants reflects the more isolated and protected lives of many disabled, who are likely to live in more restricted and intimate environments. As disabled men and women increasingly move into the mainstream, they may well become more frequent targets of stranger assaults.

Disabled Parents

Disabled parents make up a final group to consider in terms of family violence and disability. Although experts disagree on percentages, the hypothesis of intergenerational transmission of abuse does have some empirical support. For those disabled parents who are the products of violent homes or whose early years were spent in institutions where abuse and neglect were present or where parenting skills were never taught, we must recognize that a unique set of social, emotional, and financial stresses seriously affect how they raise their own children. For example, over half a million mildly to moderately retarded adults live in communities throughout the United States. With an increasing emphasis on independence and normalization, many now are deciding to have children.

The risk to a child of a mentally limited parent might spring from more than a lack of cognitive stimulation and the parent's lack of the intuitive knowledge about potential hazards that most of us take for granted. There are other concerns as well. As discussed earlier, abuse has repeatedly been implicated as a causal factor in some mental retardation; for these retarded parents, raised in abusive homes, violence may seem a normal part of child rearing. Those who were raised in institutions may have had no appropriate parental models at all. Moreover, physical and sexual abuse are an ongoing concern in a number of our nation's institutions, where some of these retarded parents as well as other disabled individuals have grown to adulthood.

Compounding this problem is the wall of isolation that separates many of these people from nonretarded community members. Retarded parents often are reluctant or unable to reach out for help. For example, Gabinet (1983), in a review of parenting programs, found that mothers with cognitive deficits were among those most likely to refuse to participate in programs. Of those retarded mothers who did consent to participate, Gabinet found that almost 60 percent were not helped and concluded that retarded mothers were one of the most difficult groups to train. Mentally retarded adults are often isolated from their extended families and are especially cautious about applying for help from agencies (Robinson 1978). Often this reflects a very realistic fear that their children may be taken from them if they seek help.

Schilling and colleagues (1982) also noted that, despite the lack of a large body of methodologically sound research, it seems that children of mentally retarded mothers are at greater risk for maltreatment. In their review of fourteen studies of mentally retarded parents, all but one study found mentally retarded parents unsatisfactory or overrepresented in abuse and neglect samples. Borgman (1969) similarly found a correlation between degree of mental retardation and inability to parent. Friedman (1972) also reported several cases in which the inquisitive behavior of children of normal intelligence made them especially vulnerable to abuse by their more limited parents.

What conclusions one can draw from these studies is not clear. Mental retardation, for example, is not an isolated condition. Other problems associated with mental retardation—such as the poorly paying job or lack of employment that often results in poverty, poor food, unsafe housing, and inadequate clothing—would increase anyone's day-to-day stress. Moreover, negative self-image and expectations of failure are associated with both child abuse and mental retardation (Schilling et al. 1982), compounding the risk for children of retarded parents.

On the whole, it is no easier to generalize about disabled parents than about those who are not disabled. Hallmarks of potential abuse and neglect, including a history of family violence, isolation, and economic, social, and psychological stress, are identified for both groups. However, disabled parents may face these stresses in a more extreme form and have fewer resources to draw on than their nondisabled peers. Of those disabled parents who were raised in violent homes, 3 to 10 percent suffered abuse that initially caused their injuries. As disabled adults, they are now paid significantly less than their peers—if they are able to find employment. Poorer food, clothing, and housing are the result. Not only are they often isolated from family and friends, but some will have physical difficulty even leaving their homes. The psychological burden of being disabled in a society where even minor physical variation is met with comment and derision compounds their problems daily. There are no data to indicate that disabled parents abuse their children any more than their nondisabled peers, but when disabled parents speak of isolation, poverty, and psychological stress they should not be dismissed. These are very real conditions in their lives that can easily lead to violence.

What Can Be Done?

Children

We can draw some inferences from the literature about how to identify and prevent abuse and neglect among the disabled. To begin, we must recognize that society places an enormous burden on both disabled individuals and their families by expecting them to function independently with little support.

Much of this burden is unnecessary and can be reduced. For those children who are identified as disabled, parents need immediate support and education. Accurate information on the current and future development of these children can help reduce frustration as well as raise realistic hopes for the future.

It must also be noted that parents' reactions to a child's disability may in some cases be complicated by the knowledge or strong suspicion that the disability was caused or compounded by their own abuse or neglect. Professionals working with disabled children and their parents should keep this in mind.

Information about the child's condition, when at all possible, should be communicated *regularly* to *both* parents. Too frequently, after initial assessment mothers are given the bulk of the responsibility for carrying out the treatment plans. Siblings should be included in family meetings whenever possible. Professionals also need to keep an eye out for the welfare of these other children in families where a disabled child is considered at risk.

Our society ignores many problems by maintaining an artificial wall of silence, portraying disabled individuals and their families as noble and brave—worthy of our pity and charity rather than our understanding. One of the implications of this distorted view is that it locks parents into a role where complaining or admitting frustration about their child or their situation—any reaction except unlimited patience and acceptance—often horrifies family, friends, and neighbors.

Often professionals know comparatively little about the families of the disabled children they serve. The financial burden alone is tremendous, even if the family is covered by insurance. For the child who needs to come to the hospital regularly, for example, parking a car may eat up several hours' hard-earned income. A direct and sincere inquiry about how a family—not simply a child—is doing should be part of every medical exam for any disabled child.

Abuse prevention is similar to that for nondisabled children. There should be mechanisms that tie parents in with others to share information and experiences. Professionals should offer services (baby-sitting, homemaking) and respite care, even part time (temporary removal of the child at home), as well as encourage activities outside the home for both parents. Such interventions may be literally lifesaving. Of special note here should be the ever-increasing number of self-help groups for parents whose children have specific disabilities. A growing number of disabled individuals have formed handicapped rights/independent living groups that offer a wealth of information to disabled persons and their families. Information on these groups should be readily available.

Finally, a parent of any child needs to be a parent first and foremost. Parents of disabled children are often asked to take on the role of therapist as well. The abuse-prone parent who is asked to help in this capacity may find such work extremely taxing, particularly if the child shows little improvement.

Adults

Almost all the literature on violence and disability deals with the abuse or neglect of disabled children. But disabled adults, particularly those whose conditions make them dependent on others for support, may be unwilling or unable to report abuse or neglect. Many fear, with justification, that they will not be believed or that retaliation will occur.

For example, social service providers and legal professionals regularly note that few courts take seriously sexual abuse or rape of mentally retarded teenage or adult women. Some in the legal system fail to distinguish between mental retardation and licentiousness—as if a lower IQ means an absence of ability to make decisions about one's own body. Others, though they are aware that abuse or rape is every bit as traumatic to a retarded individual as to others, are reluctant to bring such cases to trial, since retarded persons often do not make good witnesses on their own behalf. Disabled victims need clear explanations of the judicial process. Police, criminal justice workers, and medical personnel also need more accurate knowledge of what they can expect of a particular victim with a specific disability.

Disabled women are particularly vulnerable to situations where they not only are victims of violence in their homes but are unable to use the few community programs that exist because they are not designed for the disabled. Programs that serve battered women, including shelters, should make provision for the disabled. This need not—indeed should not—mean entirely separate programs. As Melling (1984) points out, abused women who are disabled need the same types of assistance as other victims: emergency shelter, emotional support, psychological counseling, legal assistance, job training, and housing. But staff should also be familiar with some of the very specific problems they encounter. For example, a battered women's hot line would do well to have a TTY link, printed materials might be made available in Braille and large type, group meetings should be held in places accessible to wheelchairs, and shelters should have ramps as well. A sign-language translator should be available. Indeed, some of the staff and volunteers should themselves be drawn from the disabled community.

Abusive disabled parents often find themselves with particularly few resources to draw on. It is important to emphasize that disability alone does not create this problem—isolation, poverty, stress, and personal history are usually more salient. But disability in abusive parents may compound these factors: they will tend to be more isolated poorer, and less able or willing to request help. Support groups and self-help groups may be part of the solution, but a professional awareness of the problem and identification of services that can be provided are equally important. Sustained support from both professionals and peer groups is essential.

Disabled individuals make up a significant percentage of victims of abuse and neglect. It is therefore imperative that all professionals working with family violence have some familiarity with their special needs and the resources available for helping them.

References

Aiello, D., and Capkin, L. 1984. Services for disabled victims: Elements and standards. *Response to the Victimization of Women and Children* 7(4): 14–16.

Allen, R. E., and Oliver, J. M. 1982. The effects of child maltreatment on language development. *Child Abuse and Neglect* 6:299–305.

Berenberg, W. 1968. Toward the prevention of neuromotor dysfunctions. Presidential address to the American Academy for Cerebral Palsy. *Developmental Medicine and Child Neurology* 11:137–41.

Birrell, R. G., and Birrell, J. H. W. 1968. The maltreatment syndrome in children: A hospital survey. *Medical Journal of Australia* 2:1023–29.

Borgman, R. D. 1969. Intelligence and maternal inadequacy. *Child Welfare* 48:301–4.

Caffey, J. 1964. Multiple fractures of the long bones of children suffering from subdural hematoma. *American Journal of Roentgenology* 56:163–73.

Camblin, L. 1982. A survey of state efforts in gathering information on child abuse and neglect in handicapped populations. *Child Abuse and Neglect* 6:465–72.

Chotiner, N., and Lehr, W., eds. 1976. Child abuse and developmental disabilities. A report from the New England Regional Conference, sponsored by United Cerebral Palsy of Rhode Island and United Cerebral Palsy Association.

Dimond, L. J., and Jaudis, P. K. 1983. Child abuse in a cerebral-palsied population. *Developmental Medicine and Child Neurology* 25:169–74.

Elmer, E., and Gregg, G. E. 1967. Developmental characteristics of abused children. *Pediatrics* 40(4): 596–602.

Eppler, M., and Brown, G. 1977. Child abuse and neglect: Preventable causes of mental retardation. *Child Abuse and Neglect* 1:309–13.

Friedman, R. 1976. Child abuse: A review of the psychosocial research. In *Four perspectives on the status of child abuse and neglect research*. Washington, D.C.: National Center on Child Abuse and Neglect, DHEW.

Friedman, S. 1972. The need for intensive follow-up of abused children. In *Helping the battered child and his family*, ed. C. Kempe and R. Helfer, 79–92. Philadelphia: J. B. Lippincott.

Friedrich, W. N., and Boriskin, J. A. 1976. The role of the child in abuse: A review of the literature. *American Journal of Orthopsychiatry* 46(4): 580–90.

Gabinet, L. 1983. Child abuse treatment failures reveal need for redefinition of the problem. *Child Abuse and Neglect* 70:196–202.

Gil, D. G. 1970. *Violence against children: Physical child abuse in the United States*. Cambridge: Harvard University Press.

Glaser, D., and Bentovim, A. 1979. Abuse and risk to handicapped and chronically ill children. *Child Abuse and Neglect* 3:565–75.

Groce, N. 1985. *Everyone here spoke sign language*. Cambridge: Harvard University Press.

Jaudis, P., and Dimond, L. 1985. The handicapped child and child abuse. *Child Abuse and Neglect* 9:341–47.

Johnson, B., and Morse, H. 1968. *The child and his development: A study of children with inflicted injuries.* Denver: Department of Public Welfare.

MacKeith, R. 1974. Speculation on non-accidental injury as a cause of chronic brain disorder. *Developmental Medicine and Child Neurology* 16:216-18.

Martin, H. P. 1972. The child and his development. In *Helping the battered child and his family,* C. Kempe and R. Helfer, 93-114. Philadelphia: J. B. Lippincott.

Melling, L. 1984. Wife abuse in the deaf community. *Response to Violence in the Family and Sexual Assault* 7(1): 15-17.

Morse, C.; Sahler, O.; and Friedman, S. 1970. A three-year follow-up of abused and neglected children. *American Journal of the Diseases of Childhood* 120:439-46.

National Center on Child Abuse and Neglect. 1980. *National analysis of official child abuse and neglect reporting, 1977.* Department of Health and Human Services. Publication OHDS 79-30232. Washington, D.C.: U.S. Government Printing Office.

Oates, B. K.; Peacock, A.; and Forrest, D. 1984. The development of abused children. *Developmental Medicine and Child Neurology* 26.649-56.

Oliver, J. 1977. Some studies of families in which children suffer maltreatment. In *The challenge of child abuse,* ed. A. W. Franklin. New York: Grune and Stratton.

Ounsted, C.; Oppenheimer, B.; and Lindsay, J. 1974. Aspects of bonding failure: The psychopathology and psychotherapeutic treatment of families of battered children. *Developmental Medicine and Child Neurology* 16:447-56

Pasamanic, B. 1975. Ill-health and child abuse. *Lancet,* 20 September, 550.

Robinson, L. H. 1978. Parental attitudes of retarded young mothers. *Child Psychiatry and Human Development* 8:131-44.

Ryerson, E. 1983. *Sexual abuse and self-protection education for developmentally disabled youth: A priority need.* Seattle: Seattle Rape Relief and Sexual Assault Center.

Sandgrund, A.; Gaines, R. W.; and Greene, A. H. 1974. Child abuse and mental retardation: A problem of cause and effect. *American Journal of Mental Deficiency* 79:327-30.

Scally, B. G. 1973. Marriage and mental handicap: Some observations in Northern Ireland. In *Human sexuality and the mentally retarded,* ed. F. F. de la Cruz and G. D. LaVeck. New York: Brunner/Mazel.

Schilling, R. F.; Schinke, S. P.; Blythe, B. J.; and Barth, R. P. 1982. Child maltreatment and mentally retarded parents: Is there a relationship? *Mental Retardation* 20(5): 201-9.

Silverman, F. N. 1953. Roentgen manifestations of unrecognized skeletal trauma in infants. *American Journal of Roentgenology* 56:413-27.

Toro, P. 1982. Developmental effects of child abuse: A review. *Child Abuse and Neglect* 6:423-31.

Worthington, G. M. 1984. Sexual exploitation and abuse of people with disabilities. *Response to Violence in the Family and Sexual Assault* 7(2): 10-14.

13 *A Framework for Understanding and Empowering Battered Women*

Susan Schechter

with Lisa T. Gary

We all have frameworks for understanding why women are abused and why men batter. We decide, for example, that stress, alcoholism, violence within the abuser's family of origin, or some combination of these factors causes men to assault their partners. This framework then guides our intervention strategies; we design programs to reduce the batterer's stress level, or we teach him to control his anger more effectively. Many of these interventions are· inadequate to stop the violence, and some are dangerous. They persist, however, because we unwittingly subscribe to theories that support the aggressor and blame the victim.

Definition of the Problem

Battering is created by an inequality of power within a relationship, which leads to an *abuse* of power. It is a pattern of coercive control

---

This chapter is adapted from a paper presented at the Harvard Continuing Education Course, "Abuse and Victimization," 2–4 May 1985.

that can take four forms: physical, emotional, sexual, and economic (see table 13.1). Each abusive act builds on the others. Each new act of coercion brings to the victim's mind the fear, violence, and coercion of all past acts against her. The violence has a purpose: it allows the abuser, usually a man, to dominate his partner and reminds the woman (victim) that she is subordinate.

Physical abuse takes the forms listed in table 13.1: hitting, slapping, kicking, holding a knife to the victim's throat. Many battered women

Table 13.1 Battering of Adult Women

The Forms of Abuse Women Experience

Physical	Emotional	Sexual	Economic
Hitting	Humiliation	Rape	Withholding money
Slapping	Name calling	Unwanted sexual	Lying about assets
Kicking	Harassment	practices	Stealing money
Burning	Refusing to	Forced sex with	Taking money
Holding a knife to	speak	other men	
throat		Sexual abuse of	
Destroying a loved		child	
object or pet			
Mutilating			

The Self-Reported Effects of Abuse on the Victim

It frightens me
It controls my life
I withdraw and get depressed
I lost my self-confidence
I'm nervous, get headaches and high blood pressure
I lost my home
My kids had to change schools again
I lost my furniture
I never had a moment's peace
I was always terrified
I lost my job because he called me thirty times a day at work
I lost my family because he said he would kill everyone

Gains for the Abuser—Women's Report

He got his way
He got control
He didn't have to do anything at home
He got taken care of
He felt powerful because I was frightened
He felt superior to me
He got the house
He got pity from others and respect from the guys

report that at some point in the abuse a weapon was used. But physical abuse goes beyond the actual assault. To understand its impact, we have to imagine what it is like to live with the threat of violence day in and day out.

Physical abuse also includes the destruction of the things a woman may cherish most: clothing, photographs of her family, old beloved objects, or even her pet. Although this destruction is clearly emotionally abusive, we label it physical abuse because it gives the victim a profound message about the batterer's access to her and his ability to continue his assaults. The woman learns that the abuser can control her behavior even if he is not physically harming her at that moment.

Almost any woman who has been beaten can talk about the many forms of emotional abuse. Most battered women experience constant humiliation and name calling. Some consider this more abusive than the physical attacks and more painful to resolve.

Isolation is another powerful form of emotional abuse. The abuser cuts the woman off from family, friends, and possible sources of protection. He rips the phone out of the wall before a violent attack and denies the woman access to transportation so that she is unable to talk to anyone or seek help. Threats regarding the children are common as well. Many abusers insist that they will fight for custody of the children, claim the woman is an abusive mother, and discredit her publicly to her family, friends, and the court.

Even when she lives apart from him, the abuser harasses by constantly calling the victim's home, circling the block where she lives, or persistently calling her workplace; this not only frightens her but may also cause the woman to lose her job. A Duluth, Minnesota, study found that 20 percent of the women who had been beaten lost their jobs because of persistent workplace harassment by their abusers (Pence, Lepak, and Medicinehorse 1984).

Sexual abuse includes forced sex (rape) with the abuser or his friends, constant accusations about affairs, threats of violence if the woman refuses to have sex, and threats of sexual abuse against the children.

Economic abuse takes various forms. The abuser steals money from his victim, makes her account for every penny spent, or uses her need for money (even for the children's clothing or for groceries) as justification for battering her. Dobash (1978) noted that in violent relationships this "negotiation" over resources is redefined by the abuser as "nagging." "Nagging" is then used as a rationalization to justify the assault. Financial withholding also entraps the victim, because she may not have enough money to leave the assailant. Finally, there are "contrite" abusers who, after a beating, buy the victim expensive presents, place the family in debt, and ruin the woman's credit.

To understand battering, we must consider all four forms of abuse. It is insufficient to count up the number of times there is a physical attack and call that battering. Battering is a *pattern* of coercive control. It is behavior that causes physical and emotional harm, arouses fear, prevents a woman from doing what she wants, or forces her to do something she does not want to do (Adams 1987).

Not every battered woman experiences all these forms of abuse or the same severe and continual abuse. But when a woman is battered, there is a pattern of unfair and unwarranted control being exercised over her life. Even as she resists her abuser's efforts, he continues to use coercion to dominate her. It is essential to comprehend this dynamic in order to understand why violence against a woman is so pervasive and powerful.

The Meaning of Battering

A second task in developing a framework is to assess the impact of the violence on the victim and to understand its roots. Violence against women results in *losses* for the victim and *gains* for the batterer (see table 13.1). These losses and gains are supported and maintained by the response of family, friends, and "helping" agencies.

Women who are in a violent relationship lose the basic sense of trust and safety that other people assume in daily life. Battered women say that life feels like "walking on eggs." They never know when they will be hurt again. In response to the question, "What effects did the violence have on your life?" battered women describe multiple losses. They report:

> The violence constantly frightened me.
> It controlled my life.
> I lost my self-confidence.
> I lost touch with my family and friends.
> I lost my health.
> I lost my home.

These losses are material as well as emotional—her apartment, friends in the neighborhood, clothing, and personal belongings. The desire not to leave a home that has taken ten to twenty years to create becomes more understandable if we label this as a material loss. The desire to remain at home should be interpreted as a reaction to a major loss rather than as a masochistic wish to be harmed or a denial of the danger at home.

For the abuser, the *gains* are many. He controls his partner. He gets his way. He feels strong and superior in the relationship. His partner can no longer challenge his wishes or commands for fear of harm. She may do everything necessary to please him, to try to stop the beating. Therefore he is "taken care of" as well.

The abuser creates an imbalance of power by bringing violence to the relationship. Once he chooses to use intimidating tactics, negotiation and discussion end. Domination characterizes the relationship. Clinically, therefore, we must define battering as *an abuse of power.*

Individual abusers are repeating and reinforcing cultural patterns of domination that have existed for centuries. Generation after generation, women have been the target of violence. Why? We must explain this in order to design strategies that will stop the targeting of this particular group. Theories suggesting that stress, mental illness, or abuse of drugs cause the violence never adequately explain why women have been the victims. These theories describe what is contributing to violence at a particular moment for a particular individual. They do not explain, however, why men continue day after day, year after year, to choose women as the target of their violence.

Why Are Women the Target?
The Social Sanctioning of Battering

We have inherited from Western European law and religious practice a legal, social, and moral tradition that supports the premise that the husband and wife are one, legally, and that the "one" is the husband. Until the end of the nineteenth century, less than a hundred years ago, women were not allowed to divorce, inherit property, or claim custody of their children. In practice, the husband had the right to chastise his wife when he felt she was not adequately performing her wifely duties.

Although treating a woman as a man's property is no longer legal, it remains an accepted tradition. Current evidence of this social relationship is found in statements like, "Of course I can beat her, she's my wife." It is clear that this belief endures. Approximately two million married men in the United States beat their partners every year (Straus, Gelles, and Steinmetz 1980). We can no longer dismiss this behavior as psychopathological. It must be recognized as both tolerated and approved by parts of our culture and its institutions.

The Institutional Barriers to Effective Intervention

Violence against women will continue as long as it is culturally supported and men experience no negative consequences of their behavior. This social approval reinforces the inequality of power in a relationship and gives the batterer permission to assault again. As the violence continues, the victim becomes increasingly isolated and vulnerable, remaining in the relationship without options for escape.

Institutions in the community support violence against women, creating barriers to effective intervention. In a British study of battered women, 44 percent of the sample reported that they sought medical help after being victimized but were sent back home unsupported. In this study, 64 percent of the women also found the police useless in assisting and protecting them. And 48 percent additionally reported that the social service response has been inadequate in helping them find safety and protection (Binney, Harkell, and Nixon 1981).

The strong support that the Christian church has given to marriage has left abused women further unprotected. Marriage has been lauded as a timeless, unbreakable contract, and clergy have made every effort to keep this contract intact, even when the wife has been in danger. A recent survey of predominantly conservative Protestant clergy revealed two disturbing statistics: 21 percent felt that no amount of abuse would ever justify a wife's leaving her husband; and 26 percent agreed with the statement that a wife should submit to her husband and trust that God would honor her action by either stopping the abuse or giving her the strength to endure it (Alsdurf 1985). Although many battered women have looked first to their church or synagogue for help and support, these institutions have seldom responded by condemning the violence.

The police and courts have historically subscribed to the theory that the victim is to blame—that she "likes" the violence and that she should keep her family together. As a result the woman loses her options for safety and protection, and the abuser learns that there are no consequences for his behavior: he can batter and no one—not even those mandated by law to protect the woman—will intervene to stop him (Schechter 1982).

The mental health community has also responded inadequately. Many therapeutic assumptions and practices harm battered women, keep them entrapped, and support the abuser. Rather than understand the broad social and political context through which violence is perpetuated, professionals have chosen to individualize, psychologize, and pathologize it. For example, often the effect of the violence is confused with the cause; many professionals say there is something wrong with the woman's personality and conclude that this is why she is battered. The practitioner then focuses on the victim's "pathology" instead of her need for validation, safety, and support. As the practitioner tries to transform the woman's personality, the problem—the violence—is ignored.

Therapeutic intervention with the victim and abuser has often relied upon an introspective model based on the assumption that the violence exists because of unresolved childhood conflicts or feelings of maternal deprivation. These issues become the focus of the treatment. However, there is *no* evidence that this form of therapy stops the violence (Adams 1987). Therapy designed to look at the stressors in the abuser's life, such as unemployment or his family history, is also inadequate for stopping the violence.

Couples therapy is similarly an ineffective, even dangerous, mode of treatment. Here the therapist assumes that the couple is an interacting system with two equal partners. In fact, these partners are in an unequal relationship: one is frightened, and one uses power and intimidation to control the relationship.

Encouraging a couple to negotiate about how to stop the male's violence gives the victim a false message: that she contributes to the violence, that she is responsible, and that the batterer's change is dependent on her involvement and help. A woman in couples therapy is presented with the mystifying statement that she "plays a role" in the violence. The therapist may give her tasks to carry out at home that put her in the unrealistic position of taking responsibility for the abuse. If the woman shows anger, defies her partner, or challenges his right to control a situation, the batterer and the therapist may feel that she provokes the violence. The abuser then can say, "I don't have to change; she didn't do her part" (Adams 1987). This allows him to further avoid responsibility for his assaultive behavior.

Therapists frequently misunderstand battered women's behavior. During the therapy session the woman may seem to challenge her partner, as if to bring on the violence. The therapist may not realize that the woman, in the safety of the session, wants to demonstrate the pattern of intimidating and coercive interactions that occurs at home. Instead of clarifying the situation, the therapist may misinterpret this behavior and begin to view the woman as provocative. Treatment for the couple should not begin until the violence and coercive tactics have ceased for at least one year and both parties request marital counseling. Until the batterer takes full responsibility for his violence, other therapeutic issues cannot be addressed. As David Adams, clinical director of EMERGE, a treatment project for battering men, notes:

> Often in our therapy we unwittingly give the batterer the message that his violence is negotiable. It depends on his ability to feel better about himself, it depends on his ability to develop insight, or to improve his or his wife's communication skills. We also give a message, although not necessarily ever verbal, that it is likely that he will beat *until* he can make changes in those other areas: his insight, his communication, or that he feels better. (Adams 1987)

Similarly, in the family therapy literature, violence has been described as acting "homeostatically to establish complementarity within the marital system" (Bograd 1984). In this framework, *both* partners act to maintain the violent relationship, and so *both* are held accountable and responsible for the violence.

The family systems view serves, once again, to blame the victim. Its application within mental health agencies and hospitals entraps women in abusive relationships and makes effective intervention impossible. The violence cannot be tolerated by any institution to which battered women turn for help, or women and men will both receive the message that battering women is socially endorsed.

Additional Barriers to Empowerment

Lack of shelters, safe homes, or other advocacy services means that few or no viable options are available to many women to enable them to escape their batterers. Although there are approximately seven-hundred to one-thousand shelters in the United States today (and there were none only ten years ago), they still turn away thousands of women annually. Consequently, if family and friends do not support the woman or cannot adequately house her and her children, she may be left without a safe place to live.

Lack of financial resources also haunts many women. In 1980 the median income of a full-time working woman was $11,590 (Stallard, Ehrenreich, and Sklar 1983). The medium income for black women was $10,914, and for Latinas it was $9,887. This woeful economic situation creates a barrier to independence because even if a woman and her children can find an apartment, they may be forced into poverty—an often frightening contrast to their economic status in the household of the abuser. Housing for women and their children is scarce as well, with many landlords discriminating against children. Resources—housing, jobs, welfare—give women the tools to stop the violence in their lives. Without these tools, escape becomes much more difficult.

Principles of Effective Intervention

If battering results from an inequality of power, our goal becomes to give power back to the victim—that is, empower her—and to stop the assailant's misuse of power. The essence of effective intervention with a battered woman is to help restore a sense of power, control, and dignity to her life. Her empowerment can take many forms. For example, we can encourage her to act by acknowledging her courage in reaching out for help, or we can turn her individual defeats and fears into victories by advocating for her. Empowerment means offering a woman the tools with which to better control her life.

We can intervene effectively by accomplishing three basic tasks:

1. Unequivocally reject the violence and the abuser's justification for it.
2. Support and validate the victim and ensure her safety.
3. Bring consequences to bear on the abuser and stop his abuse of power. Hold the abuser accountable and make institutions responsible for stopping the violence. (R. E. Dobash and R. Dobash, pers. comm.)

Effective intervention begins with an active, reassuring therapist/ advocate who believes the victim. Disbelief will make it impossible for the woman to trust, as this former battered woman commented to the author: "The minute I felt that the person I reached out to for help did not believe me, I stopped talking. I didn't tell the whole truth. I cut the interview short and went home" (pers. comm. 1985). Information is also empowering for the victim. By talking with other battered women or by reading a book or pamphlet on violence, the woman will learn that she is neither alone nor crazy.

Providing options for safety is an essential element of empowerment. Without safety, empowerment is impossible. The therapist/advocate must know about shelters and services for the victim and turn to them for advice. Designing an immediate safety plan with the woman is also critical. Will she go to a relative's or friend's home, go to a shelter, or remain at home to prepare further? What does she want to do? What resources does she need to be safe? As options are explored, the practitioner should focus on the woman's strength and survival skills rather than on her failure to escape. The client needs hope, the sense that she can make changes. The practitioner's task is to draw the woman out and validate what she has done to protect herself and survive. For example, one woman hid fifty cents a week until she had the twenty-five dollars for bus fare to leave town. Others had called her deceitful (as she did herself) for concealing this money from her husband. However, we should relabel this behavior as resourceful and laud it.

While it is important for practitioners to advocate for the empowerment of a woman, it is also essential that we not define empowerment in middle-class terms. For instance, the advocate may encourage a victim to call the police and prosecute the abuser. This woman may have extended family in the community who might be at serious risk if she goes to the police. Her refusal to prosecute may be not a passive gesture but one of great love and concern for others. For example, after interviewing poor women who had survived rape, social psychologist Michelle Fine (1983–84, 251) concluded:

> Poor people do assert control in ways ignored by psychologists. For many, their taking control involves ignoring advice to solve one's problem's individually and recognizing instead the need for collective, structural change. Taking control may mean rejecting available social programs as inappropriate to one's needs, or recognizing that one's social supports are too vulnerable to be relied upon.

Fine emphasizes the dilemma for victims of violence when she notes that they are reluctant to appeal an injustice. They do this, she says, because they are less likely to win such an appeal. They usually have more to lose than nonvictims who appeal. We must conclude that empowerment is still a limited concept because the social resources do not yet exist to enable all people to truly take control of their lives (Fine 1983–84).

Practitioners can also empower women by stopping the abuser. As societal institutions such as the courts and the police begin to place controls on the abuser's behavior, the victim will feel supported and protected. There is some evidence that when the abuser is arrested and forced to face consequences, there is a reduction in his violence (Sherman and Berk 1984; Galaway and Novack 1983).

Churches, synagogues, and community agencies can also take a stand against the violence. They can remove batterers from positions of authority and honor in their organizations, monitor abusers' behavior, and offer to protect victims.

After the victim's safety is assured and her batterer experiences consequences for his violent behavior, the woman can begin to take control of her life. Separate from his victim, the abuser can also change. His treatment must focus on the violence and its consequences, not on what he describes as his intention or motivation. The following excerpt from a counseling interview with a batterer illustrates the shift from discussing the batterer's stated reasons for assaulting to focusing on the effects of his behavior upon the victim (Adams 1987):

> *Counselor:* What do you think causes you to hit your wife?
>
> *Client:* Insecurity. . . . It goes way back. . . . My father was a drinker too. He was a mean drunk. He'd whack my mother for no reason really. . . . I left home when I was seventeen, got married. It only lasted two months. I've always been insecure with women.
>
> *Counselor:* This is helping me to understand why you are insecure, but not why you hit your wife.
>
> *Client:* Some times I take things the wrong way. I overreact because of my insecurity. My shrink said I was like a time bomb waiting to go off. She [client's wife] might say something, and I don't react at the time, but then the next day or maybe a few hours later I get to really thinking about that and I get really bullshit.
>
> *Counselor:* A lot of people feel insecure, but they are not violent. What I'm interested in finding out is how do you make the decision to hit your wife, to break the law—even if you are feeling insecure?
>
> *Client:* I never really thought of it that way, as a decision.
>
> *Counselor:* But you were talking just now as if your violence is the direct result of your insecurity or of something that she says or does.
>
> *Client:* Yeah, you're right, I do. But I'm still thinking about what you said about the decision. I honestly have to say that I never thought of it that way before. I mean, I'm really dumbfounded! I'm going to have to really think about that.
>
> *Counselor:* What are you waiting for?
>
> *Client:* What do you mean?
>
> *Counselor:* I mean are you waiting to stop feeling insecure before you stop being violent?
>
> *Client:* Yeah, I guess that's what I've been waiting for.

The counselor in this interview comments further:

> The above is a dialogue I had during an intake interview with an abusive husband. He had been in psychotherapy with a male psychologist off and on for four years. Though he had talked about his insecurity, his upbringing, his drinking problem, his anger toward his mother, his anger toward his father, his relationship with his wife, in great detail during his treatment, they had never talked about his decision to continually break the law by being violent toward his wife. Nor had Jack become less insecure during this time. How could he? How can a man feel secure when he has to maintain a constant vigilance and worry about losing control over his wife. (D. Adams, 1987.)

As this interview indicates, violence is a choice by the abuser; it is not a symptom of other problems. If the therapist fails to focus on the violence, it will not stop. This excerpt also illustrates that as long as the batterer is using violence to keep control over another person, he cannot be helped with other problems.

Without experiencing the consequences of his behavior, such as arrest or the woman's leaving, the abuser usually cannot be helped. In recently established programs in Minnesota, if a woman is visibly injured the police arrest the batterer and keep him in jail overnight, because he is dangerous. When he is arrested, his wife is visited by an advocate, urged to join a support group (with transportation and child care provided), and offered help in finding shelter and using the criminal justice system. In court, if the batterer is found guilty of abuse, he can be evicted from his home and sentenced to mandatory education or counseling. If he is violent again, he serves thirty to ninety days in jail (E. Pence, pers. comm.).

It is vital that the abuser begin to take responsibility for his action. However, in a recent study of fifty-nine programs working with batterers, only eight said that having the abuser take responsibility for the violence was an important treatment goal (Pirog-Good and Stets-Kealey 1985). The fifty-one agencies surveyed that did not subscribe to this goal are a danger to battered women.

Treatment of the batterer must also address stopping the entitlement to batter. Good programs for men who batter not only work to stop the violence but also challenge the assailant to give up the controlling tactics detailed in figure 13.1. These programs acknowledge that without this focus they may stop the most violent assaults yet fail to halt equally terrifying sexual and emotional abuse.

Ending Violence against Women

Intervention and change must occur not only for the victim and abuser, but also within our society. The approval and support of violence in our culture is evident on television, in newspapers, in literature, and at the movies. There must be institutional sanctions against the violence. This transformation in the courts, police departments, and religious institutions will come through education and training as well as institutional policy changes and will occur only when the community demands it. Almost every positive change on behalf of battered women has come from the pressure exerted by the battered women's movement in the past ten years. We can broaden our base and grow stronger

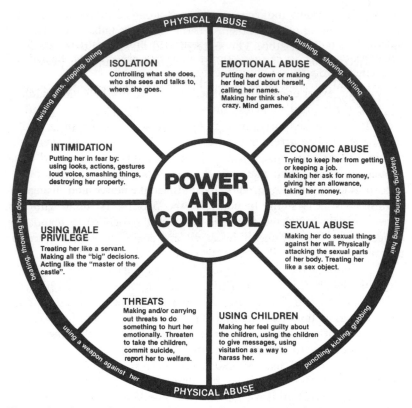

Figure 13.1 Source: Reprinted with permission from Domestic Abuse Intervention Project, 206 West 4th Street, Duluth, Minn. 55806

by lobbying, educating, and promoting programs that keep women safe. We will need continued funding and support to maintain the momentum achieved in recent years.

None of the interventions detailed here, however, will end violence against women. The abuse of power that individual men inflict on their partners will continue as long as women are treated as unequal and less important. This inequality is maintained through unfair legal and child support practices, lower pay, and discriminatory housing policies for women with children. It is also perpetuated through poverty—inadequate welfare benefits, housing, medical, and child-care services. In other words, we will end violence against women only by seeking social equality on personal, cultural, and institutional levels.

References

Adams, D. 1987. Counseling men who batter: A profeminist analysis of five treatment models. In *Feminist perspectives on wife abuse,* ed. M. Bograd and K. Yllo. Beverly Hills, Calif.: Sage.

Alsdurf, J. M. 1985. Wife abuse and the church: The response of pastors. *Response* 8(1): 10.

Binney, V.; Harkell, G.; and Nixon, J. 1981. *Leaving violent men: A study of refuges and housing for battered women.* London: Women's Aid Federation of England.

Bograd, M. 1984. Family systems approaches to wife battering: A feminist critique. *American Journal of Orthopsychiatry* 54(4): 562.

Dobash, R. 1978. The negotiation of daily life and the provocation of violence: A patriarchal concept in support of the wife beater. Paper presented at the Ninth World Congress of Sociology, August, Uppsala, Sweden.

Fine, M. 1983-84. Coping with rape: Critical perspectives on consciousness. *Imagination, Cognition, and Personality* 3(3): 251.

Galaway, B., and Novack, S. 1983. The domestic abuse intervention project: Final report. Domestic Abuse Intervention Project, Duluth, Minn.

Pence, E.; Lepak, M.; and Medicinehorse, M. 1984. Effects of battering on the employment status of women. Unpublished paper. Domestic Abuse Intervention Project, Duluth, Minn.

Pirog-Good, M., and Stets-Kealey, J. 1985. Male Batterers and batterers prevention programs: A national survey. *Response* 8(3): 8-12.

Schechter, S. 1982. *Women and male violence: The visions and struggles of the battered women's movement.* Boston: South End Press.

Sherman, W., and Berk, R. A. 1984. *The Minneapolis domestic violence experiment.* Duluth, Minn.: Police Foundation Reports.

Stallard, K.; Ehrenreich, B.; and Sklar, H. 1983. *Poverty in the American dream: Women and children first.* Boston: South End Press.

Straus, M.; Gelles, R.; and Steinmetz, S. 1980. *Behind closed doors: Violence in the American family.* Garden City, N.Y.: Anchor Books/Doubleday.

14 *The Treatment and Criminal Prosecution of Family Violence*

RICHARD BOURNE

In the management of child abuse cases, two important social policy questions are when and how the state should intervene in families. The first issue concerns family autonomy/privacy and the legal standard permitting intrusion only when parents act in such a way that government can legitimately define their caretaking behavior as abusive or neglectful. Assuming intervention, the second issue deals with whether the primary concern should be treatment or punishment of the abuser (Bourne and Newberger 1977).

Treatment and punishment, of course, are not necessarily discrete entities. A mother required by a state protective services agency to attend weekly therapy sessions, parenting classes, and medical assessments may view such "supports" as punitive despite the benign definition of professionals. In dispositional planning, moreover, the threat of criminal punishment may facilitate treatment (i.e., a prosecutor might initiate criminal proceedings if an alleged abuser fails to enter therapy), or treatment and punishment may intertwine; foster care may harm (punish) both child and parents even if benefits also result.

Though treatment and punishment are often difficult to distinguish, two intervention models exist. The first, a criminal justice model, emphasizes identifying a perpetrator, establishing guilt, and punishing a wrongdoer. The second, a clinical model, emphasizes protecting the abused child and treating both victim and abuser so that the family can remain intact without danger of serious inflicted injury.

Adherents to one or the other model approach child abuse from different orientations and assumptions and often mistrust professionals from the opposing camp. The legal definition of incest, for example, is narrower than the clinical definition. Clinicians define it as sexual exploitation by an intimate involving secrecy and misuse of authority, yet police and district attorneys may prosecute only if there is intercourse by a blood relative or family member. Though both clinicians and criminal justice professionals use intuition in case assessment, the latter are much more concerned about the quality of evidence and "proof"—it matters less whether a child was abused ("fact") than whether the abuse can be proved in a courtroom.

While clinicians may view an abuser as "sick," acting because of psychological and sociological forces beyond his or her control, police may see the abuser as a "criminal" intentionally deciding to harm a child. While clinicians attempt to understand family dysfunction, police are much more likely to adopt a dyadic, perpetrator/victim approach. While clinicians focus on a wide variety of family issues (in some families the existence of an incestuous relationship between father and daughter is only one problem, and not necessarily the major one), police focus on that problem that involves a violation of the law.

Different Responses to Family Violence

Though nonfamily and family assault are both "crimes," the criminal sanction is used more frequently with nonfamily violence. That is, a person who assaults a stranger is more likely to receive punishment than one who batters his spouse or child. Different types of family violence, however, evoke different "recommended" interventions depending, among other factors, on how the offender and abuse are defined. For example, unless a child dies or suffers permanent injury, physical abusers usually are not prosecuted. This reluctance to initiate criminal charges stems in part from the fact that such abusers are defined as "victims" of psychological stress who are doing (to a greater degree) what most parents do—namely, striking their children. Children are often seen as the "property" of their parents, and corporal punishment is considered a culturally appropriate form of discipline ("Spare the rod and spoil the child").

Sexual abuse of children is much more likely to be criminally prosecuted than is physical abuse. In a sense this punitive reaction is surprising, given that a "sickness" or pathology explanation is more common to sexual abuse. If an abuser is "sick," he is arguably less responsible for his actions and therefore should be treated rather than punished: usually the less deliberate and intentional the behavior (behavior that is beyond the control of the perpetrator), the greater the use of treatment. On the other hand, sexual abuse of a child violates societal norms to a much greater degree than does physical abuse. A father who fondles his daughter's breast is seen as much more "deviant" than a father who beats his daughter. That is, the social definition of the act and its perceived prevalence affect social response.

It is instructive to compare physical abuse and sexual abuse to alcoholism and heroin addiction. Many people drink, just as many parents hit their children. The alcoholic is seen as "sick," and his or her disease is treated; it is not considered appropriate to jail drunks unless they are committing a crime or are in need of detention for their own safety. Heroin users, often seen as coming from nonconformist, poor, or minority subcultures, are defined as "criminal" and are subject to arrest for possession of an illegal substance. This punitive response to heroin exists despite the fact that heroin, as a drug, causes much less individual and social harm than does alcohol (Bourne and Levin 1983). How "perpetrators" and "acts" are labeled clearly influences intervention.

The use of criminal prosecution with sexual abuse is encouraged by another factor. Unlike a physical abuser, who is more likely to feel remorse and admit wrongdoing, a sexual abuser often rationalizes, justifies, and denies his exploitation of a child. Only criminal sanction or its threat will keep him in treatment, for he is usually unwilling to seek help voluntarily (Burgess et al. 1978). Ironically, given the emphasis on "proof" in criminal cases, sexual abuse is much more difficult to prove beyond a reasonable doubt (the burden of proof in a criminal case) than is physical abuse. At least with physical abuse there is usually tangible evidence like burns and broken bones, whereas in sexual exploitation the only symptoms or clinical findings may be fear of men, nightmares, and stomachaches.

With wife abuse, most professionals have long encouraged criminal prosecution of offenders. Unlike the definition of physical abusers of children as "victims" or sexual abusers as "sick," wife beaters are often seen as "brutes." Though children are still the property of (within the authority of) parents, wives are no longer chattels within our culture. Husbands therefore are having an increasingly difficult time rationalizing their violence (there is no "spare the rod" justification). Along with research indicating that arrest and trial are deterrents, criminal prosecution parallels the usual clinical response to spouse abuse. Unlike physical child abuse, where the customary clinical goal is to keep parents and children together when possible, clinicians in wife abuse often urge the female victim to separate permanently from the abuser, giving little concern to family unity (Battered Women 1978).

Despite clinicians' positive response to the criminal prosecution of wife beaters, the criminal justice system has often failed to act. There are many reasons for the failure to prosecute effectively. These include male police officers' empathy with male offenders; police belief that they are dealing with a private family matter rather than a public issue requiring law enforcement; and police feelings that the victim will not "follow through" with court action (Martin 1976).

In summary, then, physical abuse cases are generally not prosecuted unless a child dies or is very seriously injured. Sexual abuse of children is much more frequently prosecuted, though often the prosecution is "unsuccessful" because of the difficulty of meeting legal standards of proof. Professionals in the field of woman abuse encourage prosecution, but the criminal justice system has traditionally failed to act, seeing the abuse as more appropriate to social welfare intervention.

The Criminalization of Family Violence

When state-mandated reporting of child abuse and neglect began, police departments had the responsibility of receiving and processing such information. Policymakers perceived family violence as a crime, with law enforcement officers expected to respond because of their twenty-four-hour-a-day availability. Soon, however, experts redefined abuse as a social problem demanding treatment rather than prosecution; hospital emergency rooms became the point of entry for serious cases, and departments of welfare (or social services) replaced police as the primary management authority.

At present many policymakers are reassessing the need for involvement of the criminal justice system. Though clinicians dealing with sexual abuse often urge prosecution of the offender (Herman 1981), those managing physical abuse generally express strong opposition to the "criminalization" of family violence. In fact an ideological war exists between "treaters" and "punishers" as to what interventions are appropriate in these cases (Newberger 1982).

What are the arguments and counterarguments made by the two groups? Though it is difficult to generalize, a debate between "con" and "pro" by criminalization experts might go as follows:

1. CON: If parents knew that bringing an abused or neglected child

to a hospital for treatment might involve the police, they would hesitate to obtain needed medical and other services because of their fear of arrest. PRO: Abusive parents often love their children despite an inability to care for them and would seek assistance because they were upset at what they had done. If concern was not a motivating force, fear would be. Delay in treating a child's medical problems would only exacerbate the family's legal and social problems. Besides, abusive parents have long known that they risk social punishment—for example, potential foster placement of a child victim by the juvenile court—and such coercive interventions have failed to deter abusers from seeking medical attention in the past.

2. CON: The possibility of criminal prosecution of abusers places extraordinary role strain on treaters such as social workers. On the one hand, such clinicians, wanting to help those in crisis, urge parents to trust them by communicating intimate family matters; on the other hand, these workers know that they may have to reveal to police all details shared in confidence. They resent that they are acting as implicit agents of law enforcement; that they may betray their clients; that with police involvement they will lose control of case management; that police are often insensitive to the psychological needs of both victim and attacker. PRO: Clinicians already operate under role strain, given the mandate to report child abuse to state authorities and the possibility of court action to remove abused children from their families of origin. They can never guarantee nondisclosure of materials and should not have such an expectation. Police are not as insensitive as the stereotype implies, and being dependent upon clinical assessments, they treat clinician collaborators with respect. If treaters are concerned about deceiving clients, they might inform them of the possible consequences of revelation, though admittedly such information may cause clients to withdraw from contact, if not to hire a defense attorney.

3. CON: In criminal court prosecutors must prove child abuse "beyond a reasonable doubt," which is difficult given that the child victim is often too young to testify, that wives may have immunity from testimony against husbands, and that inflicted injury is frequently hard to distinguish from accident or disease. Though "factually guilty," an abusive parent may be vindicated by a legal finding of "not guilty." PRO: Merely because a crime is difficult to prove does not mean the behavior should not remain illegal and subject to prosecution. Arson and rape, for example, are difficult to prove in criminal court, but few would suggest decriminalizing them for that reason. Additionally, as the public becomes more knowledgeable about child abuse and rules

of evidence grow more flexible, successful prosecution will become more frequent.

4. CON: The criminal process often causes abused children to be victimized again. They are pressured by both family and the "system" for a seemingly endless time. Police and district attorneys interview them over and over, rubbing raw the trauma they have suffered. In court, defense attorneys subject the youngster to harsh cross-examination, dealing with "embarrassing" materials in a public forum. Even if such children receive preparation and support from victim assistance counselors, they feel ambivalent about testifying against parents whom they often love, and they have difficulty accepting the burden of being responsible for a parent's incarceration. PRO: Criminal prosecution is often therapeutic for the child victim—in sexual abuse, for example, by helping to convince the abused youngster that her father is the wrongdoer (not she the seducer) and that society will not tolerate the harm she has experienced.

5. CON: Two goals of the criminal sanction, rehabilitation of an offender and deterrence of future abusers, are not achieved by successful prosecution. Few child abusers receive effective treatment while imprisoned; few potential abusers restrain their violence because others are punished. PRO: Data on rehabilitation and deterrence are incomplete. The criminal process, however, may force an offender to obtain therapy that he would not voluntarily request. It also deters an incarcerated offender from committing crimes against children. The public demands retribution for gross acts of child abuse, and this third function—punishment of a wrongdoer—is fulfilled by police action, as is the "symbolic" purpose of criminal law: a clear statement that abusive behavior is intolerable in our society.

In summary, those holding the antiprosecution position argue that the criminal justice system often victimizes children and families over again and interferes with therapeutic intervention. Those advocating prosecution argue that child abuse is a crime and that children, like adults, deserve the protection of the criminal law. Prosecution brings just punishment on those who have hurt children and, indeed, may serve therapeutic objectives for both offenders and victims.

Policy Guidelines

Though some states have adopted a "dual reporting" system—that is, all reports of child abuse go to both social service and police agencies—others have attempted to adopt criteria determining which reported cases receive treatment as opposed to punitive responses. Given the prevalence of family violence, police, prosecutors, and courts may lack the resources to process every possible referral anyway. Furthermore, since "not all abusers are alike," clinicians cannot recommend a monolithic intervention for all cases.

How, then, do policymakers decide which cases require a criminal approach? The following criteria may serve as useful guidelines:

1. Intentionality and deliberateness. An abuser who tortures a child by holding cigarette butts against flesh is arguably different from one who, under severe stress, explodes and lashes out in frustration. This distinction parallels the legal difference between first-degree murder and manslaughter.
2. Nature of the abuse and harm to the victim. Prosecutors, for example, should initiate criminal action against sexual abusers who physically harm their victims (Groth's sex force offenses; Burgess et al. 1978) and against physical abusers who cause death or substantial or permanent bodily harm.
3. Duration and frequency. Depending on other criteria, a one-time abusive episode is arguably less heinous than physical or sexual violence that continues for years.
4. Characteristics of the victim. A sexual abuser of an infant or very young child, for example, may receive a harsher response than one who has sex with a "consenting" teenager.
5. Multiple victims. The more children a single abuser hurts, the more likely is criminal prosecution.
6. Effect on treatment. Where the treatment approach has failed or is unlikely to succeed, or where the criminal process may enhance the likelihood that treatment will succeed, prosecution may occur.
7. Impact on the child. Professionals should avoid the criminal process if it will inevitably and severely retraumatize the child victim.
8. Exploitation by third parties. If a child is exploited by third parties with the full knowledge and consent of a parent—for example, in prostitution or pornography rings—or if institutional abuse by caretakers (surrogate parents) occurs, criminal prosecution requires serious consideration.

Clinicians might make a distinction between the "horrible" and the "miserable" child abuse cases, with the latter favored for treatment. Though "horrible" abuses (e.g., the torturing of a child) often receive much publicity, the "miserable" abuses (abuse triggered by the stress of poverty and deprivation) are more numerous. Lawyers, on the other hand, might distinguish "corporal punishment" or "soft" abuse cases (slapping a child for discipline or such sexual misuse as parental intercourse in front of children) from those that seem to violate the criminal law (e.g., rape of a child). Or they may choose prosecution versus treatment based on procedural requirements (Fourth and Fifth amendment constitutional questions, for example) or on the likelihood that the state can meet its burden of proof.

In part, of course, the decision to prosecute rather than to treat child abusers is a political and ideological choice made not on empirical evidence, but on personal beliefs and interests. As the political climate becomes more conservative, with calls for capital punishment and a "crackdown" on criminals, child abuse is once again becoming a "crime" rather than a "psychosocial problem."

Controversy and Reform

Sexual abuse prosecutions are undergoing reform, from eliminating competency hearings requiring young witnesses to demonstrate that they understand what it means to tell the truth before being allowed to testify to admitting children's statements on abuse in evidence as exceptions to the hearsay rule.

Both pro- and antiprosecution forces urge the criminal justice system to deal more sensitively and effectively with child abuse. For example, many clinicians believe that law enforcement professionals should receive training in the dynamics of family violence and in such necessary skills as interviewing (how to talk and listen to children): that victim-assistance counselors should prepare and support child victims; that judges should hold proceedings in their chambers or in a small courtroom and should consider excluding the public and limiting publicity in order to alleviate the child's anxiety.

However, many of the proposals to avoid retraumatizing the child are controversial and trigger constitutional and budgetary problems. Three of the most conflictful areas are the use of experts and expert testimony, videotaping, and plea bargaining.

Therapists who have interviewed and assessed child victims before trial often act as expert or fact witnesses for the prosecution. On cross-examination, defense attorneys question the therapist's background, view of abuse and victimization, and clinical techniques. Beliefs (e.g., "when children say they have been sexually abused they are almost always telling the truth") are challenged; doubts are raised about whether these experts encouraged answers they wanted to hear and whether patients gave the answers "expected" (Nurcombe 1986).

Testimony becomes an ordeal for these clinicians, who often "know" the alleged offender is factually guilty and resent the insensitivity of lawyers, the disparity between legal and clinical standards, and the difficulty of successful prosecution. Defense attorneys, on the other hand, argue that those trained in abuse management always find abuse—that prejudgment and bias affect their perception that the child was victimized.

Because of a desire to spare the victim of abuse the trauma of traditional courtroom testimony, videotaping the therapist's interviews and the child's communications is increasingly common. Prosecutors use such tapes to induce a guilty plea or, depending on state statute, as evidence against the defendant. The Sixth Amendment to the United States Constitution, however, guarantees a defendant the right to cross-examine his accuser and to confront a hostile witness; a prerecorded tape with only a child's communications cannot be so examined. If it is shown in a courtroom, therefore, the child may still have to testify personally. The tape, subject to a frame-by-frame analysis by the defense, may allow the techniques of therapist-expert (if they appear on tape) to be even more closely assessed and criticized.

Other alternatives allow cross-examination but protect the child from badgering. These include providing an attorney for the child who may object to questions that confuse or upset the witness and viewing the child through a one-way mirror. The child answers questions asked by a child therapist but propounded by a defense lawyer watching in the courtroom. Through a simultaneous electronic transmission, the attorney may probe the child's responses by speaking into a microphone hooked into the therapist's earphones.

Plea bargaining, finally, is a process whereby a criminal defendant pleads guilty rather than insisting on his right to trial. The inducement for such a plea is often a reduced charge (e.g., aggravated assault rather than rape) or a prosecutor's recommendation of a lighter sentence. The plea, if voluntary and knowingly made, is the functional equivalent of a guilty verdict and thus spares the child from the need to testify, and in this sense it is functional. On the other hand, because the charge may not reflect the actual offense and may offer a reduced punishment, a counterargument can be made that the abuser is "not getting what he deserves."

Very little consensus exists about the techniques of criminal prosecution in cases involving children. Even the "simple" matter of multiple questionings is disputed. Some experts argue that children are traumatized by having to repeat their stories over and over. Other experts feel that repetition tests credibility, allows new facts to emerge, and prepares children for the repeated interrogation of the courtroom.

Prosecutors and defense attorneys both have complaints about the present system. For example, prosecutors become frustrated if young child victims lack the ability to understand questions or to communicate. Defense attorneys also complain that they do not have the freedom to challenge child witnesses vigorously because of the jury's empathy with the alleged victim. Legal reforms will be welcomed by all involved.

However, as legal reforms are proposed and debated, both sides should maintain a similar sensitivity to the complexity of the child victim's needs. Only then will children truly benefit from the systems that are supposed to help them and keep them safe.

References

Battered women: Issues of public policy. 1978. A consultation sponsored by the U.S. Commission on Civil Rights, Washington, D.C., 30–31 January.

Bourne, R., And Levin, J. 1983. *Social problems: Causes, consequences, interventions.* Saint Paul, Minn.: West.

Bourne, R., and Newberger, E. H. 1977. "Family autonomy" or "coercive intervention"? Ambiguity and conflict in the proposed standards for child abuse and neglect. *Boston University Law Review* 57:670–706.

Burgess, A. W.; Groth, A. N.; Holmstrom, L. L.; and Sgroi, S. 1978. *Sexual assaults of children and adolescents.* Lexington, Mass.: Lexington Books.

Herman, J. 1981. *Father-daughter incest.* Cambridge: Harvard University Press.

Martin, D. 1976. *Battered wives.* San Francisco: Glide.

Newberger, E. H., ed. 1982. *Child abuse.* Boston: Little, Brown.

Nurcombe, B. 1986. The child as witness: Competency and credibility. *Journal of the American Academy of Child Psychiatry* 25(4):206–20.

Rosenfeld, A. 1982. Sexual abuse of children: Personal and professional responses. In *Child abuse,* ed. E. H. Newberger. Boston: Little, Brown.

Index

265